the Tennis Drill Book

SECOND EDITION

TINA HOSKINS-BURNEY
LEX CARRINGTON

Human Kinetics

Library of Congress Cataloging-in-Publication Data

Hoskins-Burney, Tina, 1965-
  The tennis drill book / Tina Hoskins-Burney, Lex Carrington. -- Second edition.
    pages cm.
  1. Tennis--Training. I. Title.
  GV1002.9.T27H67 2014
  796.342'2--dc23
                                          2013044762

ISBN-10: 1-4504-5992-7 (print)
ISBN-13: 978-1-4504-5992-1 (print)

The web addresses cited in this text were current as of October 2013, unless otherwise noted.

Acquisitions Editor: Justin Klug; **Developmental Editor:** Claire Marty; **Managing Editor:** Tyler Wolpert; **Copyeditor:** Joanna Hatzopoulos; **Permissions Manager:** Martha Gullo; **Graphic Designer:** Fred Starbird; **Graphic Artist:** Tara Welsh; **Cover Designer:** Keith Blomberg; **Photograph (cover):** © Human Kinetics; **Photographs (interior):** © Human Kinetics; **Photo Asset Manager:** Laura Fitch; **Visual Production Assistant:** Joyce Brumfield; **Photo Production Manager:** Jason Allen; **Art Manager:** Kelly Hendren; **Associate Art Manager:** Alan L. Wilborn; **Illustrations:** © Human Kinetics; **Printer:** Total Printing Systems

We thank Atkins Tennis Center in Urbana, Illinois, for assistance in providing the location for the photo shoot for this book.

Human Kinetics books are available at special discounts for bulk purchase. Special editions or book excerpts can also be created to specification. For details, contact the Special Sales Manager at Human Kinetics.

Printed in the United States of America   10 9 8 7 6 5

The paper in this book is certified under a sustainable forestry program.

Human Kinetics
1607 N. Market Street
Champaign, IL 61820
USA

United States and International
Website: **US.HumanKinetics.com**
Email: info@hkusa.com
Phone: 1-800-747-4457

Canada
Website: **Canada.HumanKinetics.com**
Email: info@hkcanada.com

E6008

Tell us what you think!
Human Kinetics would love to hear what we can do to improve the customer experience. Use this QR code to take our brief survey.

This is for my husband, Alan, and my mother, Barbara, who always knew I'd finish every page and every chapter on time while raising a puppy (which almost killed me), running a business, getting no sleep, and giving countless lessons. I am wholly indebted to them and to the following coaches, colleagues, and friends for their infinite energy, professional advice, loyalty, laughter, and unstinting help in the preparation of this book: Alan J. Burney, Lex Carrington, Joshua Warren, Rich Berman, David Hall, Rhoda H. Weinman, Justin Klug, Claire Marty, and the entire team at Human Kinetics. Thanks again.

Tina Hoskins-Burney

I would like to thank my lifelong coach and father, Art Carrington; my mother; my eternal companion and wife, Marria; my three children, Safiya, Noor, and Ibby; Bruce Carrington; Gale and Keith Quenneville; Hampshire College; and Michael J. Kittredge II and family.

Lex Carrington

Contents

Drill Finder

Drill Title	Level	Forehand	Backhand	Volley	Serve and Return	Lobs and Overheads	Offensive Play	Defensive Play	Mental Skills	Singles	Doubles	Page
CHAPTER 1												
1. Eastern Grip Technique	●	X	X	X	X							6
2. Continental Grip Technique	●		X	X	X							7
3. Semi-Western Grip Technique	●	X	X									8
4. Western Grip Technique	●●	X	X									9
5. Continental–Semi-Western Grip Technique	●●		X									10
CHAPTER 2												
6. Neutral-Stance Technique	●	X	X									13
7. Closed-Stance Technique	●	X	X									14
8. Semi-Open Stance Technique	●	X	X									15
9. Ready, Set, Split Step	●			X								16
10. Return of Serve	●				X							16
11. Open-Stance Technique	●●	X	X									17
12. Open-Stance Backhand Technique	●●		X									18
13. Crosscourt and Down the Line	●●	X	X									19
14. Open-Stance Backhand	●●		X									20
15. Baseline Rally	●●	X	X									21
16. Two-on-One Backhand Buster	●●		X									22
17. Buggy Whip Technique	●●●	X	X									23
18. Crazy-8 Groundstroke	●●●	X	X									24
CHAPTER 3												
19. Split-Step Attack	●			X								27
20. No-Bounce Scoring	●●			X								27
21. Approach-Volley Technique	●●			X								28
22. High-Volley Technique	●●			X								29
23. Low-Volley Technique	●●			X								30
24. No-Bounce Tennis	●●			X								32
25. Crisscross Volley Poach	●●			X								33
26. Chip Approach and Touch Volley	●●			X								34
27. Oscillation Volley	●●			X								35
28. Swinging-Volley Technique	●●●			X								36
29. Half-Volley Technique	●●●			X								37
30. Drop-Volley Technique	●●●			X								38

Drill Title	Level	Forehand	Backhand	Volley	Serve and Return	Lobs and Overheads	Offensive Play	Defensive Play	Mental Skills	Singles	Doubles	Page
CHAPTER 9												
99. Single-File Volley Approach	●									X	X	117
100. Crosscourt and Down the Line	●									X	X	118
101. Three-Hit Cycle	●									X	X	119
102. Singles Challenge	●●									X		120
103. Inside Ins	●●	X	X									121
104. Deep Shot Forehand–Backhand	●●	X	X							X		122
105. Up and Back	●●						X	X				122
106. Five-Ball Overhead Sequence	●●						X					123
107. Six-Ball Pattern Sequence	●●							X		X	X	123
108. Quick Volley	●●			X								124
109. Crosscourt Rally Attack	●●	X	X									124
110. Short Ball	●●	X	X									125
111. Rising Star	●●						X	X				126
112. Half-Court Hustle	●●						X	X				126
113. Approach Shot, Passing Shot	●●	X	X	X								127
114. Net Approach	●●	X	X	X								127
115. Attack and Smack	●●				X	X						128
116. Hot-Pepper Doubles	●●										X	128
117. Crazy-8 Volley	●●			X								129
118. Hit (the Volleyer) and Run	●●	X	X	X								130
119. Monkey in the Middle	●●	X	X	X								131
120. Doubles Hustle	●●										X	131
121. Doubles Approach Lob and Recovery	●●						X				X	132
122. Doubles Approach-Shot Challenge	●●										X	133
123. Attack and Defend Doubles Challenge	●●						X	X			X	134
124. Rotating Approach Doubles	●●										X	135
125. Australian Doubles	●●●										X	136
126. Monster Doubles	●●●										X	137
127. Quick Volley, Drop Out	●●●			X								138
128. Short Court	●●●	X	X									139
CHAPTER 10												
129. Five-Ball Recovery	●●						X	X				143
130. Serve and Approach Low	●●				X							144
131. Traction and Balance	●●						X	X				145
132. Make It or Break It	●●				X							146
133. Four-Hit Serve-and-Volley	●●				X							147
134. Three-Hit Baseline	●●	X	X									148

Drill Title	Level	Forehand	Backhand	Volley	Serve and Return	Lobs and Overheads	Offensive Play	Defensive Play	Mental Skills	Singles	Doubles	Page
CHAPTER 10 (CONTINUED)												
135. Hurricane	●●●						X	X				149
136. Mad Batter	●●●						X	X				150
137. Fast Grass	●●●				X							151
138. Return of the Big Serve	●●●				X							152
139. Hot-Pepper Singles	●●●									X		153
140. Advanced Singles Hustle	●●●									X		153
141. Four-Hit Passing Shot	●●●	X	X	X								154
142. Two-on-One Serve-and-Volley	●●●			X	X							155
CHAPTER 11												
143. Changeover	●									X		159
144. Tick-Tock	●●									X		160
145. Three-on-One Passing Shot	●●									X		161
146. Two Back–One Up	●●			X						X		162
147. Shadow Volley	●●			X							X	162
148. Everlasting Service	●●				X						X	163
149. Captain Hook Service	●●				X						X	163
150. Preplanned Set	●●										X	164
151. Hardcore Groundstroke Volley	●●●			X							X	166
152. Ball-Machine Stretch Volley	●●●			X							X	167
153. One Up–One Back	●●●	X	X								X	168
154. Volley Lunge	●●●			X						X		169
155. Serve-and-Volley	●●●				X					X		170
156. Razzle Dazzle at the Net	●●●			X						X		170
157. Patterned Net Rush	●●●			X						X		171
158. Scrambled Egg	●●●			X						X		171
CHAPTER 12												
159. King or Queen of the Court	●	X	X									177
160. Tennis Blackjack	●	X	X							X		177
161. Rotating Canadian Singles	●									X	X	178
162. Mini-Me Tennis	●	X	X									179
163. Singles Mining for Gold	●									X		179
164. Cheeseburger and Fries	●●									X		180
165. Rotating Singles	●●									X		181
166. Singles Attack	●●									X		181
167. Half Courting	●●									X		182
168. Singles Go	●●									X		183

Drill Title	Level	Forehand	Backhand	Volley	Serve and Return	Lobs and Overheads	Offensive Play	Defensive Play	Mental Skills	Singles	Doubles	Page
CHAPTER 13												
169. Knocker Tennis	●								X	X	X	187
170. Tennis Baseball	●	X	X							X		188
171. Sticky Situation	●●			X		X						190
172. O-U-T	●●	X	X							X		190
173. Shoot the Moon	●●					X						191
174. Staying Alive	●●									X		192
175. Flub or Scrub	●●								X	X		192
176. Rush and Crush	●●				X	X						193
177. Sink or Swim	●●										X	193
178. Quick Change	●●										X	194
CHAPTER 14												
179. Dingles Multiplayer Game	●								X	X		197
180. Doubles Serving Team	●●										X	198
181. Chip-Lob Return	●●				X							199
182. Rotating Doubles	●●										X	200
183. Serve-and-Volley-Volley	●●				X	X						201
184. Passing-Shot Medusa	●●				X							202
185. Half-Volley Passing-Shot Challenge	●●				X							203
186. Grip-and-Rip Overhead	●●					X						203
187. Team Merry-Go-Round	●●										X	204
188. Peg-Leg Doubles	●●										X	205
CHAPTER 15												
189. Point and Go	●●						X	X				211
190. Dark Shadow	●●						X	X				211
191. Run, Hit, and Recover	●●						X	X				212
192. Step-Out Volley	●●			X			X	X				213
193. Quick-Feet Alley	●●						X	X				214
194. Dexterity Ball	●●						X	X				215
195. Skiing for Skill	●●						X	X				216
196. Fan	●●						X	X				217
197. Shuttle Run	●●●						X	X				218
198. Court Circuit	●●●						X	X				219
199. Nonstop Rally	●●●						X	X				220
200. Spider	●●●						X	X				221

Preface

Ten years have passed since the publication of the first edition of *The Tennis Drill Book*. In that time I have grown a little older and wiser. Although my knees may not like playing on hard courts anymore, my spirit still does. As I readjust my tennis playing mentality toward my equipment, my on-court mechanics, my physicality, and my teaching methods, one fact remains constant: The fundamentals of the game are tested, tried, and eternally true.

I have witnessed tremendous changes in tennis, including the rules for tennis players under 10; the size and shape of the equipment used to train young players; the size, weight, and length of rackets for both juniors and adults; and new ways of training the body and the mind. I have witnessed serves and groundstrokes from male and female players at speeds in excess of 155 miles per hour. Balls are hitting every square inch of available court. When you think a point is over, don't blink; because of the current conditioning of players, every shot comes back harder, sharper, and with more spin than the definition of spin allows.

The United States Tennis Association (USTA) estimates that 25 million tennis players exist across 144 nations. Of these players, there are currently 1,814 registered ATP and 1,106 WTA registered professional players in the world. So should modern tennis techniques and the mechanics associated with the top pros be taught to junior or adult amateur and club tennis players? I think the answer lies somewhere within each player's needs and ability level. If you are a player with years of playing and lessons behind you and with the willingness and the ability to change old habits, then the answer is maybe. It depends on each individual player's wants, ability level, financial situation, and location. To become a world class tennis player who is making a living at playing the game is hard, and may even take a miracle. If you take the example of the Williams sisters, Venus and Serena, they had all of the cards stacked against them including locale, lack of equipment, and the financial power to travel for tournaments, but they did it anyway. Even if they hadn't become professional players, they could have easily gone to college on a scholarship or become coaches for amateur or professional students. Having a great foundation in tennis not only helps to solidify many hours, days, and years of fun exercise, but can also lead to meeting wonderful people, seeing beautiful places, and possibly lifelong job opportunities.

But first and foremost, creating a solid foundation of skills will always be the best way to help all players at all levels make tennis an enjoyable sport for a lifetime. Consistent practice using drills and games is essential for developing all players, including beginners, veteran instructors, and even ranked professionals. This book is a collection of the tennis drills, games, and tips that players and teaching pros need. Many instructors spend countless hours discussing what students will work on each week, figuring out warm-ups, and struggling to make practice effective yet entertaining so that students improve and enjoy themselves at the same time. This book frees you of that time and effort and provides you with what you need. Instructors and players don't have to buy 10 books to find 10 different types of drills or games. *The Tennis Drill Book, Second Edition,* contains a plethora of information that you can easily carry to the tennis court for a quick drill or game to suit any skill level, class size, or age group.

This book is organized so that you can quickly and easily find drills according to difficulty levels. It includes chapters covering competitive games, singles drills, doubles drills, strokes, strategy, challenging and simulated match play, and on- and off-court conditioning drills for young children, juniors, and adults. If you are a player, you can choose from a smorgasbord of drills whether you play with partners, team members, tennis friends, or the old reliable backboard. You can quickly find drills for working on a particular stroke, for practicing shot combinations such as serve-and-volley or groundstroke patterns, or for playing against a particular game style. The drills, games, and tips in this book will help you learn, teach, and even laugh at attempts to execute shots and perform. Instructor or player, beginner or professional, young or old, tennis can hook you for a lifetime, but only if you can improve, execute, and enjoy the competition.

Tina Hoskins-Burney

Key to Diagrams

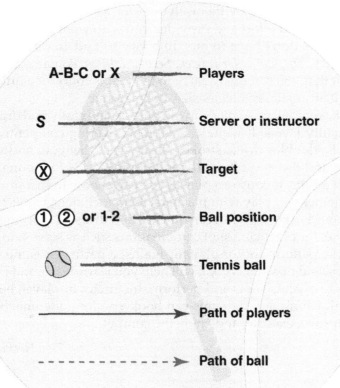

A-B-C or X ———— Players

S ———————— Server or instructor

Ⓧ ———————— Target

① ② or 1-2 ———— Ball position

🎾 ——————— Tennis ball

————————→ Path of players

- - - - - - - - - - → Path of ball

PART

I

Strokes and
Techniques

Since the turn of the 21st century tennis has made many advances. The sport includes a more diverse population, and over the years it has become increasingly exciting to watch. In the late 1990s and early 2000s, tennis enthusiasts pretty much knew who would win all of the four major tournaments; now, predicting the winner is not as clear. In recent years tennis has gained more momentum. Tennis took a dip in popularity in the late 1990s and early 2000s until the William sisters, Rafael Nadal, and a few others brought speed, agility, and color in dress, face, and play back to the game. Players are stronger, healthier, and more confident in their ability to win matches. To evolve and compete with the next generation, current players must constantly strive to upgrade their mental, technical, and fitness game.

Tennis is no longer only for athletes with natural tennis finesse; it is for everyone. The inclusion of the USTA's 10 and Under Tennis techniques and modified QuickStart Tennis equipment (shorter racquets from 17 to 26 inches in length and smaller nets), court sizes (30-, 60-, and 90-foot courts), and balls (orange, green, and red dot softer and slower balls) has encouraged more young players to begin match play. Players as young as 4 and 5 years old are playing matches and tournaments—and *crushing* the ball! Regardless of age or level, learning to master simple techniques can help players develop and improve their game. A tiny grip change can help players generate mind-blowing spins. Practicing drills can help them gain insight into how to perform the more advanced shots and strokes and, if they practice diligently, eventually put their *signature* on them. Players can only own a stroke or technique with constant practice.

Chapters 1 through 5 show players how, when, and why to use the various types of grips and stances and their vital role in applying various types of spin on the ball. Practicing the many drills and using the time-tested tips collected in each chapter will help players master the simplest and most complicated techniques. Players will also learn how to perfect their groundstrokes and volleys, how to own a penetrating overhead smash or bomb, and how to use serving styles that fit any style of play.

Chapter 1

Grips

Since the 1970s and '80s, grips and gripping techniques have changed dramatically. In those years, most players used the Eastern and Continental grips for every stroke, giving the ball lots of power but not much spin or variety. The current era of tennis commands a much more dramatic use of grips in order to stay on top of the changing pace and spin of the ball. Using semi-Western to full Western forehand and backhand grips is essential for competing against the pace, spin, and power that players use today. Changing the position of the hand or hands on the grip causes the angle of the racket face to change, thereby causing the ball to spin in a direction that creates topspin (forward), backspin (backward), or slice or sidespin (horizontal). To become more consistent and hit with controlled power, players put more topspin on the ball. To create a more penetrating and effective volley, players put backspin on the ball.

Players often overlook one aspect of gripping; that is, why the grips do what they do. Whether a player chooses an Eastern or full Western grip, the part of the hand that has greater grip control determines the depth of the shot. The palm has two ways to grip the racket: with the forefinger and thumb or with the little, ring, and middle fingers. Using the forefinger and the thumb together is called using the *pinchers*. The bottom three fingers are called the *squeezers*. To achieve greater depth with the forehand and backhand, players tighten the squeezers on the forward swing. For a sharp crosscourt shot, they use the pinchers. On the forehand, the squeezers are the ones controlling and tightening (which turns the grip into the Eastern forehand). On the backhand, the pinchers are the control fingers (index and thumb), and help add subtle underspin. For the serve, the grip is held loosely on the backswing. As the racket lifts to the point of contact, the pinchers tighten, rotating the forearm and snapping up to the ball for control, feel, and placement. For the volley, the Continental grip is preferred. However, using the squeezers (the last three fingers on the racket hand) and the pinchers changes the face of the racket.

When players investigate the various types of grips and learn how to find and use them properly, with practice they can eventually use them to build a more consistent, powerful game with reliable groundstrokes. Learning to manipulate the grips of today's tennis requires excellent timing, balance, footwork, practice, and loads of patience. When you first teach young tennis players (players under the age of 10) how to grip the racket, you'll notice that sometimes the most natural way is to use the semi-Western grip on the forehand and two-handed grip on the backhand. Let them go for it. Using QuickStart tennis balls, a mini tennis net, and smaller court dimensions, your young players will be able to hit with topspin within months instead of years. They will already have a greater advantage in the progression of their tennis game from day one.

The drills in this chapter will help players to make the small changes necessary to take their game to the next level. Above all, players must know that the best grip is the most comfortable one. The player or instructor must decide which grip works best for the stroke or spin the player is trying to hit.

Lex Carrington

Owner of Arthur Carrington Tennis Academy (ACTA)

I was a farm-raised tennis player, never receiving what I would consider a private lesson during my early years. My father was a two-time US Open Tennis competitor playing first as an amateur and then a professional. For me, tennis began at a young age. I was on the court beside my father while he taught private lessons in the suburbs of northern New Jersey. I played against the wall behind him for countless hours as he fed balls during lessons. Some of my most vivid memories growing up on the courts are of coaching my father's students on the side while my father was still coaching them. I had a different way of teaching tennis, one that seemed to work well with the players my father had been coaching for years. In retrospect, I feel like I was destined to be a coach.

I traveled down the same arduous junior tennis journey that thousands of young junior tennis players embark upon with great zeal and joy. I was ranked 35th nationally in the Boys' 12 and Under division. At that point I fully committed myself to improving my game and becoming a top national-level player. At age 15 I moved to the Nick Bollettieri Tennis Academy in Bradenton, Florida. Later I made it to the semi-finals at the USTA National Championships in Kalamazoo in the Boys' 18 and Under division, became a member of the 1992 USTA National team, and traveled and competed in all the Junior Grand Slams with the exception of Wimbledon. As a coach, the All England Lawn Tennis and Croquet Club would be on the calendar for many years to come.

Soon after leaving the professional tour I started my coaching career. One of my first students started with me at age 6 and went on to win the prestigious Les Petits As 14 and Under championships in Tarbes, France. This event is the premier international event for that specific age group. I have coached dozens of players who have gone on to play NCAA Division I, II and III tennis. I worked with and coached quite a few top-ranked professionals, including Vincent Spadea, whom I helped win two ATP Championships, achieve a career high ranking of 18, and reach the round of 16 at Wimbledon. I worked with Vera Zvonareva for 4 years and became her full-time coach while on tour for 2 years, during which time she won a Grand Slam doubles title, one mixed doubles grand slam title with Bob Bryan, and would later reach a career high ranking of 2 on the WTA Tour and compete in two Grand Slam singles finals. Yes, I am proud.

My passion has always been in junior development. I enjoy the technical side of the game and teaching the mechanics. During my 18 years of coaching, I have managed to gather together some helpful, simple, fun exercises and drills to help any player or coach achieve a better understanding of the game I love. Having had the opportunity to work with Nick Bolletieri, Stan Smith, and Nick Saviano when I was a player, I've come up with some cool stuff. I also picked up a few things from hours of practice with Andre Agassi, Jim Courier, and Björn Borg.

1. EASTERN GRIP TECHNIQUE

Objective

To learn and practice using the technique for the Eastern grip, which is the most comfortable, versatile grip for all ages and ability levels.

Description

The Eastern grip is the standard basic grip. It is good for beginners because it is the most comfortable grip to adapt to when starting out. In addition, players can use it with forehands, backhands, serves, and volleys without having to worry about a grip change. The Eastern grip is also known as the handshake grip; it is the grip most players use when picking up a racket for the first time. Players should test the grip by turning the racket so that the racket face is sideways to the net, not facedown to the court. When they grip the racket handle, they should do so as though they were shaking the hand of an old friend. Before long, the Eastern grip will become an old friend on the court!

Execution

Players hold the racket out in front in the left hand (or in the right hand if left-handed) and rotate the racket so that the face (strings) of the racket is perpendicular to the ground. They place the palm of the free hand flat on the face of the racket and move the palm toward the body, down the shaft of the racket until it hits the end of the handle (butt). Players wrap the fingers around the grip and spread the fingers slightly apart. The thumb and forefinger should lie almost directly on the top of the grip, forming a V that points toward the right shoulder (toward the left shoulder if left-handed). The thumb should lie across the top of the grip. Players should practice the Eastern grip technique not only with forehands and backhands but also with serves and volleys.

2. CONTINENTAL GRIP TECHNIQUE

Objective

To learn and practice using the technique for the Continental grip, which helps to impart various types of spin on all strokes except the forehand.

Description

Most intermediate to advanced players these days use the Continental grip, sometimes called the *master grip*, for almost every stroke in tennis except the forehand. This one grip can create monstrous topspin, slice, and backspin on all strokes except the forehand. When using this grip to hit a forehand, the racket face is wide open to the sky, and players can make only one type of shot. In addition, trying to manipulate the racket to use this grip for a forehand causes too much wear and tear on the wrist.

Execution

Players begin by forming the Eastern grip and turning the racket using the left hand if right-handed (or the right hand if left-handed). They turn the racket

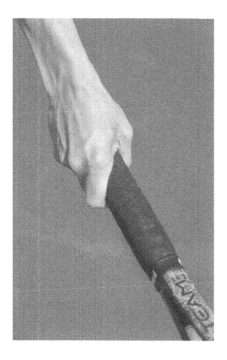

until it is perpendicular to the court or until it is in the twelve o'clock position. Now, right-handers turn the racket to the eleven o'clock position; left-handers turn the racket to one o'clock. Players wrap the fingers around the shaft of the racket and spread them slightly apart. The V formed by the thumb and forefinger should point toward the player, and the thumb should lie along the length of the handle. The bottom knuckle of the index finger should lie right on the top of the racket.

Tip

Players who are losing the ability to place the ball may be tightening the grip at the wrong time. They should check to see if they are tightening the grip just before striking the ball. The grip should tighten as the forward swing begins.

3. SEMI-WESTERN GRIP TECHNIQUE

Objective

To learn and practice using the technique for the Semi-Western grip, which helps many players more comfortably generate topspin on both the forehand and backhand.

Description

This grip helps players achieve maximum topspin and control over shots. Players at every level can use this grip because it is so close to the handshake grip. With just a slight grip change, most players can adapt to it with minimal frustration and add topspin to the ball. The semi-Western grip is also the preferred grip against hard-court baseliners because it permits quick grip changes between the forehand and backhand grips.

Execution

Players hold the racket using the Western grip and point it in the two o'clock position if right-handed, in the eleven o'clock position if left-handed. To achieve the semi-Western grip, players turn the grip back to one o'clock if right-handed, or between eleven o'clock and twelve o'clock if left-handed. When using this grip, right-handers must follow through into the left hand. Left-handed players must follow through into the right hand. The tracking hand (free hand, nonracket hand) is the hand that changes the grip. For example, right-handed players positioned to hit a forehand groundstroke when the ball is on their side of the net point to the incoming ball with the left hand, stroke the ball out to a targeted area of the court, and then complete the follow-through by swinging the racket into the left hand. Both hands should be on the racket and ready for the next shot.

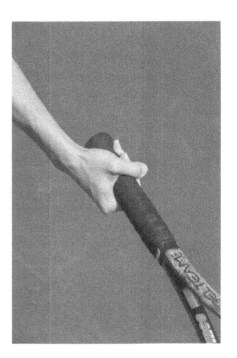

Objective

To learn and practice using the technique for the Western grip, which helps generate topspin on forehand and backhand strokes.

Description

The Western grip is excellent for the forehand and the swinging volley. Players will generate tremendous power and spin while using this grip. Because the racket face is closed, or turned down to the court, players must explosively brush up the back of the ball while hitting the ball from low to high to get it up and over the net. This kind of swing creates topspin. The faster that players swing or brush up, the more power and spin they create.

Execution

Players start by holding the racket with an Eastern grip. They relax the grip and turn the racket counterclockwise until the top of the racket is in the two o'clock position. (Left-handed players should turn the racket to the eleven o'clock position.) They wrap the fingers around the grip and space them slightly apart. The V formation should point to the right (or to the left for left-handed players), and the thumb should lie across the top of the handle. The grip should be loose until the backswing begins and then tighten when the racket strikes the ball. Keeping the grip loose prevents tension from interfering with a smooth motion.

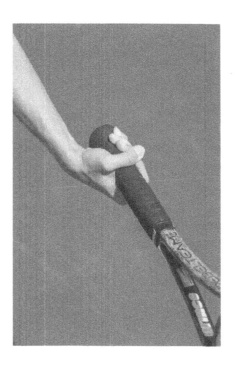

5. CONTINENTAL–SEMI-WESTERN GRIP TECHNIQUE

Objective
To learn and practice using a combination of Continental and Semi-Western grip techniques, which help to generate topspin with a two-handed backhand.

Description
When players use a combination of the Continental and semi-Western grips, they can generate heavy topspin, have maximum control, and develop wicked power with their groundstrokes. Players who prefer to hit with a two-handed backhand or forehand prefer this grip combination.

Execution
Right-handed players place the right hand in the Continental grip position and then place the left hand above the right hand on the grip. Making sure that both hands are touching lightly, they place the left hand in the semi-Western grip position. Left-handed players use the reverse process. Players must remember never to release a hand off the grip until they complete a full follow-through.

Variation
The Eastern grip, Eastern–semi-Western grip, and Continental–Eastern grip may be used for both the two-handed backhand and forehand groundstrokes.

Tip
Players may sometimes have to use different grips for the different types of balls hit at them on a particular surface, even by the same opponent. Players must be able to adapt to all situations. No single grip is acceptable at all times for each stroke.

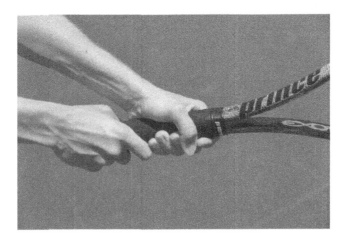

Chapter 2

Groundstrokes

When practicing groundstrokes, every player's primary objective is to work on better accuracy, control, and power. Sound groundstroking begins with the player's approach to an incoming ball. Players can use either a forehand or a backhand to hit groundstrokes from baseline to baseline or service line to service line inside of the mini-court area. Every part of the body is involved in returning a tennis ball successfully. For example, if players attempt to hit a shot crosscourt but the ball flies up and over the fence, their first thought may be that they are hitting the ball too hard or just don't have the finesse it takes to control the ball. The problem isn't too much strength or lack of finesse, it's the approach to the ball and what happens when players actually strike the ball. If players lift the chin or head while striking the ball, the ball will follow the head and fly high. If players straighten the front leg, meaning that they don't keep both knees down while hitting, chances are the ball will sail over the fence. Many factors affect the direction and control of the ball, which ultimately effects players' ability to hit effective groundstrokes. The first stop on the road to successful ground stroking is moving the feet and stepping into the ball while using the most effective stance.

A stance coupled with sound footwork is both an individual and a natural extension of a style of play. The stance for any shot is influenced by the player's position on the court, the difficulty of the oncoming ball, the grip, and the player's physical conditioning. Thus, four different hitting stances used in today's wickedly fast-paced tennis determine the player's potential level. During the 1970s and '80 s using the open stance in anything but an emergency was virtually unheard of, but the fast pace of the game today has dramatically reversed previous beliefs. One cannot play today's tennis using the stepping-across or closed-stance footwork to execute a counter against balls coming in at speeds greater than 100 miles per hour. The speed and power of professional tennis has dictated the need for players to adapt their games in an attempt to conform with and combat the intensity at which the game is now played.

Thus, the open and semi-open stances are products of today's power game. The widespread use of the semi-Western and full Western grips has allowed players to generate tremendous racket head speed from the semi-open and open stances. Players should adapt the use of both based on their personal style of play, use of various grips, movement skills, and stage of development. During match play, players must use a preferred stance and sound groundstroking in all sorts of difficult situations depending on the speed, spin, and direction of the opponent's shot. In any case, players should remember the basic rules for proper footwork and combine them with good, solid groundstrokes.

This chapter will help players become familiar with the four hitting stances. Sound groundstroking rules combined with drills will help players perfect their overall groundstroking (rallying) game.

6. NEUTRAL-STANCE TECHNIQUE

Objective

To learn and practice the technique for the neutral stance, which forms the base for all other stances.

Description

The neutral stance serves as the origin for all other stances. The neutral stance allows players in the early stages of development to experience shifting weight and body rotation toward the target area. The neutral stance provides the best foundation from which to execute follow-through and recovery from shots unless a difficult ball must be played on the run. In that situation players will most likely use the semi-open or full open stance. The neutral stance is also the preferred stance to hit both one-handed and two-handed backhands, because it allows players to move their weight in the direction of the targeted area.

Execution

From the ready position, players begin the backswing by rotating or coiling the hips, trunk, and shoulders simultaneously. Players begin footwork, stepping out with the right foot (if right-handed; left foot if left-handed) and shifting weight to the outside foot. Players step forward toward the center net tape with the inside foot (the left foot if right-handed; right foot if left-handed) and shift weight onto it before executing the forward swing. When striking the ball toward the target area of the court, they keep their weight on the front foot until after contact and remain balanced during the follow-through and recovery. Bringing the back foot forward  and around, complete with a ready hop, will help maintain a strong, balanced foundation as players rotate the shoulders and hips to recover.

Tip

Teaching or using the technique for neutral stance when hitting forehands and backhands allows players of all levels to learn how to benefit from shifting the body weight smoothly forward in the direction of the targeted area of the court. To aid in developing confidence in using this stance while practicing groundstrokes, use QuickStart court dimensions along with the orange or green balls to help slow the pace of the ball.

7. CLOSED-STANCE TECHNIQUE

Objective

To learn the technique for the closed stance and to identify the pros and cons of using this stance for the backhand or forehand groundstroke.

Description

The closed stance is the settled-upon stance when chasing down a ball on a full run for either the backhand or forehand. Players use this stance only when forced wide for a shot or when on the run and unable to set up for quick recovery.

Execution

Players should not use this stance unless absolutely necessary. The stance closes out the hips, preventing hip rotation into the stroke and precluding transfer of weight toward the targeted hitting area. This action forces players to take additional recovery steps before they can rotate their shoulders and hips into the shot. The stance also limits control of shots, reduces shot options and power, and slows recovery time significantly.

Tips

If players find themselves in a closed stance when returning a forehand or backhand, they should try hitting a lob to help recover and get back into position for the next shot. To avoid being caught off balance, which may lead to using the closed stance, players must remember to breathe. Breathing relaxes the entire body, permitting better and quicker footwork, more racket head speed through contact, and more pace and depth on shots. Breathing during and between points is the best way to combat the nerves all players feel when under pressure. Players should exhale as they begin moving the racket forward to strike the ball, and continue exhaling all the way through the shot.

8. SEMI-OPEN STANCE TECHNIQUE

Objective

To learn and practice using the technique for the semi-open stance, which is an alternative to the full open stance when time is limited.

Description

The semi-open stance is based on the same principles as the open stance. Players use this stance when they have little time to prepare for an incoming shot. Instead of stepping forward toward the net, players open up the step slightly more to the left (for right-handed players; right for left-handed players), load all their weight onto the outside hip (right hip for right-handed players; left hip for left-handed players), and uncoil explosively into the forehand or backhand groundstroke.

Execution

From the ready position players begin the backswing for the forehand by rotating or coiling the hips, trunk, and shoulders simultaneously. They step out and shift their weight to the outside foot (right foot for a right-handed players; left foot for left-handed players). As with the open stance, the key to the semi-open stance is how far players step into the court with the left foot. For the semi-open stance players step slightly to the left of the net tape with the left foot to maintain a solid foundation after striking the ball. Players should remember to keep body weight on the outside foot until after contact and remain balanced during follow-through and recovery. The slight difference between the semi-open and open stance is the length of the step forward into the ball with the left foot (for right-handed players; right foot for left-handed players) when hitting either a forehand or backhand.

Tips

For more control, players should hit the ball back in the direction it came from. Players must have confidence in their strokes to step outside the rally and change the direction, spin, and speed of the ball coming into the playing area at 70 or 80 miles per hour. To help build confidence in learning new stances, use QuickStart orange or green balls to slow the rally.

9. READY, SET, SPLIT STEP

Objective
To help players make the split step second nature.

Description
The split step is a dynamic move that takes players from the ready position to an explosive movement toward the ball.

Execution
Every time the opponent strikes the ball, players should split step, reacting as a sprinter does after the starter's pistol. The wider the split step, the better the player's balance. The player will split step (also known as a *ready hop*) every single time the opponent strikes the ball. In other words, during an opponent's serve, the returner does a split step the moment the server hits the ball. The moment the opponent strikes the ball on a forehand, backhand, volley, or overhead, the receiver should do a split step.

Tip
The split step should be performed every time the opponent hits the ball. If the player's feet lag, then they cannot get into position quickly enough to return the ball.

10. RETURN OF SERVE

Objective
To help players learn how to control the spin, depth, pace, and placement of their returns with more confidence.

Description
Practicing return of serve while using the open hitting stance will raise a player's game to new levels. This effective drill isolates this specific stroke and footwork and helps players focus on moving to the ball using this hitting stance.

Execution
Players practice hitting the return of serve using the open stance. The server hits medium-paced serves to the forehand and backhand sides. Players hit crosscourt past the service line and repeat the drill hitting down the line. Practicing hitting returns using the open-stance forehand or backhand will result in control of a higher percentage of points during the opponent's service game.

Tips
Use QuickStart orange and green balls to slow the pace so that players can more clearly see the various types of spin they impart on the ball and for the receiver to hit more accurate returns. To serve or return effectively, players should vary placement and spins. When players serve to the corners as well as down the center (T), they can keep the opponent guessing.

11. OPEN-STANCE TECHNIQUE

Objective

To learn and practice the technique for the open stance, which helps players achieve faster racket head speed to hit harder, with more spin and quicker recovery.

Description

The open stance is the greatest symbol of modern tennis. This stance is perfect for situations when little time is available to prepare; the combination of stepping out, shifting body weight to the outside foot, loading the hip, and turning the trunk lessens preparation time. Players can hit killer forehands and backhands from this stance, because they can load up on the outside hip and virtually explode into the selected shot.

Execution

From the ready position, which is the starting point on the court (usually behind the center [T] on the baseline), players begin the backswing by rotating the shoulders and hips simultaneously, stepping out to the right with the right foot (if right-handed; left if left-handed), and shifting the weight to the outside foot. With weight on the outside foot, players should remain balanced through the follow-through and recovery. Because the shoulders, trunk, and hips are coiled like a tightly wound spring, after beginning the stroke players will uncoil with tremendous speed. This uncoiling action helps players hit the ball way out in front of the body, which creates great control and power.

Tips

Players should avoid shifting the body weight too early, which results in pulling off the ball too early and causes shots to fall short in the court or in the net. Players should also remember to keep their nonhitting hand, which is commonly referred to as the *ball-tracking hand*, extended out to the targeted area of the court. This subtle but major adjustment is the key to acquiring height and depth on all shots.

Objective

To learn and practice the technique for the open-stance backhand, which helps players achieve faster racket head speed to hit harder, with more spin and quicker recovery.

Description

The backhand is the most natural motion of any of the strokes in tennis and is ideal for both single- and double-handed players. Adding the open stance to the footwork allows the backhand to become a weapon.

Execution

Whatever their size and strength, players must develop a smooth, fluid swing that is free from hesitation during any part of the stroke. The backswing should be one continuous motion, not a double pump or in some instances a double pump of the wrist. Simultaneous coiling of the hips, trunk, and shoulders produces fluidity, control, and power. Players must remember to load up their weight on the left foot (if right-handed; right foot if left-handed) and coil the hips, trunk, and shoulders. Players often transfer their weight from the left foot to the right foot too early during the stroke. This action results in pulling off the shot too early, causing mishits. To have a strong foundation, players must remember to turn the shoulder before the ball crosses the net and keep their weight on the left foot throughout the stroke. After contact they extend the arm and racket out to the target for better control and depth.

Tips

The two-handed backhand is a deadly weapon for balls that sit up (sitters). Players who prefer to play using the two-handed backhand grip should look out for sitters and then move in and crunch them. Players must refrain from peeking at their shots before they complete the stroke. Trying to sneak a look will result in loss of power and depth and may cause a mishit. No matter which stance or grip combination they choose to use, players must learn how to anticipate the direction, speed, and height of the oncoming ball. Players must be able to get to the ball faster, return the shot with a potent shot, and recover quickly to prepare for the next shot. Players will benefit greatly by using QuickStart orange or green balls to help slow down the pace of the rally.

13. CROSSCOURT AND DOWN THE LINE

Objective
To help players groove their groundstrokes, hit in a specific direction to a targeted area on the court, and focus on keeping the ball in play, thereby increasing consistency.

Description
Two or four players can perform this drill. One player hits forehands crosscourt to the other player's forehand. The second set of players hits backhands crosscourt to the other player's backhand. Then all players should switch positions so that the players hitting forehands are now hitting backhands crosscourt and vice versa. This drill isolates the forehand crosscourt shot and the backhand crosscourt shot by having a set of players hit only forehands or only backhands towards one another crosscourt.

Execution
Players take a position at the baseline or service line center (T). A server feeds balls. Players hit crosscourt past the service line to each other, remembering to rotate the shoulders, trunk, and hips together to get a smooth stroke. If there are only two players practicing this drill each player positions themselves behind the baseline or service line center (T). With a fed ball into play or a drop fed ball by either player, each player aims to hit the ball crosscourt to the other player's forehand side. Once players accomplish hitting 10 forehands in a row crosscourt, then players switch and direct the ball to the backhand side. They try to make as many shots as possible out of 10 and then repeat the drill hitting down the singles sideline.

Tips
Use QuickStart orange and green balls to slow the action down until players can get a sound rhythm going. A serious tennis player must have a potent forehand. At the same time, not every forehand must be hit at 200 miles per hour. The forehand should also be used as a controlling tool to manage the tempo and pattern of a point. A player can hit 5 or 10 or more shots to set up the point and then unleash the forehand weapon!

14. OPEN-STANCE BACKHAND

Objective

To improve timing and impart power and topspin from the fast uncoiling action of the lower body.

Description

When using the open stance and executing the backhand groundstroke, players must prepare quickly to set up for the incoming ball. This drill helps players accomplish a quick setup and an explosive follow-through.

Execution

Players take a position just inside the baseline and use the open stance while a partner serves from behind the service line. Players bend their knees and coil the upper body with their weight on the hitting-side leg. When working on quick hitting and recovery, players have little time to step into the ball. The open stance allows players to contact the ball sooner and farther in front of the body, leaving no time for an opponent to hit a return.

Tips

Use orange and green QuickStart balls to slow the pace. Good running shots are as much about timing and athletic ability as they are about textbook ground-stroke construction. When on the run, players should play it safe. A backhand topspin lob or passing shot may offer the best chance to stay in the point.

Justine Henin

Little Lady, Lethal Backhand

Justine Henin was born in Brussels, Belgium on June 1, 1982. She is 5 feet, 5.5 inches (166 centimeters) tall, which is considered short in stature compared with today's top 10 women's players. She plays right-handed and has a one-handed backhand. Justine was ranked number 1 in 2003. She won 43 Women's Tennis Association (WTA) singles titles and 7 Grand Slam singles—4 French Open titles, 1 Australian Open title, and 2 US Open titles. She retired once in 2008 only to return to compete again, but subsequently lost in the finals of the Australian Open due to an elbow injury in 2012.

Many top pros have described Henin as the best female athlete they have ever seen, the best one-handed backhand in tennis, and one of the most talented women to have played the game ever. In 2011, *Time* magazine included Justine in their "30 Legends of Women's Tennis: Past, Present and Future" issue. She is brilliance wrapped in a tiny package. In 2008, women's tennis welcomed in a new era of pure brute strength coupled with elegance from players such as Venus Williams, Serena Williams, Maria Sharapova, and Kim Clijsters. Justine still stood head and shoulders above the pack with her game style and fluid stroke elegance combined with an icy mental toughness. Justine had a devastatingly beautiful one-handed backhand and was like a chameleon in that she had the ability to unleash dizzying topspin, severely sharp angles, masterful slice, and wicked drop shots without the blink of an eye.

15. BASELINE RALLY

Objective

To learn to control the depth and speed of shots while in the open hitting stance.

Description

This simple, effective drill takes the pressure off players as they learn to control the depth and speed of their shots in an open stance. Players practice hitting past the service line, keeping weight transfer into the ball consistently forward and learning to keep shots deep in the backcourt rather than in the midcourt area where the opponent can move in and take control.

Execution

When rallying with a partner from the baseline while hitting the forehand in an open stance, players learn how to execute the open-stance footwork. Players should try rallying crosscourt, hitting forehands in an open stance, and remembering to hit the ball past the service line to prevent the opponent from moving in and smacking a winner. They should repeat this drill down the line. After mastering the stance, players can play out a few points. The first player to 21 wins.

Variation

To help slow the pace and to aid in developing a steady rhythm, use QuickStart minicourt dimensions for a 60 foot (about 18 meters) or 78 foot (about 23 meters) court along with the orange or green balls. Players can then practice returning serves using the open stance technique for both the forehand and backhand return of serve and the swinging volley technique while learning to control the ball in the midcourt area. Players should try to keep a continuous rally of 10 or more balls in play while using the open-stance technique on both the forehand and backhand groundstrokes.

Tip

Simultaneous rotation of the shoulders and hips creates tremendous power. When they set up to hit a forehand or backhand groundstroke, players should imagine that the upper torso is a tightly coiled spring. When the spring releases without hesitation, a smooth, powerful stroke results. If players interrupt the uncoiling by breaking up the fluidity of motion, the stroke will be choppy and cause an uncontrolled return.

Objective

To improve players' shot tolerance (how many types of shots a player can hit consistently), depth, and ball control off the backhand side.

Description

This simple, but disciplined, technique helps players develop a sense of ball control, direction, depth of shot, and stamina, while helping to develop a killer stroke by isolating the backhand groundstroke and forcing the footwork necessary to hit consistently crosscourt and down the line.

Execution

Players A and B start at the baseline on one side of the court, and player C begins on the opposite baseline. Targets should be placed wide and 3 or 4 feet (about 1 meter) inside the baseline in front of players A and B. This gives player C a visual target to hit toward in order to keep the ball deep in the backcourt. Any player can put the ball in play and only the singles court is used. Players A and B hit shots to Player C on the backhand side exclusively. Players A and B should have an imaginary line extending from the center service line to the baseline in order to segment the backhand side. Imagine a line drawn from the service line center (T) to the baseline center (T) on the opposite side of the court. This imaginary line will segment the court to help keep the ball on the backhand side of the court. Player C should hit backhands to both sides of the court, crosscourt and down the line. Play out the drill for 5 minutes, then rotate players.

Variation

Players can spice up this drill by requiring a set number of shots to be hit in the targeted area of the backcourt. This results in player A fully concentrating on footwork to maintain good positioning on the court and to obtain maximum depth on each backhand shot. Players try 5 shots to the backhand side of the court, then 1 shot to the forehand side. Repeat until the point ends.

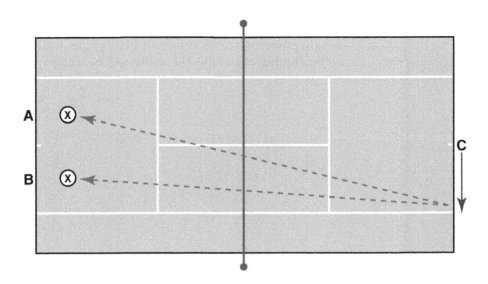

Objective

To learn and practice the technique for the buggy whip to impart topspin on the ball.

Description

Not for the faint of heart, this shot imparts tremendous topspin on the ball. Maria Sharapova, Rafael Nadal, Pete Sampras, and a whole host of players have hit the buggy whip, also called the reverse forehand. This stroke can be particularly effective when players have been stretched out wide and have no time to step into the incoming ball or shift the body weight forward. In this situation players must hit a shot from behind the hip and follow through along the same side of the body. Right-handed players normally follow through on a forehand out in front and to the left side of the body and into the left hand. With the buggy whip, the follow-through whips up past the right ear, which is on the same side as the forehand stroke. It's called the buggy whip because players have to boogie to get to the ball and then whip it to get it up over the net. This shot is also tremendously effective in helping a player dig or lift up a low, slow sliced shot to either the forehand or backhand.

Execution

The point of contact is late and low, so instead of driving completely through the shot, the racket comes up and over the same shoulder. The ball must be hit from an open stance or it won't work. Most of the body weight is on the back foot, and little weight transfer occurs because the stroke is wristy—just a whip of the racket. Players are on a full run, with no time to stop and set up, so they must whip quickly to lift the ball over the net.

Tips

Holding the finish is key. Players must use a semi-Western or full Western grip for maximum spin and control. Players must keep their eyes on the ball, focusing on its spin. If they don't focus long enough, they will mishit. To get a good look at the ball, players must keep their heads down and steady while focusing on the ball, not peek at the location where they want the ball to go. Lifting the head, chin, or eyes while stroking the ball will cause a mishit on groundstrokes, so players must keep the head up and watch the ball.

Objective

To build players' confidence, consistency, ball control, and stamina while using open hitting stances.

Description

Two to four players can do this drill. Players get a sense of how to move side to side while using the various hitting stances and directing the ball to a designated area of the court. No scoring is needed; this drill is for learning, not competing.

Execution

Players A and B start at the center baseline (T) at opposite ends of the court and start rallying. Player A hits every ball down the line, and player B hits every return crosscourt. The players try to keep 20 balls going without missing. They should not compete, because this is a learning drill that should be performed free of stress.

Variation

To slow the pace of the drill, use orange and green QuickStart balls. Player A takes a position at the baseline or service line. Player B is up at the net. Player A hits every ball down the line, and player B hits every volley crosscourt. They try to keep a steady, consistent pace on the ball, no winners. To improve consistency and ball control, they hit as many balls as they can. After 10 minutes they can switch directions. Players do not use scoring for this drill.

Tip

Players should try to kiss their shoulders. This technique has been phrased in many different ways, but the outcome is the same. They must continue stroking until they place the racket (grip) into the nonhitting hand and their shoulder and chin or lips have met (kiss) after the finish stroke. Players often fail to complete the stroke after hitting the ball. They think that once their rackets connect with the ball, that's all there is.

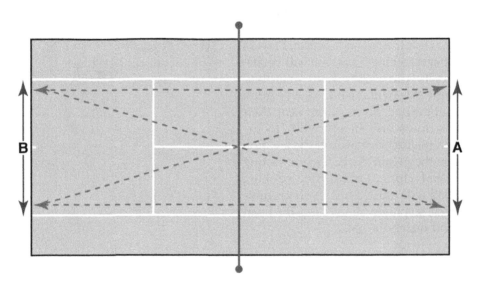

Chapter 3

Volleys

When two or more players are rallying back and forth across the net from baseline to baseline and a player achieves the goal of gaining control of the net by hitting an approach shot off the opponent's short shot, the next shot up at the net will be the volley. The volley is less technically complicated than the forehand, backhand, or even the serve, but being exact is extremely important. Volleying is about precise timing, footwork, and maneuvering.

Volleying used to be as easy as putting one foot in front of the other. The technique just wasn't as complicated as the many different steps needed to hit groundstrokes. The stroking technique of the basic volley is the same on either side of the body, except that on the backhand, as on groundstrokes, contact must occur further out in front of the body than it does on the forehand. When hitting the volley, a good initial split step is key to a player's positioning and balance on the court. The split step readies the player to react to the oncoming passing shot in any given direction. Nowadays given the excessive spin and speed of most shots, it will take more than a split step, cross step, and short, abrupt punch to return shots effectively.

The adjustments needed to hit an aggressive volley must be quick and precise. Once players commit to volleying, they must follow it through. If players back away from the net when in position to hit a volley or overhead, they will almost always lose the point. Players need to have confidence in their footwork and strokes to be successful when hitting this aggressive shot. The wrist and grip should be strong for a put-away volley; the grip loosens slightly for a drop volley. This is not a powder puff push or rally shot. The objective is not trying to keep the ball in play; it is to end the point—hit a *winner*. This chapter explains the styles, describes the technique, and offers drills that will help players successfully integrate volleying into their game.

19. SPLIT-STEP ATTACK

Objective

To help players acquire good volleying form, learn to anticipate the opponent's next shot, and react aggressively.

Description

To perform the split step, players bring their feet together momentarily as they determine the direction of the opponent's shot.

Execution

Players observe the position of the opponent's shoulders and speed and direction of movement. Players then split step so that the feet touch the court when the opponent strikes the ball. The key is figuring out whether the opponent is going to pass down the line, hit crosscourt, or lob. If players hit to the opponent's forehand, the opponent will be running parallel to the net with the shoulders sideways and set up to hit a passing shot down the line. If moving fast, players may hit a lob because they will be unable to generate power. On a short approach shot or first volley, the opponent will be moving forward with the leading shoulder pointed crosscourt. A crosscourt shot is likely. When the opponent moves back to cover a deep shot, players should move up to cover the net because the opponent's shot will be weak enough for players to close in and smack a winning volley.

20. NO-BOUNCE SCORING

Objective

To encourage aggressive play that will solidify volleying techniques used in doubles or singles.

Description

This drill creates monstrous confidence and anticipation of shots. When playing singles or doubles, players can score a point only by hitting a volley of any kind or an overhead. The ball may bounce to set up the points, but players score a point only if they take the ball out of the air.

Execution

Players play a regular game of singles and serve in the court they are serving in until the first point is successfully won. The serving player must continue serving until winning the service game. The first game may take up to 10 minutes. Players can play an entire set this way.

Variation

Players can play a 12-point tiebreaker or doubles using this method.

Objective

To give players extra practice on the split step before they hit the approach volley and help develop the feeling of closing in on the net.

Description

The approach volley can be hit on either the forehand or backhand side of the body. The approach volley is sometimes known as the *transitional volley* because in attacking the net, players may be faced with a first volley that they are not in position for or are not ready to end the point with. Players usually encounter this volley at the service line while attempting to charge the net either after a return of serve or after they serve and attempt to rush the net.

Execution

The approach volley requires an instant grip change to the Continental grip. When approaching the net, players should split step to stop the body from moving and hitting while running. They should step into the shot, keep the hips and knees down, keep the head steady throughout the stroke, and volley the shot well out in front of the body. Players should use the opponent's power, maintain strong footing, and direct the ball down the line or, if in the center of the court, down the middle. They close in and look to finish the point with the attack volley. An approach volley requires perfect balance and timing. Players can practice a series of serve and approach volleys or a return of serve and a move up to hit the next shot as an approach volley. They should try 25 serve and approach volleys and 25 return of serve and approach volleys.

Tip

When players are attempting to hit the approach volley, they must stutter step to slow their feet down. If they continue to run through this or any other volley, they will lose control of the ball, its direction, and the shot.

Objective

To differentiate between high volleys and overheads and to learn how to hit a high volley.

Description

Is it an overhead or high volley? It's somewhere in between. Taken on either side, forehand or backhand, a common mistake on a high forehand or backhand volley is to swing at it. When players are positioned at the net they must punch through this volley. They must be careful in swinging at this sneaky shot, or they will knock the ball right out of the tennis court.

Execution

The player takes a position up at the net, and a practice partner takes a position behind the opposite service line or baseline. In learning how to identify the high volley, players should alternate playing low volleys, shoulder-high volleys, and then high volleys, which they can reach without having to back up or jump vigorously. They should try to hit 50 low volleys, 50 shoulder-high volleys, and 50 high volleys, alternating between the forehand and backhand volley. They should then try a set of 150 alternating volleys, concentrating on moving forward so that they can successfully hit through the shot. They should keep the grip tight, the wrist cocked high, and the left hand out in front for balance if right-handed (right hand if left-handed). Players then punch or block the incoming ball.

Tips

Players should keep the racket cocked high above the wrist and lock the wrist to keep it firmly in place. Players should also keep their nonhitting hand extended out in front and finish into that hand after they hit the volley, mimicking a clapping motion. This action aids in balance and tracking of the ball and will keep the high-volley stroke short, sweet, and crisp.

23. LOW-VOLLEY TECHNIQUE

Objective

To help players develop the feel and confidence needed for hitting low volleys.

Description

This volleying technique and practice drill is for forehand, backhand, and two-handed backhand volleyers attempting to retrieve and hit an effective low volley. This technique takes patience, balance, and good hand–eye coordination. Just getting down low enough and holding the body steady while moving forward is hard enough. Players must combine all that with an effective return so that the opponent won't eat up the return volley.

Execution

If time is available, players should step forward into this volley using a neutral stance. A strong foundation with a deep knee bend is key to getting down to the level of the ball. Keeping the upper body straight will improve balance and allow players to use little or no backswing on the low volley. Before contact, the racket face is slightly open, using the Continental grip, to help lift the ball over the net with backspin. The backspin (also called *underspin*) will help the ball die when it hits the ground. The opponent will have trouble trying to get under the ball if the shot has a lot of backspin. The shot should have little or no follow-through. If players swing, they will hit the ball too deep and the opponent will be able to get to it and hit a passing shot. The racket should remain above the wrist throughout the shot for optimum control. Dropping the racket head will put the ball in the bottom of the net.

Tip

When faced with retrieving a low volley, players should try to hit high, deep lob volleys right over the opponent's backhand side. If the opponent is able to return it, the player who hit the lob volley should be up at the net waiting to take advantage of the attempted return and cream the put-away volley.

Bob and Mike: The Bryan Brothers

Twin Turbo Chargers

It's been said that the volley has become the dinosaur of singles in 21st century tennis. Because the game is so fast and players are hitting more stinging and precise passing shots, volleys—along with the serve-and-volley strategy—have all but disappeared except in doubles.

Bob and Mike Bryan are twins who were born on April 29, 1978. They are known as the Bryan brothers—and the best tennis doubles team in history. They have won multiple Olympic medals, 82 tour titles surpassing the legendary Woodies (Todd Woodbridge and partner Mark Woodforde, previously the best team in the history of men's doubles), a career Golden Slam, 12 titles overall, and ATP Team of the Decade (2000–2009). They will finish the 2013 ATP year as the number 1 team for a record of 8 times with more games, matches, tournaments, and grand slams won in the history of the game.

The Bryan brothers are known for their excellent net play, footwork, conditioning, rhythm on and off of the court, and their famous victory *jump bump*. I remember watching Bob and Mike when I was growing up playing on the tennis circuit down in Georgia. They were always full of energy, funny, loud, and just plain fun to watch. They would exhaust me before I played my matches. Their matches were so intense, on several occasions I felt sorry for their opponents. The brothers had unique way of controlling the court. They controlled the ball with soft, magical hands, as if they were born with rackets for arms. If their opponents made the mistake of hitting the ball short in the court, they were all over that ball and would dominate the net. No one could pass them up at net. No one could lob them easily. If by chance a lob did manage to reach heights that their long arms couldn't reach, they would just scramble back, retrieve the lob, and win the point anyway.

24. NO-BOUNCE TENNIS

Objective

To improve reflex action at the net, footwork, dexterity, and confidence in attacking the net. Players learn to create and recognize opportunities to attack and be successful at the net.

Description

This twist will sharpen players' attacking skills and force them to approach the net, because they can't score a point unless they hit a volley successfully.

Execution

Player A is positioned on the service line in the center, and player B is positioned on the opposite service line in the center. Player A starts the point by drop hitting the ball to player B. Each player serves 4 points or an entire regular-scoring game. The ball can bounce only on the serve. Players win points only by hitting a volley, swinging volley, or overhead. Servers switch after every game or every fourth point, and the game is played to 16 no-bounce points.

Variation

Use QuickStart orange and green balls as a warm-up or to slow the pace of the drill. Players position themselves on the baseline, serving in the regular overhand way to start the point. They can play doubles using this technique.

Tip

Serve-and-volley is an aggressive tactic that helps players get quickly up to the net to end and win the point. Quick hands and quick feet produce crisp, sweet volleys.

25. CRISSCROSS VOLLEY POACH

Objective

To develop poaching and volleying skills in doubles play.

Description

The term *poaching* means intercepting the receiver's return of serve. When attempting to poach or bluff and steal the volley in doubles, players must communicate with their partners and be proficient at volleying.

Execution

Players form two single-file lines behind the service boxes next to the center (T). A server feeds a volley to the first player in one of the lines. That player volleys down the line or crosscourt, then immediately crosses over from the right side of the court (if right-handed) to the left side of the court for a backhand poach volley and hits it crosscourt. If left handed the shot will be a forehand poach volley. Players should move diagonally forward with a quick split step for the poach shot. After completing the poached volley, they go to the end of the opposite line.

Variation

This drill can be used in cardio tennis training. Players divide into two lines behind the baseline center (T). Two servers feed wide forehands to one side and wide backhands to the other side (simultaneously). Immediately after hitting, players crisscross to the end of the opposite line. The server must keep players moving by feeding both sides at the same time.

Tip

The player at the net can bluff by pretending to intercept the return of serve but then return to the usual position. The bluff can elicit a down-the-line shot right back at the bluffer, who can make an easy volley.

26. CHIP APPROACH AND TOUCH VOLLEY

Objective

To introduce the beginning stages of finesse skills and in time create the rhythmic footwork needed for those kinds of shots.

Description

Touch shots (finesse shots) in tennis require players to develop a sense of being able to feel the ball on the racket. Developing good touch (feel) adds a new dimension to any player's game. This technique affords players more placement strategy than just plain smacking the ball 100 percent of the time. Placement more than power wins points, not the other way around.

Execution

Players form two lines—one line behind the deuce court and the other behind the advantage-court. The first player in the deuce line hits an approach shot fed in by a server down the singles sideline. The player then moves diagonally forward to approach the net and hits a touch volley. The player then proceeds to the end of the advantage-court line. One side hits a forehand approach and a backhand touch volley crosscourt, and the other side hits a backhand approach with a forehand touch volley. Players can start the drill slowly and gradually increase the pace of the rotation to work on developing a quick split step and close in diagonally to the net to hit the volley.

Tip

All players should remember that developing a touch game or finesse game makes any player a smarter and more dangerous competitor to reckon with.

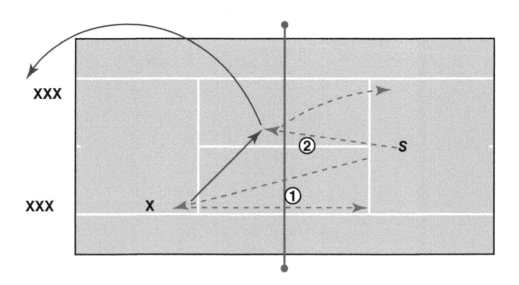

Objective

To develop quick rhythmic footwork, fast reaction to the ball, change of direction with recovery, volley placement, and sound groundstroking.

Description

Running wide for alternating forehands and backhands is called *oscillation*. This drill helps players improve volley skills, groundstroking skills, footwork, and consistency.

Execution

Player A takes a position behind the baseline, and player B plays the net. Player A hits groundstrokes down the line only, and player B, the volleyer, hits crosscourt only. Both players move with the ball or shot. Player A hits a forehand down the line to player B's backhand volley (if player B is right-handed). Player B volleys crosscourt to player A's backhand. Player A returns a backhand shot down the line to players B's forehand volley. Player B volleys this shot crosscourt again. They keep this pattern going as long as they can. Because this is a consistency drill, players do not keep score. Rotation is optional.

Variations

Player A is behind the baseline, and player B is up at the net. Both players use only one side of the court and return to the center (T) each time after hitting. The volleyer hits forehand volleys to the baseline player's backhand. They rotate positions. Another variation is for the player or players in line behind the baseline to start at the center (T). A server positioned at the net on the other side feeds alternating shots to the player's forehand and backhand.

Tip

The racket face controls the direction of shots. The ball goes in the direction the strings are facing, because it bounces off the racket at right angles.

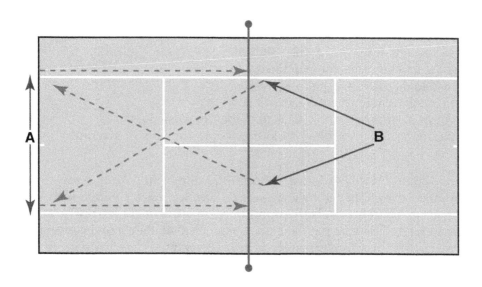

28. SWINGING-VOLLEY TECHNIQUE

Objective

To learn to hit swinging volleys aggressively, with topspin and power, when trying to hit an outright winner.

Description

Not for the cowardly, this aggressive and offensive forehand and backhand weapon occurs out of a rally when players step into the area known as no-man's-land to pick off a deep groundstroke in the air. The difference between this shot and the classic volley is that the racket head is not cocked high above the wrist and the shot is hit with tremendous topspin. It's easier to think of this shot as a groundstroke from the midcourt taken out of the air before the ball bounces, and hit only with mind-numbing speed, topspin, and confidence.

Execution

The grip should be semi-Western to full Western. When moving into the mid-court area to attempt this stroke, players should not hesitate in coming forward. Right-handed players attempting to hit a forehand swinging volley should coil the shoulders, trunk, and hips while moving forward. They position the left hand out in front to track the ball and keep weight and momentum moving forward. The right elbow should be close to the body to shorten the backswing. The racket face is slightly closed; the top of the racket head is lower than the wrist. Once within hitting range, players should go ahead and let loose into the ball, remembering to keep the wrist loose to put lots of topspin on the shot. Players should accelerate on contact way out in front of the body with a complete follow-through. If they push the ball from inside the baseline area, the opponent will have a field day. Because of the aggressive nature of the technique, confidence is key.

Encourage players not to hold back once they've mastered the basics. After hitting the swinging volley, players close to the net for a possible return.

Tips

Players should remember to use the semi-Western or full Western grip when hitting this stroke. They should be sure to practice this technique with both forehands and backhands. Perhaps most important, acceleration is a must! No bones about it, if players pat the ball or push the ball, they may be eating the ball later. After the swinging volley is hit, players must close in on the net for a possible return shot.

Objective

To develop the timing, footwork, hand–eye coordination, and confidence to hit the half volley.

Description

The half volley, especially the forehand half volley, is one of the most difficult shots in tennis. The half volley is a stroke that players are forced to hit when the ball is aimed at their feet. It mimics a hard-hit grounder in baseball that bounces at the feet of the shortstop. The half volley is somewhere between a volley and a groundstroke. Essentially, this means that players take neither a full groundstroke swing nor an abrupt punch-volley stroke. Players normally don't choose to hit this shot. It chooses them, so they must be prepared!

Execution

Usually this shot happens when players are moving forward to hit an approach volley, but it can happen anywhere on the court. Players must move to the ball and not wait for it to come to them. They must keep their eyes locked in on the ball and not look away as it lands immediately in front of the feet. The shot demands perfect timing and must be hit in front of the body. Players should be positioned as low as the ball is and hold the position until the ball leaves the racket. Attempting to stand up or lift up while executing this shot will cause the ball to go into the net. By staying down and steady, players will never be surprised by the half volley.

Tip

Because the half volley is a defensive shot, the best play is to block the ball back deep and then move closer to the net. Players should hit the shot out in front, stutter or split step, and keep moving to the ball.

Objective

To develop the finesse and footwork needed in order to hit a drop volley.

Description

For forehand, backhand, and two-handed volleyers, the drop volley can be a valuable shot. This volley is especially useful when the opponent takes a position deep behind the baseline or uses an extreme Western grip and has trouble switching or moving forward. A drop volley works very well because it forces the opponent to respect the player's use of finesse and touch shots in the short court area.

Execution

For this volley, players must incorporate the catch concept. Just as a baseball glove absorbs the pace of the ball on a catch, the face of the racket can absorb the pace of the ball. Players must be prepared at the contact point for the volley and eliminate any forward movement that would create a follow-through. When contacting the ball, players should allow the grip and wrist to flex with just enough power to send the ball a few feet over the net. Players should practice using the technique for the forehand and backhand drop volley by hitting sharp angles  to a specified area on the court. Attempting to use this technique before gaining confidence when executing the drop volley may lead to a mishit and will allow the opponent to move in and take advantage of the attempted shot and point. This shot requires a lot of practice to build up the confidence and touch needed for successful execution.

Tip

The drop volley is one of those finesse shots that take many hours of hitting to perfect. The key to hitting an effective drop volley is to loosen the grip just before impact and make sure that the opponent is way off balance. Otherwise, the opponent will read the shot and blast a passing shot for a winner.

Chapter 4

Serves and Returns

In a big match no shot is more important than the serve. It is the stroke that puts the ball in play and is the quickest, most devastating way to win a point. Executed properly, it is a valuable offensive weapon. To be successful in tennis, players must have an effective serve. The more points players win with the serve, the harder it will be to beat them. For example, a well-placed serve up the middle of the service box dictates where the opponent will most likely hit the return. A wide serve to the forehand or backhand can open the court up for an easy volley winner.

Unfortunately, players generally spend little time developing this important stroke. The most successful servers on the professional tour have put in thousands of hours practicing every aspect of serving from tossing, standing, bending, and exploding up and into the serve to experimenting with grips. These players all use a similar technique that helps them generate unbelievable spins and speed. By arranging their bodies under the toss and angling themselves as if they were throwing an upward pitch with an explosive drive up to the ball, they lean into the court using their entire body weight and snap the wrist to produce thunderous power. No matter the level of player or style, the serve can be the crucial key to determining the outcome of a closely contested match. Players should perfect each tiny step from ball toss, knee bend, launch, and wrist snap to the often-overlooked placement of the serve. Remember, the serve is the only shot in tennis that all players have complete and absolute control over, so it must be used skillfully!

The first and most important adjustment that players must make to learn correct service technique is the grip, which provides support to players' wrist when they are learning the basic service motion. Applying spin to the serve will help players control the ball and put a higher percentage of serves into play. Good servers also know that the contact point commands the successful serve and that by varying the contact point they can achieve different types of serves and spins. Players can use the clock method as a tool to compare where the toss should be visually (see figure 4.1). This example is for right-handed players; left-handed players use the reverse pattern.

Before mastering the techniques of the most successful servers, players must first learn the fundamentals of the stroke, consistent placement, depth, spin, footwork, and power. The accuracy that comes from intense practice is a critical building block in perfecting any type of serve. Developing a successful serve will take many hours of repetitive practice, drilling, and playing enjoyable, pressure-free games. Because the serve is so important, players must spend as much time as they can to perfect it.

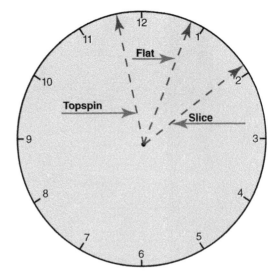

Figure 4.1 The clock method is a valuable tool to determine where a ball should be tossed on a serve.

Objective

To develop the foundation for all service technique.

Description

The flat serve is the basic service motion. The setup for this serve is the foundation for the more advanced serves. When placed accurately, the flat serve often results in a service winner, a weak return, or an ace! The tradeoff is that it offers less control.

Execution

Players take a position at the baseline with the feet shoulder-width apart. The lead foot is at a 45-degree angle to the baseline, and the rear foot is parallel to it. The hands are relaxed and at waist level. Players hold the ball lightly in the left hand with the fingertips and use the Eastern grip. With the ball facing up in the palm, players lower the arms, simultaneously taking the racket back and transferring weight to the rear foot.

While reaching up to toss the ball, players continue to move the racket back. At the end of the backswing, they release the ball with the tossing arm fully extended and fingertips pointed upward. The face of the racket makes contact directly behind the ball. Right-handed players strike the ball when the toss is in the one o'clock position. Left-handed players use the eleven o'clock position. As the forward swing begins, body weight shifts forward. As players complete the weight transfer, they hit the ball while simultaneously rotating the shoulders and hips forward to add fluidity and power. To add speed, they accelerate the wrist by snapping through contact. Players follow through by hitting up and out, letting the racket head come down across the body to the left.

Tip

To establish a rhythm, players can say "Toss" to themselves when releasing the ball and "Hit" at contact.

32. FLAT SERVICE

Objective
To solidify the grip and footwork needed for the flat-service technique.

Description
Players learn how to create more speed and power in the flat-service technique.

Execution
To get more speed with the flat serve, players take a position a few feet behind the service line. They serve the ball into the service box using the flat-service grip and the correct ball toss (one o'clock for right-handed players and eleven o'clock for left-handed players). Players practice increasing racket-head speed by accelerating up and into the ball and then out to the target that they have set up. Serves go to all target areas—down the center (T), down the middle of the service box, which jams the opponent, and into the far corner in both service boxes. The feet stay stationary except that the rear foot rises up onto the toes on and after contact with the ball. The face of the racket makes contact directly behind the ball. Complete the follow-through. Players serve at targets positioned at the center service line (T) 15 times, down the center of the service box 15 times, into the corner of the service box 15 times, and near the service line sideline 15 times using 75 percent power. Then complete the same exercises in the advantage court.

Tip
Tossing and balance are two essential ingredients for executing an effective serve, whatever the style.

33. SERVICE REPETITION

Objective
To develop footwork, dexterity, and coordination in all service techniques.

Description
Practicing the serve is crucial, and repetition is the key to having a reliable, consistent serve. When players do a task repeatedly, they can make it become second nature. In this drill, players pick areas in the service box to serve to and vary the types of serves to each area.

Execution
This service plan should be part of a tennis workout: Players designate a target in the service boxes to which they will hit spin, flat, slice, and kick serves. Players should warm up either with QuickStart orange and green balls or regular tennis balls, slowly increasing racket head speed as they warm up from the service line or baseline. They should try to hit 25 spin, flat, slice, and kick serves to each target in each box. Once they have mastered a skill level, players should increase the number of each type of serve.

34. SERVICE BREATHING

Objective

To help players create a fluid motion when striking the ball.

Description

Breathing is the key to promoting two good habits during any stroke. First, when breathing through the serve, players avoid the tendency to hold their breath, which can lead to overall tightness of the muscles in the arm, wrist, and elsewhere. Breathing helps relax the entire body, allowing more racket-head speed through contact and creating more power. Second, breathing during the point and taking deep breaths between points is the best way to combat the jitters players may feel under pressure.

Execution

Players can use this simple exercise while hitting groundstrokes or serving. Every time they strike the ball they should exhale. While playing out a point, they try to focus on their breathing. Slow and steady breathing is best. The rhythm I use for my students is the bounce–breath technique. They say "Bounce" to themselves when the ball bounces, and they breathe out loud when striking the ball. Maria Sharapova makes that sound when she's striking the ball.

35. SERVICE GEOMETRIC

Objective

To help players see the court differently while drilling and learning to hit to specific areas on the court.

Description

While learning to direct the serve, players need to visualize the service boxes as quadrants, or many different slices in one box. Visualizing a pizza pie is an entertaining way to accomplish this task.

Execution

When serving into either service box, players should visualize the box as half of a large pepperoni pizza; the pepperoni marks each target they want to aim for. To force the opponent out of the court, players serve wide to the slice closest to the doubles alley. Or, to play it safe, they serve to the second slice, which gives more room for error within the service box. If the opponent is preparing to receive wide, players serve to slice number three, straight down the middle of the service box (T). Players should serve 25 serves into each section of the service box on both the deuce and advantage sides of the court.

Tip

Players should remember that the follow-through is a natural continuation of the stroke. The racket should be moving toward the target area of the service box before its descent past the left side of the body (for right-handed players; right side for left-handed players).

Objective

To learn the importance of balance when serving.

Description

Without balance, players can't recover from hitting shots and will be unable to control weight transfer into serves, groundstrokes, or volleys, or recover after hitting overheads. Loss of balance also hinders the learning process, potentially causing frustration and loss of confidence.

Execution

Players take positions at the baseline or service line center (T). They stand in the natural service stance (flat-service stance), begin the serve, and check to see if the racket arm is raised in a back-scratch position; the nonracket hand is limp at the side. In this position the body is not in balance. Both arms should work together. Players should practice pushing upward with the nonracket hand after performing the ball toss. The racket should be raised and in the back-scratch position at the same time. This move will help keep the racket and players' head up and the body flowing together. Players should practice pointing or lifting up with the ball after tossing to hit a serve. Players serve 25 serves into the deuce service and repeat into the advantage service box.

Variation

Players can perform this exercise without the use of the tennis racket. Right-handed players should pretend to salute the back of their head with the right hand (left hand for left-handed players). The right palm faces the back of the head and right elbow is lifted above the right shoulder, while simultaneously lifting the ball-tossing hand (left hand if right-handed; right hand if left-handed) to get both arms working together. Players should then rotate their shoulders, trunk, and hips together and catch the tossed ball at the peak of the toss with their racket hand (right hand if right-handed; left hand if left-handed).

Tips

Pointing at the tennis ball is one of the most important things players can do to improve the accuracy and balance of the serve and groundstrokes. To maintain balance and keep momentum moving forward throughout the stroke, players should use the nonracket hand as the tracking and balancing hand. They keep it out in front of the body to track the incoming ball and push outward to move the body forward. They then follow through out to the target and into the nonracket hand and complete the follow-through. Players should also watch to ensure that their feet are shoulder-width apart. Most amateurs tend to stand with their feet too close together, resulting in poor balance and loss of power. Practicing the serve and chosen service style helps build the stroke and confidence needed to execute under competitive pressure. Practicing is the only way to make good technique permanent.

37. KNUCKLE BALL

Objective

To help players isolate the most important part of consistent serving—the toss and release.

Description

This tossing drill came by way of a former baseball fanatic turned tennis fiend. She suggested to one young girl who kept tossing balls behind her head to hold onto the ball with her fingertips to produce a smooth, fluid motion. By focusing on the fingertips and holding lightly onto the ball, she stopped using her fingers to manipulate the ball and toss behind her.

Execution

Upon releasing the ball, players should imagine that their fingers are a gentle water fountain spouting up and out at the height of the extension. They gently hold the ball in the tossing hand and lift up the tossing arm. At full extension they release the ball with the fingertips and hand, palm up. If they curl the fingers or hand while tossing, they will toss the ball behind the head. For maximum net clearance and control, players should remember to focus on the ball and keep the head up when tossing and hitting. Trying to sneak a peek at the serve will cause the head to drop too soon, resulting in a mishit. Players should commit to 10 tosses before each serve to start the point.

38. SERVICE MOTION

Objective

To help players acquire the fluidity needed for good serving.

Description

When serving, a fluid motion coupled with a high arc on the ball is important. A choppy service motion causes loss of power, poor placement, and lack of control.

Execution

Players begin developing the service by practicing throwing the ball into the opponent's service box. Either service box will do while players are standing on the service line. After achieving a reasonably high arc of clearance, players work their way back toward the baseline and notice the smooth, fluid rhythm that they need to toss higher so that they can get the arc necessary for maximum net clearance. When they are ready to practice the service motion, they start with the racket already in completion of half of the backswing. They start with the arm and racket above the dominant shoulder, (right shoulder for right-handed players; left for left-handed players), with the top of the racket head pointing toward the sky. They toss the ball and accelerate the racket head up and out on contact. After striking the ball, the lead foot should follow through naturally past the baseline. Making the ball and racket dance together is tough in the beginning, but practice will develop a more rhythmic feeling. Players should practice the full-swing motion first from the service line and slowly work their way back toward the baseline.

39. SERVICE FOOTWORK

Objective

This drill helps players release the rear foot more naturally, improving the rhythm of the weight transfer needed for good serving.

Description

The throwing motion used in playing catch mimics the serving motion. When throwing a ball to acquire depth, the release from the throwing hand is higher. Likewise, to get more height and depth with the serve, players must swing or snap up with the racket head and hit out using the same throwing motion. Players must remember to shift their body weight from back to front when tossing and then striking the serve.

Execution

Players position the feet in the natural service position, shoulder-width apart. In throwing a ball to a partner, they will notice that the rear foot wants to come forward with the body. They should go ahead and let the back foot come around, transferring their weight toward the target. By tossing the ball out in front and making contact with the hitting arm fully extended, they can bring the back foot around into the court after contact, naturally transferring body weight toward the target.

Tip

Rhythm isn't just for singing and dancing; players need it for the serve, too. Every step of the serve must work together like a well-oiled machine. If the service motion is jerky, then serves will be erratic—one in, one out. There are many techniques to help with maintaining your rhythm in tennis such as yoga or breathing exercises to help relax. The biggest key to maintaining good rhythm is learning how to control your nerves and to breathe smoothly through every stroke.

John Isner

The Big Fella

John Isner was born April 26, 1985 in Tampa, Florida. In March of 2013, he was the highest ranking American male tennis player. John's highest singles ranking as of March 2012 was number 9. He has had victories against players such as Roger Federer, Novak Djokovic, and Andy Roddick. He defeated Nicolas Mahut at the 2010 Wimbledon Championships, where he played a mind-blowing 11 hours and 5 minutes over 3 days with a score of 6-4, 3-6, 6-7(7), 7-6(3), 70-68 and racked up a total of 113 aces.

It has become known as *The Match*, and so far it is the longest professional tennis match in the history of the game. John's ability with the serve comes from his physical attributes and his hard work. It doesn't hurt that he is 6 feet, 7 inches (about 200 centimeters) tall with strong legs and a long reach with his racket. His wrist snap creates an intense kick to his serve. However, John attributes his serving success to his hard work and strong belief in his game. His ability with the serve comes from continuous practice, continuous match play, and many hours spent practicing his serve, which is his weapon of choice.

40. SERVICE TOSSING

Objective

To isolate the service toss and practice tossing at proper height.

Description

The toss is the most crucial part of the serve; it directly affects the success of the serve. A low toss can result in loss of power and little, if any, net clearance. Many players think a high toss causes loss of control, so they toss too low. They must practice this drill to obtain proper height.

Execution

Players hold the ball lightly in the fingers and smoothly move the arm downward and upward. They release the ball when the arm is at full extension; the fingertips point upward. The tossing arm should stay up a fraction after releasing the ball. Letting the tossing arm collapse too quickly after the toss can result in loss of power and short serves into the net. Players should practice the three types of tosses—topspin, slice, and flat—and try to use them during practice matches and real match play. See the diagram at the beginning of this chapter for reference.

41. WIDE SERVICE INTERCEPTION

Objective

To train players to move diagonally forward to return wide-hit serves.

Description

A serve hit into the corner of a service box will pull a player wide, off the court. This drill gets the feet moving in the correct direction so that players can counter the wide-hit serve and quickly recover to prepare for the return.

Execution

To return wide serves, players intercept the ball diagonally forward rather than sideways. When they incorporate the ready-hop (split-step) technique into the footwork, players will be able to move their feet diagonally forward to cut off the ball. When the opponent strikes the ball, players should be ready to attack the serve by giving a quick ready hop and a forward explosion into the ball at the same time. This move will cut down on the angle of the serve by taking it before it moves even wider. Taking the ball early also puts pressure on the opponent. The player's weight should be moving forward rather than sideways, thus giving more power with little or no extra effort. Players should serve 25 serves to the forehand side of the service box, 25 serves down the middle of the service box, which jams the receiver (opponent), and 25 serves down the center line (T).

Objective

To develop the correct toss, grip, and service motion to put sidespin on the ball when serving.

Description

The slice serve gives players more spin and control than the flat serve does but less power. The bounce is low and curves away from the opponent in the same direction as the spin. Players hit the serve with the face of the racket making contact at the two o'clock position (for right-handed players; ten o'clock for left-handed players). The slice is produced when contacting the back side of the ball, in this case with the racket face moving from inside to outside on a diagonal path when viewed from behind. When the ball hits the court, it will kick to the left (for right-handed players; right for left-handed players) and will stay lower than a topspin or flat serve does.

Execution

Players position themselves in the flat-service position and mirror the steps they take when serving a flat serve. When hitting a slice serve, players make contact by hitting the top right section of the ball. They place the toss out in front and slightly to the right of the body at two o'clock (for right-handed players; ten o'clock for left-handed players). After striking the ball at its highest point, they complete the follow-through.

Tips

If players are having trouble defending against a slice or spin serve, check their court positioning when they're returning this slippery service style. Players may be standing too close to the service line center (T), which opens them up to a serve sliced or spun wide.

Many players don't spend enough time developing the serve, let alone a spin serve. Working on the correct positioning of the ball toss and understanding where in the air the racket face should make contact with the ball will help players see and feel the classic spin serve. Players should watch the ball spin after they make contact and watch what happens to the ball once it leaves the racket and hits the court. The ball should cut into the opponent's body if the server is right-handed or cut out wide if the server is left handed.

Objective

To help players put a slice (sidespin) on the ball.

Description

Like the flat power serve, the slice serve can be an offensive service weapon.

Execution

Players take a position at the service line and stand in the flat-serve position. Using the semi-Continental grip, they toss the ball forward and a little to the right (if right-handed; to the left if left-handed), and turn the hitting shoulder away while transferring weight onto the lead (left if right-handed; right if left-handed) foot. They keep the hitting elbow higher than the hitting shoulder as the racket head falls deep into the throwing position. With weight shifted forward and the body held upward as the knees straighten, they throw the racket head edge on to the ball while pronating the wrist (turning the wrist and forearm together), shoulders, and hips simultaneously. Contact with the ball occurs at two o'clock, and the racket head accelerates on contact. The racket head, not the arm or elbow, must lead the downswing. When hitting slice serves, players must not toss the ball too far to the right (for right-handed players; left for left-handed players), because doing so will put too much spin and height on the ball. Players then complete the follow-through. Players should serve 15 slice or spin serves down the center (T), 15 slice or spin serves down the middle of the service box, 15 slice or spin serves into the corner of the service box, and 15 slice or spin serves on the deuce service box sideline. Then switch service boxes and repeat the same pattern of slice or spin serves in the advantage service box.

44. WALKING SERVE

Objective
To help integrate the entire body into the service motion.

Description
The serve requires total body integration between the upper and lower parts as well as between the left and right sides and a continuous throwing motion with the racket in hand.

Execution
Players hold two balls. They start in the alley in a comfortable shoulder-width open stance position; both feet point directly toward the net. Players begin the motion at the same time as stepping onto the throwing foot (right foot for right-handed players; left foot for left-handed players). Players proceed with normal service motion as the other foot comes forward in a normal walking stride. Smoothly after the second step comes down, players make contact with the ball. Upon completion of the first serve, players morph their follow-through into the next serve to be delivered; they go into a figure 8 motion, which takes them back to the starting point of their motion. It is crucial that at no point prior to reaching the starting point of the second serve should the racket stop moving. This insures that the toss is hit at the optimal point for players to maintain a smooth, continuous and balanced delivery. The second serve to be hit will begin in the same manner as the first, except the feet will now be in a walking stance (left foot in front for right-handed players; right foot in front for left-handed players). Motion begins once again at the same time as taking a step onto the throwing foot, and it continues on as the other foot comes forward, smoothly thereafter making contact with the ball. After the initial serve is hit, the players should feel a flowing sensation that naturally propels them into the next serve. The placement of these serves should be between the service line on the other side of the net and the baseline. The more advanced the players, the closer to the service box the ball should bounce, and it should bounce directly in front of them. Players are not aiming for the proper service box but rather the one directly in front of themselves on the other side of the net.

Variation
In order to really get the feel of a continuous flowing motion it is sometimes helpful for someone to walk alongside the server as they proceed, enabling them to hit numerous serves. One way of doing this is for players to begin at the back of the court, starting the walking serve with the intention of hitting their last serve from their normal starting position.

Tip
Players should hold the number of balls that are appropriate for them. Usually taller players have longer fingers, so they can comfortably hold up to four balls and still toss accurately. Some smaller and younger players with tiny hands and shorter fingers may only be able to hold up to two balls.

Objective

To work on quick reflexes, quick footwork, and anticipation skills when returning serve.

Description

When players are waiting to return serve, they must keep their feet moving in order to be able to react to any type of serve no matter where the serve lands. This drill helps players to anticipate what type of serve the opponent will hit, predict where the serve will land, and solidify the split step forward movement necessary to hit an offensive shot off the return of serve.

Execution

Two players, A and B, are serving to the returning player, C. Player C is standing 2 feet (about half a meter) inside of the baseline on the deuce service side of the court. Players A and B are positioned on the opposite side of the court facing player C. Player A is positioned in the corner of the service box diagonally across from player C, and player B is positioned just behind the service line center (T) behind the same service box as Player A. Players A and B take turns serving to all areas of the deuce service box toward player C. Player C must hit 21 service returns to a designated area of the court. Once 21 shots are achieved, players should switch service boxes and do the same drill in the advantage-court.

Tips

When returning serve, players should work on shortening their backswing on both the forehand and backhand. A shorter backswing helps players hit the ball off the rise as opposed to waiting for the ball to drop slightly, consequently pushing the returner back and off balance. Players must remember to keep the feet moving and the eyes forward and on the opponent's toss and racket head.

Objective

To learn technique for the kick serve, which offers more clearance and spin, helping to cut down on double faults and throw opponents off balance.

Description

The kick serve occurs when the racket face brushes the back of the ball with the wrist snapping out in a left-to-right motion (for right-handed players; right-to-left for left-handed players).

Execution

Players position themselves at the baseline in the flat-service position. This setup mirrors the flat serve with a slight twist. The upswing and the contact point with the ball are different. Players brush up the back of the ball while snapping the wrist up and out in a left-to-right motion (if right-handed; right-to left if left-handed). The toss should be placed at twelve o'clock right above the head. This location offers enough net clearance, leaving a slight margin for error. Players should remember to continue the snapping-up or brushing-up motion after striking the ball to give the ball net clearance and the topspin that causes the ball to kick up and over the opponent's head.

Tips

Backswings have all sorts of variations from how low to drop the racket head to how high above the head players should stop the racket head from dropping. No matter what, players must have the correct timing and motion to serve successfully. Players should remain relaxed from the start of the serve through impact and the finish. If players tighten up at any point during the progression stages of the service motion, they are thwarting their potential energy up through the racket and into the ball. This tension equals no power into the serve. Players should think of their arms as loose spaghetti or whips when transferring potential energy up and out through the racket and into the ball.

Objective

To take the basic flat serve to new levels by adding powerful lower-body technique to the mix.

Description

While tossing the ball and shifting body weight forward, players step up to the baseline with the back foot and launch up and into the ball with both legs together. This action helps generate a tremendously powerful serve.

Execution

Players take a position at the baseline or the service line center (T) and start from the natural service ready position. They mirror the steps of the flat serve but after transferring body weight forward, they simultaneously step up with the back foot while tossing the ball, place the back foot next to the lead foot, bend both knees, and launch up and out with the legs together. This sequence produces tremendous power from the lower body. Players strike the ball at the peak of the toss for net clearance and control, and then land on the lead foot. They complete the follow-through and recover.

Tips

The accuracy of the toss is especially important when adding fancy footwork to the serve. After players toss the ball, it essentially stays stationary, but the body will be moving all over the place. Players must therefore place the toss in the same location every time. They must practice tossing the ball at least as much as they practice serving the ball, if not more. A great way to learn how to hit up on the serve is by sitting or kneeling on the baseline or service line next to the center (T). This type of positioning forces a player to really extend the racket head up and into the ball before swinging out to the service-court area. Players who crave more pace and depth on the serve should try exhaling to help prevent a choked stroke and to smoothly accelerate up and through the ball.

Objective

To add power to the slice, flat, or kick serve.

Description

This serve is for players who prefer their weight under them and their feet close together. It is an explosive service style that allows players to utilize their lower body to the max during the service motion. This utilization of the lower body gives the squat launch serve its power.

Execution

The squat launch is a sweet addition to the basic service motion. Players follow the flat-service procedure but during the backswing of the racket, they bend the knees, launch off the balls of the feet, and hit the ball. They simultaneously toss the ball and bend the knees into a semi-crouching position. They begin the forward swing up to the ball and launch off the balls of both feet. At contact the body should be fully extended, the shoulders and hips should be rotated forward into the serve, and the feet should come up off the ground a couple of inches, not feet. Players land on the lead foot and complete the follow-through. This combination of steps creates an explosive serve and is thus an excellent technique for all players to have in their repertoire.

Tip

For the more advanced serving styles, players must learn to use their legs, hips, shoulders, trunk rotation, and wrist snap to generate powerful, aggressive serves. The squat launch serve motion is the ingredient that can change a mediocre serve into a powerful weapon. Once the rhythm of combining the footwork, legs, hip rotation, shoulder turn, racket pronation, and wrist snap is established, players are able to generate the speed and spin with added control and confidence to place the ball in the desired area of the service box.

49. CROSSOVER LAUNCH SERVE TECHNIQUE

Objective

To develop good timing, patience, and balance to provide more spin, power, and accuracy.

Description

This serve is the basic flat-serve motion with fancy footwork to provide more spin, power, and superb placement.

Execution

Players position themselves at the baseline next to the center (T) and begin in the flat-service stance. Players begin the forward swing while bending the knees and simultaneously shifting body weight forward. After completing the weight transfer, they launch off the lead foot and strike the ball at the peak of the toss for maximum power and control. Players kick the lead foot back, scissor the rear foot forward, and then land on it. They bring the back leg forward as they contact the ball and complete the follow-through to recover.

Tip

The Continental grip is the preferred grip for the crossover launch serve because it allows players to use racket-head speed more effectively and helps create the super spin that makes this serve unique.

50. KICK SERVICE

Objective

To help players learn how to hit an effective kick serve.

Description

Once mastered, this serve is extremely reliable because the spin creates a dipping flight that allows high net clearance. This serve is also an offensive weapon that players can use for a first service.

Execution

Players position themselves on the service line standing in the flat-service stance. A few targets are set up anywhere inside one of the service boxes. Players toss between twelve and one o'clock if right handed and twelve and eleven o'clock if left handed to achieve proper balance with the kick serve. If players have poor balance during the serve, the toss will probably be too far to the left (for right-handed players; right for left-handed players) and behind them. They start the downward swing and rotate the hitting shoulder while tossing the ball. As their weight transfers forward onto the lead foot, both knees bend and the racket head simultaneously drops behind the head. Players thrust the body upward while throwing the racket head up and brushing up the back of the ball. They snap the wrist up and forward so that the racket face connects with the ball crisply. After completing the snap-up-and-across action, the racket leaves the ball and arcs up and out to the right as the rear foot swings across the service line. Players complete the follow-through with the racket coming down past the right side of the body. The back foot comes down inside the court. Players should serve 15 kick serves down the center (T), 15 serves down the middle of the service box, 15 kick serves into the corner of the service box, and 15 kick serves on the deuce service box sideline. Then switch service boxes and repeat the same pattern of kick serves in the advantage service box.

Tip

Those having trouble getting kick action on the ball should hit left to right (right to left if left-handed) with pronation, be sure to use the legs, and really accelerate the racket head.

Objective

To help players learn how to use their legs to create powerful serves.

Description

The thrust launch service motion is the basic flat-service motion with some fancy footwork to help create power.

Execution

Players start in the natural service position (flat-service position), standing on the service line and keeping the feet comfortably shoulder-width apart for maximum balance and a strong foundation. While tossing the ball and shifting weight forward, they step up to the service line with the rear foot and bend both knees, because they must spring into this serve. Using the semi-Continental grip, they whip the racket head through the ball. They sit with the toss and then launch up and into the ball with both legs together. This action will generate tremendous power. Players should first practice this footwork pattern without the ball and racket to get the feel and timing of the thrust launch. Players should serve 15 thrust launch serves down the center (T), 15 thrust launch serves down the middle of the service box, 15 thrust launch serves into the corner of the service box, and 15 thrust launch serves on the deuce service box sideline. Then switch service boxes and repeat the same pattern of thrust launch serves in the advantage service box.

Variation

Players should practice by positioning themselves at the baseline and slowly starting to coordinate the swing motion with the use of the legs so that the left foot lands well inside the baseline. Finally, they use the legs and incorporate racket-head speed with the thrust.

52. SQUAT LAUNCH SERVICE

Objective

To help players learn to use their legs, hips, shoulders, trunk rotation, and wrist snap to generate powerful serves.

Description

This service motion adds pepper to the basic service motion by allowing players to use the lower body to the max during the service motion.

Execution

This serve is all about precision, so practice should first occur without a racket or ball. Players take a position at the baseline center (T), starting in the natural (basic) service stance. The lead foot should be at an angle to the baseline, pointed in the direction of the net post for both right-handed and left-handed players, and the rear foot should be parallel to the baseline. The arms should be at waist level; the ball is held lightly with the fingertips in the tossing hand. Players simultaneously toss the ball and bend the knees into a squat position. They begin the forward swing up to the ball and launch off the balls of the feet. At contact, the body should be fully extended, and the shoulders and hip should rotate into the serve. Players land on the lead foot and follow through. Players should serve 15 squat launch serves down the center (T), 15 squat launch serves down the middle of the service box, 15 squat launch serves into the corner of the service box, and 15 squat launch serves on the deuce service box sideline. Then switch service boxes and repeat the same pattern of squat launch serves in the advantage service box.

53. CROSSOVER LAUNCH SERVICE

Objective

To help players develop superb racket head speed, pronation of the forearm with a pronounced wrist-snapping action, and a better feel for using the Continental forehand grip; and, most important, to develop both the timing and the footwork rhythm needed to solidify the crossover service technique.

Description

The footwork is the most important part of this serve, and the recommended grip for intermediate and advanced players is the Continental forehand grip. Practicing the crossover footwork pattern from the service line helps develop the timing and footwork rhythm needed to make this advanced service motion more natural.

Execution

Players position themselves at the baseline and stand in the natural service stance (flat-serve position) using the Continental forehand grip. While tossing the ball, players simultaneously begin the forward swing while shifting body weight forward. As they complete the weight transfer, they launch off the lead foot and hit the ball at the peak of the toss for maximum power. They kick the lead foot back, scissor the rear foot forward, and land on it. Players complete the follow-through and recover. Players should serve 15 crossover launch serves down the center (T), 15 crossover launch serves down the middle of the service box, 15 crossover launch serves into the corner of the service box, and 15 crossover launch serves on the deuce service box sideline. Then switch service boxes and repeat the same pattern of crossover launch serves in the advantage service box.

Variation

Players progress to the baseline and continue to serve to targeted areas within the service courts. They practice their second serves from the baseline, using less spin but never forgetting the launch movement. The second serve should be almost as effective as the first serve. Players should do as the pros do—serve big, first and second.

Tips

Players should avoid lowering the dominant arm too quickly or bringing the front foot up to the baseline too soon. This action results in faults, mishits, and loss of power. The dominant arm should stay up longer to ensure high net clearance. The back foot should come up to the baseline simultaneously with the toss so that the hips and shoulders rotate smoothly and together. For maximum power, the dominant foot must land inside the baseline. Players should remember to complete the follow-through. This crucial tactic helps players recapture good balance and effectively get back into position and be ready for the return of serve.

Chapter 5

Lobs and Overheads

How do players counter an opponent who hits those annoying lobs? The answer is this: They must simply make the overhead a weapon, and they'll never be annoyed by those pesky lobs again. Lobs are a versatile and underused shot. Many players just want to hit every ball with as much power and spin as their racket, wrist, and bodies will allow. It takes hitting a few balls into the net or past the baseline to shake up some players and actually cause them to use finesse shots to change the tempo of the match.

The lob neutralizes power by immediately slowing the pace of the ball and changing the rhythm of the rally. It could be the single solution to more problems than any other individual shot. The doubles team of Paola Suárez and Virginia Ruano Pascual used this shot to help them retain the number 1 WTA doubles position for 3 consecutive years and rank second on the list behind Martina Navratilova and Pam Shriver for appearances in nine Grand Slam finals. The team used this shot to fend off the game's greatest doubles net attackers and powerhouses such as Rennae Stubbs, Lisa Raymond, Venus Williams, and Serena Williams.

In singles, the topspin lob is an offensive shot usually requiring excellent footwork on the executer's behalf and exploitable positioning or balance on the recipient's behalf. In the past 10 years, it has not been as big a part of the singles game as it was during the 80s and 90s, when serve-and-volley style players and net attackers such as John McEnroe, Stefan Edberg, Hana Mandlíková, and Patrick Rafter dominated the game. The game's best executioners of the lob were Chris Evert, Steffi Graf, Björn Borg, Mats Wilander, and Andre Agassi.

The lob does have its place in today's game. Players such as Rafael Nadal and Novak Djokovic often use this shot on the backhand side when seemingly completely out of a point and their opponents are in a finishing position at the net. Lobs can and should be used in an offensive and defensive way to change the rhythm of a point, game, and possibly the match. A defensive lob simply pushes the opponent back to the baseline to force the point to continue. An offensive lob can devastate even a top touring pro. A lob hit with major topspin can win a point, a game, and even the match; the ball may look as though it's going sail high and out, but it quickly and wickedly drops inside of the baseline and kicks up higher than the opponent can comfortably reach.

The overhead, a shot that is often overlooked by many coaches and instructors, should be addressed in almost every practice session at all ability levels. Players should first practice the smash with a bounce, then hit from all areas of the court. Then players can slowly introduce hitting the ball out of the air from all areas of the court.

Today, the lob and the overhead are weapons to be reckoned with. Lobs and overheads are no longer primarily doubles shots, and although the lob isn't used as much as it is used in doubles, singles players are using both shots to put tremendous pressure on servers, volleyers, pushers, and the baseline counterpunchers. Because of this, players must not neglect to drill the lob and overhead. They need to learn when to use the lob during points. Players need to learn how to build points—hit balls to designated targets on the court during a point to help create the opportunity to set up their opponent for a devastating overhead smash.

When they practice both strokes in gamelike situations, players will develop the confidence to use these master strokes whenever they need an easy point or need to change the rhythm of their opponent's game. Lobbing and hitting overheads can be a lot of fun, especially when players know when and how to perform the strokes. The drills in this chapter will help players develop tactics to use when building the perfect game plan for their style of game.

54. RIGHT EAR, LEFT EAR

Objective

To help players generate maximum topspin with the forehand and backhand lobbing technique.

Description

Players get the feel of the quick, wristy motion they need in order to hit this shot.

Execution

With racket and ball in hand up at the net, players attempt with the racket strings to press the ball against the net strap and brush straight up the back of the ball. The follow-through should stay on the same side of the stroke. For right-handed players hitting a forehand lob, the follow-through continues past the right ear. For the backhand lob, the follow-through continues past the left ear. The opposite is true for left-handed players. The quick-snapping, brushing-up motion will make the ball spin forward with tremendous velocity.

Variations

Players hold a ball several inches from the net strap and bounce it on the ground. As it reaches net height, they make the identical brushing motion and follow-through. Next, they back up a few steps, open up the racket face slightly, and repeat the motion and follow-through. The ball should have plenty of topspin and clear the net by 10 feet (about 3 meters). Players can also hit a topspin lob off a volley from a partner, attempting to clear the net player's outstretched racket by at least 10 feet (about 3 meters).

55. DEEP LOB

Objective

To help players learn how to lob high over any opponent.

Description

The deep lob is also called the *point-saving lob* or *defensive lob*. Two types of lobs exist—the defensive lob and the powerful offensive lob. This drill focuses on making them interchangeable.

Execution

Player A stands 4 feet (about 1 meter) behind the service line and feeds balls to player B at the opposite baseline. After hitting to player B, player A extends the racket overhead. Player B then tries to lob over the outstretched racket but within the boundaries of the court. Player A may move laterally but not backward. If player A is able to touch the ball, or if the ball is out, he or she wins the point. If player B hits the lob over player A and in the court, he or she wins the point. The players switch after 15 points.

56. OVERHEAD SMASH

Objective

To help players establish a rhythm for hitting effective overheads, and to learn to smash the overhead for a winner rather than merely put the ball back into play.

Description

This drill helps players learn the techniques needed to identify an overhead versus a high volley and to hit consistent, effective offensive overheads.

Execution

Players line up on the side of the court near the net post. One at a time, they sidestep out to the middle of the court, touch the net with the racket, and shuffle backward for an overhead hit by a server. After successfully hitting the overhead, they must close back in to the net, touch the net, and hit a second overhead. As the hitters develop more confidence and a good rhythm, they use oscillation and deeper overheads, gradually moving into randomly directed overheads. Hitters should always return to home base with a good split step (ready hop). Players should repeat this drill often to develop confidence and good footwork for hitting overheads.

57. LOB AND PASS

Objective

To help players learn how to respond and recover after failing to hit a lob high enough over the opponent.

Description

Learning how to recover from a poorly executed lob attempt while placing players in a gamelike situation helps to build the confidence necessary for defensive tactics.

Execution

Player A is positioned at the net, and player B is on the baseline of the opposite side of the court. Player B hits the ball to A, who must hit it back to player B, who, in turn, must hit a lob. Player A attempts to put the overhead away, and player B then tries to win the point with lobs or passing shots from the back-court. They play 15 points and then switch.

Tips

When hitting the overhead, players must not let the ball drop too low. The higher they make contact, the less likely they are to hit into the net. Also, players should always track the ball with the free hand.

58. TOPSPIN FOREHAND LOB TECHNIQUE

Objective

To help players learn how to hit topspin lobs off the forehand side.

Description

Hit properly, the topspin lob can be the most devastating stroke in tennis. It is usually a winner every time it is hit. Once it clears the racket and hits the court, it's virtually impossible for an opponent to run down the ball. By mixing up passing shots and topspin lobs, players will keep even the best net rushers guessing and off balance.

Execution

To hit an effective lob, the racket must make an extreme low-to-high motion and meet the ball in front of the body. The follow-through should finish behind the ear on the racket side of the head like the buggy whip stroke. This swing will generate the spin that's necessary to bring the ball down quickly once it clears the volleyer. The racket face should be slightly open with the bottom edge of the frame just in front of the top edge. Players should tilt the shoulders back a bit to ensure that the ball gets the necessary height. Generating topspin with a slightly open racket face works because this low-to-high motion is so pronounced.

Tip

A good topspin lob will come in handy on many occasions, but it's most effective when the opponent is serving and volleying or after the opponent makes an approach shot. The golden key to successful lobbing is how to properly disguise the stroke. Players should set up to hit the lob exactly as they would for any groundstroke and remember to use this calculated shot sparingly. If players overuse this strategic shot, their opponents will be more adept at reading when they are about to unleash it, and will be better prepared to run down the lob and counterpunch the attack.

59. BACKHAND LOB TECHNIQUE

Objective

To help players learn how to hit a topspin backhand lob.

Description

The backhand lob can be effectively hit with either a one-handed or two-handed backhand. The two-handed backhand topspin lob is particularly effective because it's almost impossible to read. Although players who use a two-handed backhand are usually more effective at disguising the lob, those who use the one-handed backhand can also be successful with this shot. Players who use the one-handed backhand can use the same routine in practicing their backhand lob as they do with the forehand, but they need to pay closer attention to the way they hold the racket.

Execution

Players with one-handed backhands don't seem to be as willing to hit topspin lobs as players who use two-handed backhands are. For a one-handed lob, the grip must be a full Continental backhand grip. The more exaggerated the grip and the more players roll the hand away from the forehand grip, the easier it will be to hit with topspin. After making an exaggerated low-to-high swing, players should finish the long follow-through next to the ear on the dominant side of the body. As with the forehand, players should tilt the shoulders back and open the racket face slightly while making contact. This action will get the ball in the air quickly. For a two-handed backhand lob, the preparation and the way players hold the racket in making the swing should be identical to what they use for the regular groundstroke. Although the low-to-high motion will be more exaggerated, players should finish in nearly the same follow-through position as they would on a backhand groundstroke.

Tip

Disguising the lob is key. The preparation should mirror the preparation for the passing shot. At the last moment, the player hits upward to give extra lift.

Objective

To help players recognize when a shot should be hit using the overhead as opposed to letting the ball drop and hit the court for a lob retrieval.

Description

The first component of an effective overhead is recognizing and reacting quickly to the opponent's lob. The basic strategy of the overhead is to win the point outright. Players can do this by simply overpowering the ball or by executing this technique with precision.

Execution

Players establish a solid position at the net and hold the racket with a Continental grip. An advantage of using the Continental grip when volleying is that when lobbed, players don't have to change the grip to hit the overhead. When the ball approaches, players drop the right foot back and begin to turn the hips and shoulders sideways. After completing the body rotation, players should be at a 90-degree angle to the net. Turning sideways when hitting an overhead allows players to uncoil, rotate the hips and shoulders, and then make a smooth, powerful swing. Keeping the feet close together will allow a quick jump up to the ball. When leaving the ground and exploding upward, players focus on the ball and start to bring the right arm up to make the swing. At this point players start to rotate the shoulders. The position of the racket and body closely resemble the position used in the serving motion. Players must keep the ball slightly to the dominant side (in the two o'clock position if right-handed or the ten o'clock position if left-handed). With the ball high above the head, they keep the arm loose and the grip relaxed so that the wrist can snap at contact. The wrist snap generates racket-head speed and brings the ball down into the court.

Tip

By studying the techniques of the Bryan brothers' overheads it has helped my game and my students' games reach newer levels. Watch video of their games to study their technique.

61. DROP AND LOB

Objective

To help players learn to lob after hitting a drop shot.

Description

Doing this sequence of shots repeatedly in a match can cause an opponent to fall apart. By using a drop shot and then a lob, players can force the opponent to sprint forward and try to hit an effective return and then backward to try to hit another. With the opponent then out of steam, the player should be able to hit an easy winner.

Execution

Players position themselves at opposite ends of the court on the baseline and begin rallying. Player A hits a drop shot on player B, who attempts to recover the drop shot. After player B retrieves the drop shot, player A should hit a lob over player B. They repeat this sequence 10 times and then switch positions.

Variation

This drill can be done using the mini court section, using QuickStart orange and green balls, and using the lob volley technique. For this variation, player A starts on the service line. The feeder player (B) hits a drop shot, which player A retrieves by hitting a volley. Player B lobs the next shot over player A's head, and player A retrieves it. Players repeat the sequence 10 times and then switch positions.

62. APPROACH SHOT, VOLLEY, OVERHEAD

Objective
To help the intermediate player (3.0 to 3.5) develop quick thinking and quick reflexes during match play simulation.

Description
This drill slows the action a bit. By isolating specific strokes and combining them into a pattern, players learn when and where to hit offensive shots during singles or doubles match play competition.

Execution
Players take positions behind the baseline. A server hits a ball to the first player in line, who must return it with a forehand or backhand approach shot down the line. Immediately, the player moves to the net to prepare for another ball from the server and must return it using a forehand or backhand volley. For the next hit, the server throws up a lob, and the player must shift diagonally and backward across the center service line and return the ball using an overhead. The player moves to the end of the line, and the next player waiting moves up to play.

Variation
A server feeds balls to the two players who are positioned on the baseline. The baseline players try to drive the ball past the two opponents up at the net on the opposite side of the net. Players can use any combination of shots to play out and win points. They play 11 points and then rotate clockwise one position at a time.

Tips
Players should use the approach shot when the court surface is fast to put pressure on the opponent, who will have less time to prepare to return the shot. Also, a wind at the player's back will add speed to the shot and cause the opponent to rush shots.

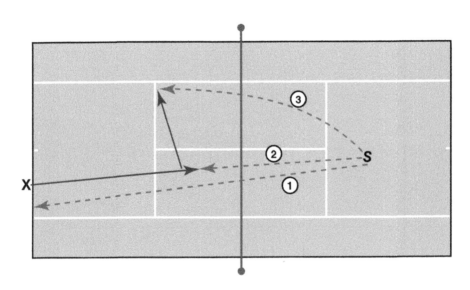

63. LOB VOLLEY TECHNIQUE

Objective

This drill helps players develop the disguised lob volley shot and learn when and where to hit it during a simulated singles or doubles match.

Description

The lob volley, a rewarding and spectacular shot, has been described as a reverse overhead smash. It's a sneaky shot that players must practice in game situations. The stroke itself is a low volley that is suddenly lobbed with either topspin or slice, usually from inside the service-court area.

Execution

Players A1 and B1, who are positioned on the service line, move out wide toward the single sideline. The server feeds to player A1, who volleys the ball to player B1. Player B1, positioned opposite player A1, lob volleys the ball over player A1 to player C1, positioned on the baseline at the center (T). Player C1 finishes the sequence with a lob over player B1's head to the baseline.

To spice things up a bit, four additional players can join in on the opposite side of the court and make this a doubles drill. Players A1 and A2 are positioned on the service line. Players B1 and B2 are positioned on the opposite service line, facing players A1 and A2. Players C1 and C2 are positioned on the baseline behind players A1 and A2. Two additional players wait to replace any player who flubs a shot. Player D1 waits off the court next to the baseline on the side of players C1 and C2. Player D2 waits off the court behind the opposite baseline. Players play 21-point games using this drilling method to start the points. Play doesn't start until the sequence of shots is successfully completed. After player C1 (or players C1 and C2) hits the lob over player B1 (or players B1 and B2), players are permitted to play out the point.

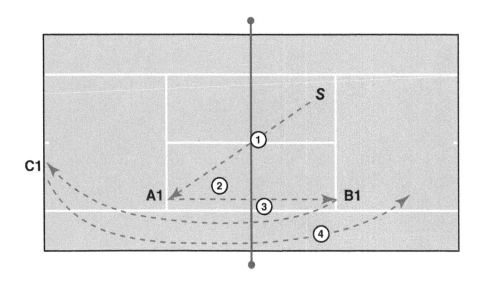

Tactics and Strategy

To play aggressive singles or doubles tennis, players must keep their cool. Players must take advantage of every opportunity to attack the net and capitalize on the opponent's mistakes. They must be prepared to counterattack when the tide turns against them, but how do they do it? What type of strategic game plan will work best? What *is* a game plan? Brad Gilbert wisely summed it up for James Blake when he said that every player has a style, learn it, study it, absorb it; every style has a weakness, find it, and exploit it.

Regardless of age or skill level, every player can play aggressive tennis. For example, one of my students marches his way onto the court in his size 3 tennis shoes and shouts, "Bring it on!" I've been coaching him for 5 years, and he's good, really good (for a 7-year-old). He approaches our game with the tactic of trying to run me into the ground, using a combination of shots that we have worked on in our practices. He is patient, waiting until he creates an opening to finish me off. He plays every ball as though it is the last ball of the match, and he never lets me see him sweat. There's no hesitation, no sign of nerves, just pure confidence. And even though I crush him, he plays as if he is winning.

All players young or old must come to each match with a game plan in mind. People never enter a sales meeting without a plan of action, so why would they play a club match or tournament match without one? The next few chapters explain how to develop a game plan for singles or doubles. Players learn how to play offensive and defensive tennis and practice the drills that will help them hone a signature style of play so that they will never be caught off guard.

Chapter 6

Offensive Play

Attack the net. Play the percentages. Take control of the point or the game—and win the match! The tactics and strategies available to tennis players are boundless, but how do players determine what is offensive tennis and what is defensive tennis? How do players control what happens with their shots or their opponent's shots? Before stepping onto a court, players must have a game plan in mind, a signature winning strategy designed specifically for them. A plan can be as simple as hitting a combination of shots to open up the court or as complex as attacking the net off every odd-numbered service point. Players should include in their plan ways of building up points to use their strengths, specific style of play, mental approach, and physical conditioning. In developing a master game plan, players should remember that offensive tactics in tennis are the ones to use when they clearly have the upper hand during the course of the point and defensive tactics are the shots that help them get back into the point or game—survival shots. Understanding various tactics, strategies, and styles of play will help players determine which tactic to use in any given situation. Observing those tactics, strategies, and styles in their opponents helps players know how to respond to them. For example, the following text lists some types of players and explains how to adapt to their style of play.

• **The sloth.** The slothful player is likely to have difficulty reaching the wide-breaking serve, so players should put more spin on the slice serve. This type of player hates to move, so players should really try to move him or her around. The crosscourt down-the-line pattern or drop shot–lob pattern can be effective. Whatever the pattern, players should be patient and remember that the sloth is a slow mover. Rushing their own play will only cause unforced errors.

• **Speed demon.** Variety is the key here. Players should keep this kind of player off balance by mixing up placement and spin types. Speedy will overrun balls, trip over his or her own two feet, and hit crazy, unpredictable shots. Players should keep this kind of opponent guessing and periodically throw in some soft stuff. An effective tactic is the three-to-one pattern—three shots to one side and then a step in to hit the fourth in the opposite direction. Players can run this pattern until the opponent is exhausted.

• **The hulk.** This type of player usually has slow reflexes because of big, bulky muscles. Players should try to hit flat, hard serves or slice the serve right into the body. This player can't move well because of bulky muscles, so any combination of shots hit far enough away should do the trick.

Players should develop game plans to deal with the styles of these kinds of players. The stronger a player's game and game plan, the more likely he or she is to succeed in upcoming matches. Players should be aware of their strengths and weaknesses and plan their strategy accordingly.

In the game of tennis, winning depends not only on how well players perform but also on how well they customize a strategy and overall approach to the opponent. When developing a game plan, players should keep in mind five basic offensive shots. When players develop each of the following shots, they will have a package of offensive strengths with which to build an overall offensive game plan.

• **Crosscourt shot.** To get the opponent moving right away, players should start the point with a crosscourt shot. The opponent will have to run more, because a crosscourt shot can be hit at greater angles. The more the opponent must run for a ball, the less chance he or she has to get set and transfer weight into the shot and the greater the chance of a weak return. By hitting to a strength with a crosscourt shot, players may expose a weakness to the other side on the next shot. By returning the ball crosscourt when out of position, players will have four or five fewer recovery steps to take to get back to home base.

Players should remember that the racket face controls the direction of shots. The ball will always go in the direction that the strings are facing, because the ball bounces off the racket at right angles. For example, when the racket face is facing diagonally across the net, the ball will go crosscourt. When the racket face is facing squarely at the net with the strings parallel to the net, the ball will go down the line.

• **Down-the-line shot.** The opponent who hits down the line will have to move a considerable distance to get to a crosscourt return. If the player can return the down-the-line shot with an aggressive crosscourt, he or she has an excellent chance to win the point outright.

On the down-the-line shot the ball travels a shorter distance and over a higher part of the net than it does with the crosscourt shot, so players must allow more leeway for error. They should hit this shot to change the routine of the basic crosscourt pattern, to hit at the opponent's weakness, or to hit behind an opponent who is running fast to cover the opposite side of the court.

• **Short shot.** The opponent who has an aversion to approaching the net probably suffers from net jitters, the tennis version of stage fright. Players can take advantage of this opportunity by hitting a short shot to draw the opponent in to the net. Players may also want to return short if the opponent is pulling them up to the net and lobbing over their heads or aggressively passing them. Players who are not effective when pulled up to the net may want to bring the opponent to the net first by using a soft, short ball instead of an approach shot. When the opponent hits a short ball (weak shot) and players must move into the midcourt offensive zone to return it, they can play it as a drop shot, which tends to pull the opponent up and out of position. In addition, short shots following high floaters can be effective change-of-pace shots.

• **Passing shot.** The most important principle in the use of passing shots is keeping the ball low so that the net rusher will be forced to hit it up, decreasing the opportunity to make an aggressive volley. Topspin balls drop faster than flat or underspin balls do. Therefore, players should know that most passing shots hit with substantial topspin are effective.

• **Drop shot.** Players who are comfortable with all the preceding shots have collected a formidable set of weapons of court destruction. Now they should learn to use one of the smallest yet most powerful shots in tennis. The drop shot can be extremely effective when playing against a baseliner who refuses to come up to the net, or off a return of serve (second serve) as long as the server habitually stays back. Players can also try it off a short ball that the opponent hits to them. Normally, players return deep, which is what the opponent expects, so the drop shot can catch the opponent by surprise. The drop shot can also work well off the opponent's drop shot, as long as the opponent is reasonably far back or off balance. If the drop shot is not a surprise, it won't work.

The drills in this chapter will help players build on their strengths and clean up some of their weaknesses so that their offensive game plan can take them to the finals of many tournaments to come.

64. ALLEY RALLY

Objective

To learn direction and complete control over ball placement, and to enhance the tight footwork needed to play tennis successfully.

Description

By isolating the playing area to rallying in the doubles alley only, players are forced to move with tight, tiny footsteps in order to keep the ball within the doubles alley.

Execution

Players A and B take a position at opposite ends of the court. Each player is positioned behind the baseline doubles alley. Player A drop feeds a ball within the doubles alley deep in the court (past the service line) to player B. Players try to keep 10 balls in play using forehands and backhands.

Tip

Being able to hit the ball to any place on the court takes hours of practice and confidence. Rallying in the doubles alley helps players concentrate on hitting to specific points and to acquire great touch or feel.

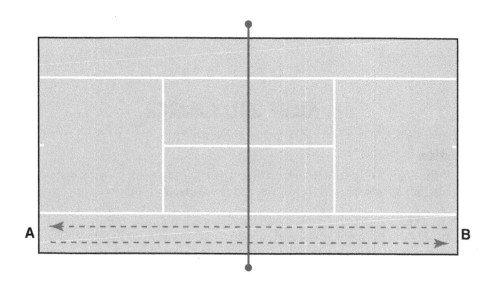

65. BALL FEEDING

Objective
To help players to learn how to shorten the backswing and create racket-head speed with control.

Description
Players who have watched teaching pros feed the ball have probably noticed that they seem to be able to do it all day without their arms falling off. They can perform the feed almost forever because they use a shortened backswing, trunk rotation, and fluid stroking. Feeding balls is a great way to get the feel of the fast, shortened movement of the racket head.

Execution
Players take a ball hopper onto the court and practice feeding to a partner, alternating between topspin, slice, and backspin and sending balls to various targets. They start by setting up cones or markers across the service line, and they try to hit each cone using all types of spin. They continue until they're accurately hitting most of the cones. The harder they hit, the shorter the backswing will become.

Variation
Once players are comfortable feeding to one player, they add more players and try to keep them moving and hitting without allowing them to stop. Players who can rhythmically feed several other players are on their way to racket-head speed perfection!

66. ALLEY RALLY MATCH

Objective
To take the Alley Rally drill to the next level by incorporating playing out points and using all tennis strokes like volleys, overheads, and lobs.

Description
Players play out points, games, and matches within the doubles alley. By isolating groundstrokes and footwork to the doubles alley, players gain a sense of control over ball direction and enhance footwork skills.

Execution
Player A takes a position behind the baseline doubles alley, and player B takes a position behind the opposite baseline doubles alley. Player A drop feeds or serves traditionally into the service box to player B. Players play out a regular scoring game—15, 30, 40, game, set, and match. Players should use all strokes in their repertoire.

Tip
In order to see improvement in their tennis strokes, players should practice low-pressure exercises correctly and consistently. Practicing point play and match play in the alley will reinforce focus, footwork, and aiming techniques.

67. ALLEY OVERHEAD ATTACK

Objective

To isolate the hitting area, lobbing area, and point playing area in order to enforce better focus, confidence in strokes, and footwork dexterity.

Description

This drill places player A up at the net in an offensive position while player B is at the baseline in a defensive position. Both players are playing in the doubles alley and must recover from the groundstroke, volley, overhead, or lob that the baseliner is striving to hit past the net player.

Execution

Player A is positioned up at the net in the doubles alley facing player B, who is on the opposite baseline. Player A feeds the first ball to player B deep in the doubles alley court. Player B must hit the first ball back to player A. Once Player B hits the first ball back to player A, the point starts and anything goes. The object is for player A to win the point with an overhead or volley, and for player B to recover from this defensive position by hitting a lob over player A's head and taking over the net to hit an overhead winner. Play 15 points then players should switch positions.

Tip

This drill is perfect for working on that devastating topspin lob and hitting topspin passing shots. When a player puts topspin on the ball, the ball dips down low because of the forward spin on the ball, which causes the opponent to bend lower than desired to lift the ball up, allowing a prime opportunity for the player to move in and crush the ball.

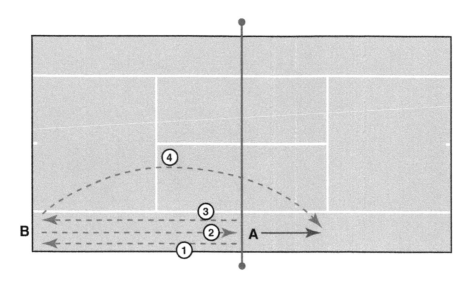

68. FAST SWING

Objective

To help players create a shortened backswing and higher racket-head speed for maximum power and control.

Description

To create lots of topspin with tremendous power, players must shorten the backswing to catch the ball earlier and farther out in front of the body.

Execution

Players begin with the racket head back as though they are about to hit a forehand. They hold the racket in a semi-Western or full Western grip. The wrist should be loose, but the grip should be tight. Players should practice whipping the racket head and snapping the wrist up and out through the hitting zone as fast as they can until they become accustomed to the feel and the motion has become fluid. Next, they incorporate rotating the upper body, the trunk, and the hips with the swing. Rotating the upper body smoothes out the stroke, allows an early catch of the ball, and creates tremendous momentum in the stroke.

Variation

Use QuickStart orange and green balls to slow the action down. When using the lighter-weight QuickStart tennis balls, players can actually see the spin of the ball because the racket stays on it longer.

Serena Williams

Voted the best woman tennis player in the world 2012

Serena Williams was born on September 26th, 1981. She is 5 feet, 10 inches (about 170 centimeters) tall and plays right-handed with a two-handed backhand. She has earned 30 Grand Slam titles and has become the only female tennis player to have earned over $40 million in prize money. Serena has 15 Grand Slam titles in singles, 13 in doubles with her sister Venus, and 2 in mixed doubles with various partners. At the time this book is being written, she is the most recent player to have held all four Grand Slam singles titles simultaneously (2002-2003) and only the fifth woman ever to do so. Her total of 15 Grand Slam singles titles is sixth on the all-time list and fourth in the open era behind Steffi Graf (22 titles) and Chris Evert and Martina Navratilova (18 titles each). Today, Serena holds the most Major titles amid singles, doubles, and mixed doubles. In doubles, she and her sister remain unbeaten in Grand Slam finals. Serena Williams is three-time winner of the WTA Tour Championship, and she has won four Olympic gold medals—one in women's singles and three in women's doubles. Serena ended the 2012 season with a WTA ranking in the 3rd position after a spectacular comeback from injuries and a life-threatening blood clot in her lungs.

All her life, Serena has been a fighter on and off the courts. She has been a spectacular focal point for female tennis players, taking women's tennis to levels some never thought possible.

Objective

To help players learn how to control the ball, feel the ball, shorten their steps, and to learn the short backswing it takes to create power and even more control.

Description

If players have trouble controlling the pace of the ball or are unable to keep the ball in play within the boundaries of the minicourt area, then they will likely not be able to sustain a full-court rally. Players must learn to develop the muscle control it takes to change the spin and speed of the oncoming and outgoing ball. People say that Monica Seles did this drill for an hour at a time when she was training at the Bollettieri Tennis Academy. This drill is one of the best ways to develop good ball sense, racket-head speed, confidence, and effective trunk and hip rotation.

Execution

Players are positioned on opposite service lines. They try to stay at least 2 feet (about 2/3 meter) back from the service line area so that they will have room to step into the ball. Players should have about the same relative ability. They try to hit the ball back and forth, keeping it inside the service-court area. Players will notice that to keep the ball in play, they must shorten the backswing, get underneath the ball, and use a tight brushing-up motion on the ball. If they try to use all arm with no racket-head speed, the ball will hit either the net or the curtain on the opposite side of the court.

Variation

Use QuickStart orange and green balls to slow the action down. Using light-weight QuickStart tennis balls helps players keep their racket on the ball longer, and because the balls are lighter in weight, players are able to see the direction the ball is spinning. Players should first work on consistency, so they should try to keep at least 25 balls in play. Players should then focus on placement by hitting consistent crosscourt shots. After players can keep 25 or more crosscourt shots in play, they should try to hit only down the line consistently for 25 or more shots. Once players build confidence and gain good ball sense, they should try a combination of the crosscourt and down-the-line rally within the minicourt area only. Players should practice this exercise until they can maintain any set of rally combinations with confidence, consistency, and control. They then progress up to playing points, games, and then an entire match.

Tip

This drill isn't for the unconditioned player. Players must be in good shape to execute this drill effectively and play the games within this area. For conditioning drills, see the chapters in part IV, Court Movement and Conditioning.

Objective

To help players who use a two-handed backhand learn how to transition between slice, topspin, and drive strokes.

Description

For many players who use a two-handed backhand, alternating between a slice backhand, drive, or topspin backhand can be a difficult transition. This drill will help players who use two-handed strokes alternate smoothly between the two while attempting to hit a slice, topspin, or drive backhand. Even though a player may use two hands on a drive or topspin backhand, most players use a single hand to hit a slice.

Execution

Player A stands at the net, and player B stands on the baseline on the other side of the court. Player A feeds the ball to the backhand side of player B. Player A maintains a rally with player B, who alternates between hitting a one-handed slice and a two-handed drive. Player A should start in the center of the court, just in front of the service box. Next, player A moves to the middle of the singles ad-court and finally to the middle of the singles deuce-court. This will allow for player B to successfully hit alternating slice and drive backhands and to work on hitting both shots down the line, crosscourt, and through the center of the court.

Variation

Player A and player B should switch positions to give player B a chance. This drill can also be performed using a two-handed or one-handed volley.

Tip

Players who use a one-handed backhand can execute all the same exercises simply alternating between slicing and driving.

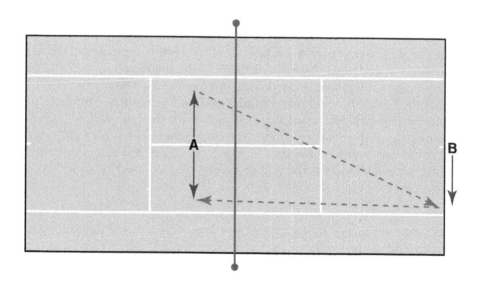

71. INSIDE-OUT FOREHAND

Objective

To develop the footwork needed for running around the backhand and hitting the inside-out forehand.

Description

The inside-out forehand is an aggressive shot that takes exquisite footwork, loads of confidence, and perfect timing. It is spectacularly devastating when hit correctly at the right time. In this drill, players learn and practice the footwork needed to make this shot effective.

Execution

Players work in pairs. Player A feeds a ball out wide to the forehand side. Player B takes a position at the center baseline (T). Starting from that position, player B hits the ball down the line with heavy topspin. The next feed is to the backhand side but a little closer to the center T and just inside the baseline. In a game situation, the opponent will think, *Aha! My opponent is going to hit a backhand.* But alas, the player runs around the backhand and hits an inside-out forehand into the backhand side of the court on the opposite side.

 72. SPANK THAT BACKHAND

Objective

To help players develop an aggressive pattern to add to the game plan.

Description

This drill isolates a killer tactical pattern. It specifically addresses how to use the backhand as a weapon. By setting up patterns for delivering every shot, players can dictate when to unleash the backhand to finish off the point.

Execution

Players work in pairs. Player A takes a position on the opposite side of the net from player B and starts by feeding balls to the backhand side of the court. Player A begins by hitting a few inside-out forehands. The next feed is to the backhand, closer to the center and a little inside of the baseline. This time Player A steps into the ball and spanks a backhand down the line. This pattern helps players open up the court by forcing the opponent to run wider and wider to retrieve the inside-out forehands. Once the court is opened up enough, players can smack a backhand for the win or run around the backhand and spank a forehand up the line.

Tip

Players should practice footwork drills to master the athletic dexterity it takes to run around shots, hit sharp angles, and recover.

Chapter 7
Defensive Play

Defensive tennis is all about the voice in the player's head. The most prominent voice in my head was my first coach and biggest fan—my father—until I met and worked with Arthur Carrington of the Carrington Tennis Academy, who is the father of Lex Carrington. I was lucky to have two wonderful tennis mentors there, and they are still in my life today. My father would always say the same thing to me before every match, and I still play by those same words of wisdom: *Have a purpose and a plan in mind for every ball you hit.*

Defensive play in a tennis match is a combination of good tactics, effective strategy, and true effort. You are not fooling anyone but yourself if you only give half effort. Players must be able to take advantage of their strengths, knowledge of their game, and knowledge of their opponent's' games when things go awry. They must create a defensive game plan that will allow them to make the most of all their strokes and tennis know-how. The more information players can gather about an opponent's capabilities, the easier it will be for them to select a strategic defensive game plan to attack the opponent's weaknesses.

Players should keep in mind that strategies or game plans must be flexible. When forced into a defensive situation, players should have two goals: Get the opponent's aggressive shot back in play, and give the opponent as little chance as possible to be aggressive on the next shot. The drills in this section provide some alternative actions for the defensive game plan to help get players back onto the road of playing their game. To paraphrase the saying, *Where there's true will, there's a way.*

73. WINDY DAY

Objective

To help players learn how to defend against the wind and play effectively on windy days.

Description

It's been said that windy day tennis is the great leveler of different ability levels. On a windy playing day a less skilled player and a highly skilled player may appear to be equal unless one of the two players learns how to use the wind to his or her advantage. The secret to playing on a windy day is that players shouldn't fight it—they should let the wind work *for* them, not against them. Whether playing with the wind or in a crosswind, players must alter their playing style to be successful.

Execution

When the wind is with players (at their back), their shots go deep while the opponent's shots are shorter. Players can be more aggressive in going to the net. When serving and volleying, they can attack second serves and go to the net. Using the offensive lob and following it to the net or using the defensive lob crosscourt adds to the margin for error. Players should anticipate shorter, slower shots from the opponent, especially on lobs, slices, and drop shots.

When the wind is against players, their shots will tend to fall short. Players should try to hit the ball a little harder than normal to keep the ball deep. They can use drop shots for an element of surprise, and they should avoid the lob, which may land short and produce an easy put-away for the opponent. A crosswind can dramatically change the path of the ball, so players must concentrate on their footwork and get into proper position for each shot. Finally, players must adjust the aim of their shots (left or right) to compensate for the crosswind.

Players should practice hitting topspin and backspin lobs, drop shots, and recovery shots. Players A and B take a position on the baseline opposite a feeder. The feeder starts by hitting high lobs to both players, one high lob to player A on their backhand side and one high lob to player B on their forehand side. Both players attempt to hit 10 topspin lobs crosscourt then switch positions. Then, players should hit 10 backspin lobs crosscourt. After each player completes 10 sets of hitting topspin and backspin lobs, the feeder should hit a combination of one lob and one drop shot. Both players A and B will hit a topspin or backspin lob, sprint forward to recover a drop shot, and sprint back to retrieve another lob and hit a lob with topspin or backspin. Try this drill 5 times in a row then switch positions.

Tips

On gusty days players should let high-hit lobs or overheads bounce before attempting to hit them. The wind will cause the ball to take all sorts of frustrating twists. Players must modify the service toss when playing on windy days. Patience, dexterity, and a mind of steel are just a few of the ingredients needed to tackle serving and hitting groundstrokes on windy days.

74. SUNNY DAY

Objective

To learn how to adapt individual playing style on bright, sunny days.

Description

Trying to serve or hit an overhead when looking directly into the sun can be painful and frustrating. However, methods are available for players to use on those beautiful sunny days so that they can still play an enjoyable game of tennis.

Execution

If the sun is directly overhead when players are trying to serve, they must alter the toss. They can try moving the position of the toss until they can see it, or they can toss slightly lower. When deciding who will serve or receive first and the opponent chooses to serve first, players should allow the opponent to serve first on the shady side so that they will have to serve only one game in the sun and can serve the second in the shade. When receiving an overhead, players should let it bounce. Players in control of the ball and on the shady side of the court should hit lots of lobs and attack the net often.

Players A and B take a position on the baseline opposite each other. Player A feeds a ball into play which must pass the service line to player B. Player B must attempt to hit a high ball—not a lob but a ball that will force player A to move forward to hit an overhead. Player A must let the ball bounce before hitting the overhead. Play 15 points using this method with player A starting the feed each time then switch servers.

Tips

If players are tempted to complain about bad weather, they should remember that conditions are the same on both sides of the court. When tossing to serve on a bright, sunny day, players should try tossing the ball at these points out in front: twelve o'clock, one o'clock, or two o'clock for right-handed players and the reverse for left-handed players. They shouldn't go for power, but more spin for consistency, and they should remember to take their time when serving. In a match, players have 30 seconds to serve both the first and second serves.

75. TIEBREAKER

Objective

To help players learn how to identify and execute defensive strategies to pull out one more point during match play. This can be key when playing a nerve racking tiebreaker.

Description

When players are faced with either winning or losing a match because the score is tied, they must play a 12-point tiebreaker. This drill helps players develop the fortitude it takes to compete in a high-pressure game situation.

Execution

Players must play points following the standard USTA-approved 12-point tie-breaker format. Players take positions and play a regular tennis match. Player A serves the first point into the deuce-court. Player B starts the sequence of two serves per point. Player B serves the second point into the advantage-court and the next point into the deuce-court. The next two serves go to player A, who starts the next serve into the advantage-court. When the players reach the sixth point, they switch sides. No rest period occurs during tiebreaker play. The player who reaches 7 points first, wins the game and the set. Note that the player who serves the last point of one of the 6-point segments serves the first point of the next one from the deuce-court. Players should practice this method until they are comfortable when playing close matches.

Ivo Karlovic

The Doctor of Defense

Word around the tennis world is that Ivo is the greatest server of all time (as of 2013), not just because of his 6-foot, 10-inch height but because of the many, many hours he spent practicing his serve.

Ivo was born February 28, 1979 in Zagreb, Croatia. In 2012 he was one of the oldest professional players on tour. Ivo's serve has been officially clocked at 156 miles per hour. He had held the world record for the most aces hit in one match at 77 aces on first serves until his record was beaten by John Isner during an epic 3-day-long match against Nicolas Mahut; Isner hit an extraordinary 113 aces, and Mahut hit 103.

Ivo is 6' 10" with arms and legs that stretch as far as the eye can see. Players must work hard to keep him off balance if they hope to gain a point. But Ivo is able to bend low to retrieve shots that hope to tangle his long stride and wide reach. He uses his powerful legs to spring up and nail the ball at its highest peak on his serve and overhead, and with just a few steps, he can cover the width and length of the court to return powerful forehands, backhands, and volleys.

76. CHOKE SYNDROME

Objective

To help players develop a defensive plan of attack that not only helps a player find their way back into the point, game, or match, but also helps them refocus.

Description

Choking is when players are overwhelmed by feelings of nervousness or anxiety that distract them and diminish their level of play. Choking on court happens even to the best players. Building psychological strength is crucial to avoiding choking. When players choke, they may become so nervous in the middle of a match that they can't breathe, let alone hit a little yellow ball over that gigantic net. Breathing helps players relax their nerves or anxiety, and it allows the body to work synchronously so that players can focus on the game instead of on their fear. Players who feel fearful should try this exercise to help them relax, focus on the ball, and take their time.

Execution

When they incorporate these tactical moves, players can conquer the opponent and feel as if they're the king or queen of the court again. They should try to focus only on the ball, not the opponent, and make a conscious effort to breathe out or grunt every time they hit the ball. When they use that method, they will find it almost impossible to play a short, jerky stroke that will cause them to lose control over their shots. A choked stroke results from the choppy stroke that players use when they suck in their breath. Players should breathe out as they swing and continue until they have followed through. If players feel as though things are spinning out of control, they should stop themselves and take a moment to collect their thoughts. They should think about their game plan, what they can do to alter it, and then just do it. The choke syndrome should vanish, and players will be on their way to playing to the best of their ability.

Tips

Here are a few tactical tricks players can incorporate into their game plan: Players should focus their nervous energy into getting more of their first serves in. They should recognize and accept their pre-match jitters, then move on from there. They should never let the opponent see them sweat. They should keep their on-court composure and play one point at a time. They should never look one point back or one point ahead; they should just play the point they're faced with at the moment. Finally, players should stick with the game plan but be flexible enough to adjust it if they must. Players rarely play the match the way they warm up, so they need not psych themselves out by an opponent's stinging forehands and big serves before the match starts.

77. CONCENTRATE AND PLAY GREAT TENNIS

Objective

To help players identify and develop a game plan to get back into the point, game, and match. To learn that they are playing the ball, not their opponent; and to help players understand the concept of *being the ball*.

Description

The power of the mind is apparent at each stage of a tennis player's development. When players stop trying to beat their opponents and just stick to the game plan, they can play better tennis. Learning how to *be the ball*, meaning focusing only on the ball, playing only the ball, and hitting the ball to targeted areas of the court no matter where the ball comes from, helps create a barrier in the mind and on the court; players can't and won't be persuaded to play their opponent's game.

Execution

Players should concentrate solely on the ball from the serve to the conclusion of the point, to the degree that the background from where it came will be blurred or unseen. They should not look for the opponent when hitting a passing shot; they should focus only on the ball. They should watch the ball before, during, and after the bounce and all the way into the racket strings, which helps to block out any attempt to see where the opponent is on the court. Players should hit the ball better than required to win the point, and they must remember to consider the spin and pace of the approaching ball. This strategy separates the players who win from those who don't. When players are rallying from the baseline, topspin gives the best control and leeway for safety. Intense spin means less pace. The less the spin, the greater the potential pace. Varying the spin is best. Players play 11-point games and incorporate the preceding strategy.

Variation

Players can add this time-tested concentration trick to the drill: While returning serve, players should focus on straightening out the strings in their racket. They should watch their opponent's ball toss, and when the racket strikes the ball they can say, "Hit." When the ball bounces in the players' service-court area, they can say, "Bounce," and when they hit the ball they can say, "Hit." The bounce-hit tactic can be used with every stroke and is a fantastic tool for keeping the eyes and mind focused on the action at hand instead of on what happened two shots ago.

Tip

As players gain experience, they learn to anticipate what type of return shot to expect from most opponents. Concentration equals smarter anticipation and smarter shot selection. Players should be patient and build points up to hit winners. Ten or 15 shots may be required before players get to the one that has their signature on it. Learning to read the opponent's body and racket position will help players identify various types of shots and spins.

78. SINGLES AND DOUBLES OVERHEAD SMASH

Objective
To teach players how to defend against the overhead smash.

Description
This fast-paced drill creates an exciting, fun way to learn how to counter the overhead smash if they hit a weak lob that the opponent turns into an overhead.

Execution
Player A takes a position behind the baseline center (T). Player B takes a position up at the net facing player A. A feeder or instructor stands off to the side of the court on player A's side of the court. The feeder hits a difficult ball resembling a low lob to player B. Player B hits the overhead trying to win the point outright against player A, who is on the baseline. Player A attempts to return the overhead. The players play out the point. Player B attempts to win 11 points, then both players switch positions.

Variation
This same drill can be performed with two players on the baseline defending against two players up at the net. Players attempt to win 11 points, then they switch sides.

Tips
Player A should try to block the overhead smash using the pace and power generated from the overhead hit by player B instead of taking a full backswing. Player A should try to hit a high lob or a passing shot. If player B hits a weak overhead, player A should take advantage of this weak shot and go for the passing shot. Both players must remember above all to never get caught flatfooted; they must keep their feet moving.

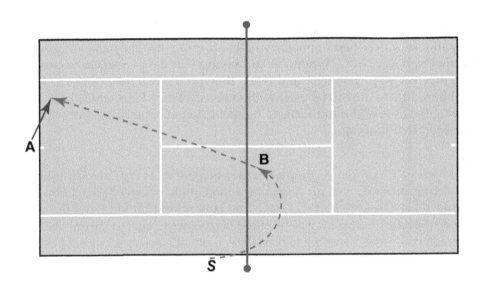

79. SINGLES AND DOUBLES GO

Objective

To place players in a defensive position at the onset of the point, testing and training their shot tolerance, retrieval, recovery, and footwork.

Description

This drill immediately puts players into a defensive position to work on their singles and doubles skills, footwork, teamwork, strategy, and defensive skills.

Execution

For singles play, player A stands behind the baseline center (T). Player B takes a position up at the net on the opposite side of the court. A feeder starts the drill by sending a challenging overhead. If player A wins the point, the feeder or instructor yells, "Go," and player A runs around to the opposite side of the court while player B also runs to the opposite side of the court to take player A's position on the baseline. At the same time both players are running, the feeder sends up a very deep lob for player A. If player B wins the point, they stay up at the net to try to rack up as many points as they can trying to achieve 11 points to win the drill.

For doubles play, players A and B are on the baseline, while players C and D are up at the net on the opposite side of the court. Play commences as described in the Execution section of this drill.

Tip

The feeder should give both (or all) players enough time to reach the other side of the court before sending up the offensive lob. All players should work on how to get back into the point after being pushed back off of the net and put into a vulnerable position by chasing down a deep lob.

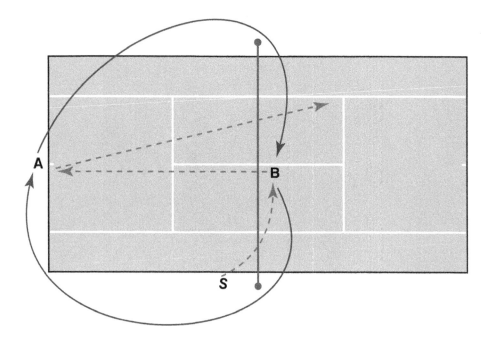

Objective

To help players develop quick bursts of speed and intersperse them with the step-slide (a sideways gallop across the baseline where a player takes a wide step sideways and then brings the feet together) to allow recovery into proper position to hit the next shot. Stroking the incoming ball effectively requires the body, legs, and feet to be in the best position possible.

Description

The ability to recover effectively after running down a shot determines whether a player will be able to stay in the point or lose the point. If a player is still trying to regain balance after hitting the first shot, he or she will probably lose the point.

Execution

Player A takes a position up at the net, and player B is positioned at the intersection of the opposite baseline and sideline. Player B must make a recovery to this area after each groundstroke by step sliding. Player B may hit shots down the line, crosscourt, or a combination of shots. Player A hits the first ball to player B, the second to the center of the court, and the third to the far sideline. They keep this drill going until player B hits a set of shots without missing. They then switch positions. Players can rotate after each sequence of shots.

Tip

This drill qualifies as a cardio tennis drill because of the exhaustive court movement. Conditioning and balance are crucial in tennis and key to conquering this drill. When they incorporate the step-slide into their recovery, players can move in any direction.

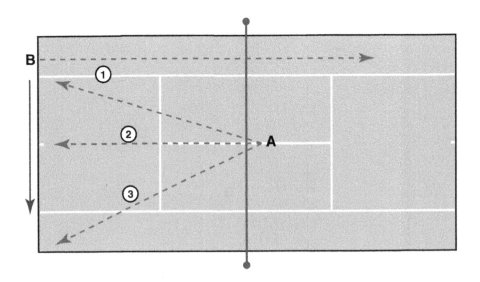

81. NEUTRALIZE THE BIG SERVE

Objective

To help players learn to recover and get back into the point after a big serve knocks them off balance.

Description

This drill helps players return the big serve; they use their opponent's serve against them by counterattacking or neutralizing the pace and angle of the serve.

Execution

A server stands on the service line opposite the returner. The server should serve a variety of power serves, kick serves, spin serves, and flat serves to various targets within the service box. The returner should hit every serve back using a chip or slice return. This return uses the pace from the serve and the returner's forward momentum to neutralize the pace of the serve. The chip and slice return takes the bite off of the pace off the ball so that the returner can get back into position, and it takes the server out of the offensive position and balances the match. After 20 serves in the deuce service box, players should switch positions; the server becomes the returner, and the returner becomes the server. After 20 serves and returns, both players should switch service boxes.

Tip

The returner should not give the server a ball that he or she can move forward inside the baseline and hit; the returner should force the server to stop or even back up to play the next shot.

Objective

To teach players how to defend against various types of ball spin.

Description

When faced with a ball that has topspin, slice, or a mixture of both, players need to learn how to counterattack with a shot that is effective and can help get them back into an offensive position.

Execution

Player A is positioned behind the center baseline (T), and player B is positioned behind the opposite baseline center (T). Player A starts the rally down the middle of the court to player B, hitting a flat ball (a ball without spin). Both players must use topspin when hitting deep balls in the court. If one of the players hits the shot short, then the receiver of the short shot must use slice to hit the ball back. Both players must hit deep shots with topspin and short shots with slice. Players should keep the ball in play for 3 consecutive shots (balls that are in the singles court and deep beyond the service line) before the point starts. They play six 15-point games.

Tips

Players should try to attack topspin shots with a topspin return. If allowed to hit the court and rise high up, a ball hit with topspin will push a player backward, thus causing the player to hit off of the back foot and put the player in a defensive position. The player must attack a topspin shot with topspin while catching and hitting the ball as it is rising, not as it is descending. Players should return slice shots with slice returns until they are able to hit an aggressive topspin shot to put them back in an offensive position.

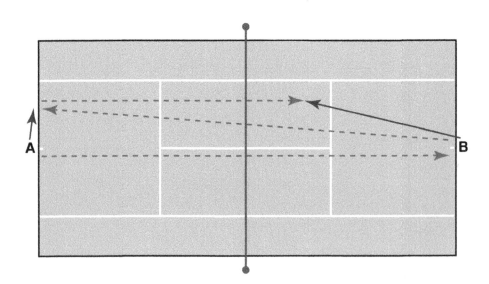

Objective

To helps players learn to fight for every ball, forcing the opponent to hit one more ball.

Description

Players work on never giving up on the ball; they try to hit every ball back into play to give the opponent one more chance to miss.

Execution

Players A and B take opposite ends of the court competing against each other. Player A serves traditionally or drop feeds the ball into play. If the server elects to drop feed the serve, the ball must go beyond the service line. If the drop-feed serve fails to pass the service line, then the server loses the point. Once the serve is in play, players must keep the ball in play four times before the point starts. When the server serves the ball and the returner returns the serves, players should start the four-ball pass count on the opponent's return (1), then continue with server's return (2), the returner's return (3), and the server's return (4); then the point starts. Players play 15 points with the server serving all 15 points. Then players rotate the serve.

Tip

Although a player can appear to be in a defensive position when on the full run off the court or when lunging for a passing shot but barely getting the ball back over the net, this player is really in an offensive position because they are willing to hit one more ball than the opponent which gives them the upper hand. Players should try to always run every ball down, get every ball back, get every serve, and make the opponent hit one more ball.

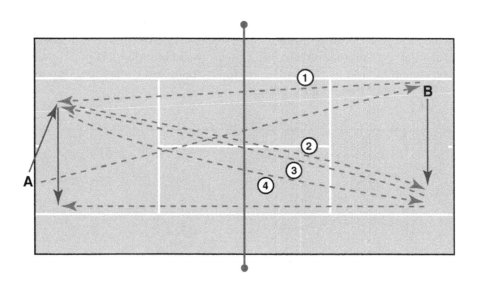

Objective

To help players develop a higher level of shot tolerance—the number of shots they are able to hit effectively during any given point when tired, excited, or when feeling outplayed.

Description

This drill will help players to expand their shot tolerance (number of balls they are able to hit effectively in a single point). In addition to helping them enhance their mental and physical stamina, this drill will enhance their ability to recover after several long points and their resistance to allowing opponents to win several points in a row.

Execution

Player A begins behind the baseline on one side of the court, and players B and C begin behind the baseline on the opposite side of the court. The point is confined to the singles court only for all players, but players should us all groundstrokes, volleys, overheads, and lobs. Players B and C are trying to win 4 consecutive points. Once they win 4 consecutive points, the players rotate. The objective for player A is to last as long as possible without losing 4 points in a row.

Variation

For a more competitive drill, player A should keep track of the points won prior to losing 4 in a row. Player A attempts to reach a predetermined number of points at which time players switch positions or rotate sides of the court if player A does not lose 4 points in a row first. Players can also time individual turns and compete to see who lasts the longest.

Tips

Players of all levels should keep in mind that being consistent, using the whole court to play, and recovering well after long points can be a lethal weapon. Also, when a player is in better tennis shape physically it helps build confidence in a players mind. A player starts to really believe and achieve a level of play where they can reach further, sprint faster, get to any ball, and outlast the opponent, which leads to more mental toughness.

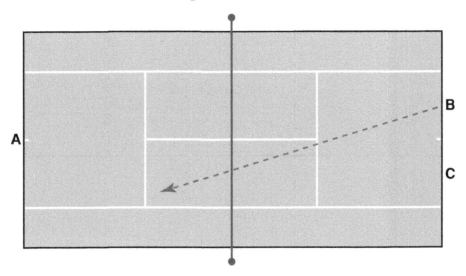

85. LOB AND LIVE

Objective

To teach players how to recover from being forced into a defensive position.

Description

Players learn how to hit a defensive lob during point play when forced to run down hard to get to shots.

Execution

Player A takes a position behind the center (T) on the baseline and player B takes a position on the opposite baseline center (T). Either player feeds a ball into play with a drop feed or with a traditional serve. Players play out the point crosscourt using the doubles alley as well. If either player hits the ball short (within the service-court area), the receiver of the short ball must hit an approach shot and follow the shot up to the net. The player who hit the short shot must lob to the player who is approaching the net. The player who hit the lob must attack the net. If either player fails to move in the prescribed manner, that player loses the point. Players play 21-point games crosscourt on the forehand side and then on the backhand side of the court.

Tips

When the lobber's opponent is up at the net looking for a volley or overhead smash, the lob becomes an offensive weapon in that the lobber can hit severe topspin or underspin and completely throw the opponent off balance and win the point outright. When the lobber is on the run and out of position, the lob is a lifesaver in that the lob, when hit high and deep in the opponent's court, can give the player who hits the lob those precious few seconds needed to recover and get back in the point.

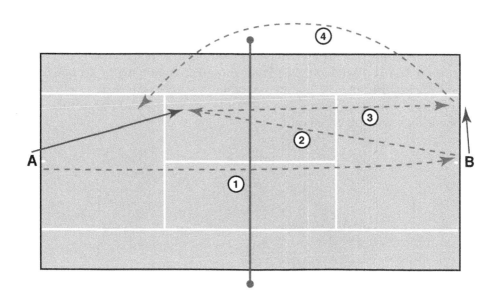

Objective

This drill helps develop stamina, consistency, and footwork for defensive play.

Description

Having to play hard-to-reach balls in different areas of the singles court allows players get a sense of court coverage and build confidence in their ability to run down any shot that may come their way. This type of drill also helps players develop the graceful footwork needed to be able to move side to side and up and back at any given moment during defensive match play.

Execution

Players take a position behind the baseline in single file. One player steps up to the center (T) on the baseline. A server feeds balls anywhere on the singles court, feeding forehands, backhands, drop shots, and lobs. Players must hit 10 consecutive shots in play. For every shot each player misses, the server deducts 1 point. For example, if the player hits 5 consecutive shots and misses shot number 6, he or she drops to number 5. The goal is to reach 10 consecutive shots without missing. Later, the goal can increase to 15 or 20.

Variation

One player starts behind the baseline, and two or three other players play the net. A server starts each point by feeding the ball to various places on the court, and the baseline player tries to win the point. The volleyers try to stop the player from winning. Players can move anywhere to retrieve the shots hit by the singles player, but they must return to their position up at the net after the point ends. Play continues until the player wins 20 points. Players rotate so that each takes a position up at the net. Players can also try a 50-point drill. The player receives 2 points for every outright passing shot but only 1 point for a point won by having to play it out.

Tip

If at any time during match play a player is required to retreat back to the baseline to recover a deeply placed lob, the player should start moving for the ball *before* the ball reaches the net tape. Taking a moment to process the action will mean it's too late, at which point the player should just forget it and congratulate the opponent for a well-placed shot.

Chapter 8

Equalizing Game Styles

Developing a wide range of playing styles, including serve-and-volley, master baseliner, hacker extraordinaire, and rock-solid lobber, is essential for being successful in match play. Tennis commands everything a player has to offer—dynamite strokes, wicked strategy, and a fitness level that can sustain hours, even days of playing without a lot of recovery time. Gone are the days when a player could specialize in one particular style of game; today's players must become tennis chameleons. However, every player will have a favorite style that functions as the catalyst for setting up winners. Within each player's style of game is that player's own individual style, which opponents must get to know. Every time players step on the court, they should be able to identify the opponent's game style and be able to confidently execute their own style.

Serena Williams, arguably the most dominant player in the history of the game and unquestionably the greatest server ever in the women's game, still bests her opponents off of the ground the majority of the time. Roger Federer has used the widest array of groundstrokes going drive for drive at the US Open, exchanging heavy topspin on the red clay at the French Open and executing a flawless slice backhand on the grass at Wimbledon, drawing most opponents out of position. Both of these players have different game styles and techniques, but the one thing they share with top player Novak Djokovic is superior court movement skill. When a coach designs a plan to develop a player's game style and playing technique, drilling groundstrokes and basic court exercises is essential for preparing the player for proper shot execution, placement, spin, optimal foot speed, positioning, and integrated full-body movements.

Players should take a close look at the various game styles and tactics they can use to counter each style of play. No one style of play exists that can dominate another, but incorporating some of the tools into the game plan enables players to prepare to play and counter almost any style. Players should learn how to counterbalance (equalize) styles of play by making small changes in their game plan, such as a grip change, so that they will be able to stick with their style of play. They should also learn how to balance game styles of different ability levels by using various methods of scoring and game handicapping, such as the stronger player may start at a 30-love deficit in each game of the set. This chapter introduces several tactical maneuvers to help players become better and smarter competitors.

87. COURT HANDICAP

Objective

To help equalize different ability levels so that players can compete against each other.

Description

A stronger player can get a great workout by playing half-court and full-court tennis with less-skilled players. Conversely, a weaker player can learn a lot by playing against a stronger player. Using this method, two unequal players can be made more equal.

Execution

The stronger player (player A) plays into the midcourt or half-court area, while the weaker player (player B) plays into the full-court (singles or doubles court) area. Player A is positioned behind the baseline center (T), and player B is positioned behind the opposite baseline center (T). Player A starts the rally or point with a drop-feed serve to player B. Player A's shots may only land within the service-court area, while player B may hit shots anywhere within the boundaries of the singles court. These rules make the game challenging for both players, and players can play an entire match this way. This drill can also be played as doubles.

Variations

Adding the alley to the stronger player's singles court widens the play area for the weaker player, allowing more area to hit in. At the same time, lessening the playing area for the stronger player places the focus on controlling shots within a smaller area. This approach creates an interesting match for the weaker player. A less-skilled player can request that the stronger player hit all balls past the service line in a baseline drill. This twist puts pressure on the stronger player to hit the ball deep in the backcourt, thus giving the weaker player an advantage. These are just a few examples of ways to even the playing field, but many more exist. Be creative; come up with variations that cater to the players' specific strengths and weaknesses.

Tips

To help equalize levels, players can use QuickStart orange and green balls. Allowing weaker players to use the two-bounce rule, where the ball is allowed to bounce twice before it is hit over the net, helps to increase their on-court footwork, dexterity, and hand-eye coordination.

88. STROKE HANDICAP

Objective

To help balance two players of different ability so that players at different levels can compete against each other.

Description

Playing a weaker opponent's strongest shot can provide the advanced player with a challenging match. The weaker player has more confidence and consistency on the stronger side and thus can give the stronger player more balls to hit.

Execution

After deciding which side of the weaker player's game is stronger (forehand or backhand), the stronger player delivers all shots, including serves, to that side. Another method of handicapping is to not allow the stronger player to put the ball away against the weaker player. By requiring the stronger player to hit every ball back to the opponent, the weaker player can give the stronger player a challenging match. Players should try to play individual points, games, and then an entire match using this method.

Variations

To further develop a weaker player's game, both players can use a particular type of spin on all shots. For example, hitting a slice shot off both sides can even out an otherwise lopsided match. The stronger player or players may only win points by hitting a specific stroke to end the point. For example, the stronger player may only hit a volley, forehand, or backhand to end the point. The stronger player may be required to hit a certain number of balls in play before the point officially starts. For example, the stronger player may be required to hit five shots over the net before the actual point begins. Another way to stroke handicap a stronger player is to allow the weaker opponent to win a point automatically if he or she is able to keep a certain number of balls in play against the stronger player. For example, if the weaker player keeps six balls in play before missing, that player automatically wins the point.

Tips

Players can use QuickStart orange and green balls to help equalize the game. Also when competing against a weaker player, a stronger player can apply pressure by maintaining concentration and playing a little faster than the opponent, or vice versa if the weaker player has trouble keeping up.

89. SCORE HANDICAP

Objective

To equalizes different game styles by giving a score advantage to the weaker player.

Description

This method puts mental pressure on the stronger player, making him or her play tighter and harder to win the game, and it gives the weaker player the confidence to play well against the stronger player. A common way to handicap the game is to spot an opponent points in a game at the onset of the game or match, such as 15-love or 30-love to start. It helps motivate the player who has fallen behind.

Execution

The weaker player or team receives a certain number of points before the first point of the game is played. For example, the weaker player or team is given a 2-point lead or a 2-game lead. Giving a combination of games and points can even out almost any match. For instance, a player who is two to three levels less advanced than the opponent could receive 4 games and a 30-love lead in every game. The stronger player can also start with negative points. The stronger player or players must fight back from a deficit. An expansion of this method is to spot the losing player points. For example, the less-skilled player receives a 15-love or a 30-love lead only after starting to fall behind in the set. When a player falls behind or is losing, the player who is winning will spot the player who is losing a point or two per game until that player can catch up in the game, set, or match.

Variations

Play 11-point games, and spot the weaker player 6 points to start with. The stronger player can also be required to achieve a certain number of points before the weaker player acquires a certain number of points. For example, players may play a 15-point game and if the weaker player acquires 3 points before the stronger player acquires 15 points, then the weaker player wins the match. Another possibility is if the weaker player wins 2 points in a row, then the stronger player must forfeit 2 points. If the weaker player wins 3 points in a row, then the stronger player forfeits 3 of his or her points. Players may set their own score handicap before the game or match begins. Try to think of other variations on the score handicap as well; these are just a few examples.

90. DOUBLE CUBE

Objective

To help motivate a losing player or team to play harder.

Description

The doubling cube used to wager in backgammon can put a twist into a set of tennis. The cube should double the stakes every time the stronger team wins.

Execution

Players may elect to play 2 or 3 sets. Players may set a wager (bet) from the beginning. For example, if player A can start by saying that if player A breaks player B's serve, then player B must do two shuttle runs at the end of the game. Additionally, if player A breaks player B's serve, player A may elect to double the stakes (two shuttle runs at the end of the set could be the wager, and the double would make it four shuttle runs). If player B continues the set, he or she may have an opportunity to redouble player A by making a comeback and getting into a position to win. If player B redoubles, the wager becomes eight shuttle runs—four times the original stakes. Pressure can sometimes equalize ability levels; when a bet is on the line, most players play more cautiously.

Variation

Players can play an eight-game pro set. If the weaker player wins three or four games before the stronger player wins eight, the weaker player wins the match.

91. SMALL CHANGE

Objective

To make just one small change in a stronger player's game to equalize a match between players of different ability.

Description

Coaches or players can make small changes that will make tennis more fun and increase participation. The small changes in this section handicap a stronger player's game and help a weaker player.

Execution

Each one of these techniques should be used in no particular order. Based on the level of player, coaches can pick and choose between handicap styles.

- Eliminate the third set, and play a tiebreaker instead.
- Eliminate side changes and change only at the end of the set.
- Eliminate let serves and first serves so that all shots will be played the same, including the serve.
- Eliminate the singles sticks so that net height will be the same for both singles and doubles.
- Play the best of four- or five-game sets.

Like other sports, junior tennis must have special concessions for participants' age, skill, and ability level.

92. POWER PLAYER EQUALIZATION

Objective

To help players learn how to neutralize the power player's game.

Description

Power players usually have a favorite side, so players should look for them to work the point to set up that weapon. This drilling tactic will help players identify opportunities to attack a power player's weakness and then take advantage of it.

Execution

Players should try to throw off the power player's game with different shots and different types of spin, including nontraditional shots known as *junk shots*. An example of a junk shot is a shot with severe backspin or slice on the ball. Those tactics will drive a power player crazy. Patience is the name of the game. Players must try to slow the game in order to throw the power player out of rhythm, which often causes power players to rush and make mistakes. Power players thrive on power. The harder their opponents hit, the harder they hit.

Tips

Players must avoid falling into the trap of playing the power game. It's enticing to want to serve the ball hard and hit the ball as hard as you can. But if that isn't your game or style of play, you will not be able to do it consistently, and the power player will notice this and encourage you to play to their style of game. Also, players must avoid changing their game style to either play more aggressive or more slowly. Doing so takes the player away from what they do best. The match will be over before they can ask, "What's the score?"

93. HACKER EQUALIZATION

Objective

To learn tactical methods that help players think and play the ball instead of the opponent, make smart shot choices, and become better at ball placement.

Description

Patience is the name of the game when playing hackers. If they are allowed to rule the match, their unorthodox mechanics will drive opponents batty. Players should avoid playing the hacker's game by pushing the ball back to him or her; it is like feeding spinach to Popeye.

Execution

The winning bet in dealing with hackers is to move them all over the court by using every stroke known to tennis. This maneuver forces the hacker's game plan to fall apart. Because of the hacker's unstable hitting positions, weird grips, and wacky uncontrolled spins, players must be ready to move quickly for balls that are spinning in all sorts of ways. Players should be aggressive but avoid going for winner after winner. Building up the point and creating opportunities is an effective approach. Players should be patient; they should wait for the right ball, and then attack.

Tips

Players must avoid being caught up in watching the hacker's unorthodox ways of executing strokes or shots. Watching the show will pull players into the hacker's trap. Players should use combo shots and stick with their game tactic; they must not hesitate or deviate from their game plan. Players should keep cool and keep the ball going until the hacker is so tired from hacking and chopping their shots that they leave an opening for players to move in and finish the point.

94. PUSHER EQUALIZATION

Objective

To help players make smart, aggressive shot selections when faced with the pusher game style.

Description

Few defeats are more agonizing than one administered by a pusher. Sometimes called a human backboard, a pusher can keep the ball going all day long, usually with very little pace. The following tactical solutions will help players learn how to build the point to hit aggressive winners, build the point to cut down on unforced errors, and create opportunities to open up the court and end the points early.

Execution

By forcing opponents to play extra balls, a pusher tempts players to overplay their shots (going for the line instead of a safe leeway inside or next to the line). To avoid this trap, players should play smart and be patient. Unless a player is rated a 5.0 or above, trying to overpower a pusher is a poor idea. A smart tactic is to hit lots of volleys with angles and hit behind a pusher, thus wrong-footing the pusher. A pusher has a way of softening shots and slapping them back, so a good pattern to establish throughout a match is to create gaps on the court by taking advantage of angles. Hitting the ball wide forces the pusher out of the comfort zone, making errors more likely and creating opportunities to take advantage of the pusher's weaknesses.

Tips

Playing against the pusher can cause players to choke. They may be overwhelmed by thoughts such as *Oh no, what will people think of me if I lose to this player?* Here a few player-tested strategies to incorporate into your game plan:

- Players must approach the pusher with respect but not be overwhelmed by the pusher's strategy.
- Players should play their game and play aggressive at the appropriate time during the point, remembering to play the ball, not their opponent.
- Once the match starts, they must close their mind to all outside or inside distractions and stay centered in the moment.
- They should play point for point, not one point in the past or one point in the future, and stick with their game plan, tweaking only when necessary.
- Finally, players must be careful when hitting a ball behind a slow opponent, because the opponent may still be there. Players instead should try hitting more to the open court area that they have created.

Objective

To learn tactics that will neutralize master baseliners' games and force them to play out of their comfort zone.

Description

Baseline masters lock themselves 3 to 5 feet (about 1 to 1.5 meters) behind the baseline and can hit and run until the cows come home. They are in top physical condition, and they can run down every shot thrown their way. Their strategy is to keep the ball coming back with high net clearance, to take few chances, and to wait until the opponent makes the first mistake. These drills help players develop ways to draw baseliners out of position and capitalize on their weaknesses, thus neutralizing their strengths.

Execution

The following drilling tactics should be on the court with every player who has encountered the baseliner game style. Players should hit drop and angled shots any time the baseliner hits the ball short into the player's court. This tactic will force the master baseliner to move up to the net where the player can take advantage of the situation with a passing shot or lob. The serve-and-volley tactic is a great way to draw this anchor up off the baseline and force him or her to make different shot choices. Players should play a set using this method of counterattack. When players meet a master baseliner in a real match, they will be prepared.

Tips

Patience is the key to this drill. Players must learn to build the point one shot at a time. They should try different spins, sharper angles, drop shots, and lobs, and they should approach the net whenever possible. Players must take the master baseliners out of their game by drawing them up to the net and then sending them scrambling back to recover a deeply hit lob. Any shot combination that incorporates the use of short shots, angles, lobs, and volleys will cause master baseliners to lose their focus and fall off balance. Players must never fall into the trap of trying to out-rally a master baseliner. Instead, they should mix up their shots to force the baseliner out of position, or else bring a sleeping bag, oxygen, and a night light, because they could be out there a long time.

96. NET RUSHER EQUALIZATION

Objective

To give players options for handling an opponent who likes to rush up to the net and end the point early.

Description

How does a player return serve against the net rusher? The primary goal of the receiver is to return the serve low and at the net rusher's feet, forcing him or her to volley up so that the receiver can move in and crush it.

Execution

When an opponent takes control of the net, players can try passing down the line or lobbing over the opponent's head. They can pick on the opponent's weaker side up at the net or, if the opponent is a great wide volleyer, try to smack it right up the middle. Players should hit the ball off the rise so that they can close in faster than the opponent can and use tremendous topspin. Players can keep the opponent from moving in too close by attacking the ball in this manner. Above all, if players are unsuccessful in returning one way, they should change and try something different.

Tip

Players should tweak the game plan to adjust to different styles of play. They shouldn't completely abandon their plan; they should just adjust it until they find their groove again.

Novak Djokovic

The Terminator: He Doesn't Stop!

Novak Djokovic was born on May 22, 1987 in Belgrade, Serbia. He has grown into a 6-foot, 2-inch (180-centimeter) tennis legend—dubbed the Terminator or Cyborg because of his relentless playing style. Neither an offensive nor defensive player, his game has been characterized as that of a shape shifter. As an all-court player, he has weapons to use against any playing style. Novak can adapt to any style of play and play his opponents' style better than them. He's also the definition of hitting the last ball because he never quits. In his mind, it doesn't matter who the player is or what the style of game is, he is only playing a game with the tennis ball.

He has won 6 Grand Slam singles titles combined at the Australian Open, Wimbledon, and the US Open. His rivalry with Rafael Nadal is considered one of the greatest rivalries in tennis according to ATPworldtour.com because of the sheer number of matches played and because of the fact that Rafael Nadal and Novak Djokovic have met and played in all 4 Grand Slam finals and 19 Masters Series matches. In 2012 Novak met Rafael yet again in the finals of the Australian Open. Djokovic and Nadal battled for 5 hours and 53 minutes, setting a record for longest Grand Slam final ever; in the end, Djokovic prevailed.

97. BASELINE COUNTERPUNCHER EQUALIZATION

Objective

To help players identify when the opponent is about to unleash a weapon.

Description

When ready to strike, players position themselves just behind the baseline. They then step inside the baseline to catch the ball on the rise and smack a winner. They don't just sit back, push the ball, and let the opponent make the mistake. They take the initiative by building up the point to where they can attack.

Execution

When encountering a baseline counterpuncher, players should take some pace off the ball but keep the counterpuncher deep in the backcourt. Counterpunchers flourish off power, so players should hit behind them to offset their balance and rhythm. Players should mix up their shots and bring counterpunchers to the net to open up their weaknesses. Counterpunchers love to use the open stance coupled with heavy topspin and can usually place the ball with severe angles. They dislike stepping into the ball, so slice shots and drop shots can be effective. Above all, players must not let counterpunchers dictate the pace.

Tip

Players must mix up the pace and not try to overpower the counterpuncher.

98. TENNIS FOOTBALL

Objective

To develop footwork, dexterity, hand–eye coordination, fast reaction to the ball, and rapid change of direction.

Description

Football terminology gives an entertaining twist to this offense–defense drill. The drill requires players to win three consecutive points to score a game point. The game is over when a player or team scores 11 points.

Execution

Players A and B are positioned on opposite baselines. The *football* (tennis ball) starts at the 50-yard line (the tennis net), where a server feeds the ball. Whichever player wins the point serves until a point is lost. Then the opponent serves. Each time a player wins a point, the player moves up 10 yards (about 9 meters) inside the court area up to the service line. When the opponent wins a point the football (tennis ball) and players move back to the baseline. *Field goals* (clear winners) can be *kicked* (hit) only from 30 yards (about 27 meters) out or closer (inside the service boxes). Extra points after the *touchdown* (winning shot) also require another point to be played. If the extra point is won, the winning player or team collects the first game and the game continues.

Strategic
Game Planning

Executing and consistently practicing strategic drills can sometimes be boring. However, practicing a drill over and over is part of developing the muscle memory needed for the body to respond to new and familiar situations as they arise during match play. The sole purpose of practicing specific drills such as the Deep Shot Forehand–Backhand drill is to isolate the part of the game a player needs to work on. Only through specific and repetitious practice can players build on their strengths and improve their weaknesses. The stronger their game, the more likely they are to succeed with a strategic game plan in a match.

Drilling with a purpose in mind helps players improve, correct weaknesses, learn new skills, and understand how to incorporate them into a strategic game plan for competition. Drills are routines that allow players to hit a large number of balls in short periods, thus helping them use their court time efficiently and effectively. Drilling reinforces proper stroke production, allows players to groove their shots, improves overall court movement and physical conditioning, and allows players to practice situations that occur frequently during match play. A drill or game may be entertaining, exciting, and complicated, but if it doesn't closely simulate the shots or situations that occur in a match, it is a waste of time. Drills should be simple, specific, entertaining, exciting, and educational. Most important, they must simulate situations of actual match play.

This chapter is filled with effective drills that can sharpen playing skills. Drilling will help players prepare for the pressure of singles and doubles during tournament or practice match-play competition.

99. SINGLE-FILE VOLLEY APPROACH

Objective

To slow the pace so that players can learn how to approach the net and set up to hit a volley.

Description

This drill allows players to focus on developing smart midcourt play.

Execution

A server takes a position on the service line, and players line up behind the opposite service line. One at a time, players close in to the net, split step, and then hit a forehand or backhand volley. After volleying, the player backpedals to the end of the line, and the next player moves forward. The server can increase the number of volleys or mix up forehand and backhand volleys.

Variation

Players line up at the net post, and a server hits balls from the opposite side. The first player in line sidesteps to the center of the court, taps the center net tape, turns sideways to sidestep backward, and then returns a ball by hitting an overhead. The player then closes to the net to return another ball using a volley.

100. CROSSCOURT AND DOWN THE LINE

Objective

To practice depth control, footwork, consistency, ball direction, and on-court conditioning.

Description

Isolating any stroke helps solidify it. This drill forces players to use good footwork, the split step (ready hop), quick recovery skills, and racket-head control to hit to a designated area of the court.

Execution

Players position themselves on the baseline. Player A hits forehands crosscourt to player B's forehand. Both players hit toward the deuce-court area and use doubles alleys to create sharper angles and more hitting room. While players A and B are hitting crosscourt, two additional players can hit crosscourt toward the advantage-court area. One or two balls can be in play at the same time. Players rally crosscourt or down the line and work on consistently keeping the ball deep past the service line.

Variations

Players can try having only one ball in play. Two players hit only down the line, and the other two hit only crosscourt. Or one player can return every ball crosscourt, while the opponent returns every shot down the line. The first to 11 points wins. Another variation is to have one player put the ball in play with a groundstroke. Players then attempt a continuous down-the-line or crosscourt rally while using all stances, spins, power adjustments, and angle placement. Targets may be placed on the court for better concentration and target control. Players play to 11 points.

Tips

To help slow the pace of the ball and drill, use QuickStart orange and green balls. Precision footwork and conditioning gained through drilling crosscourt and down-the-line groundstrokes or volleys will help players of all levels physically and mentally outlast many long, grueling, closely contested matches. Players must learn that there is more to tennis footwork than just running after the ball. This drill will also get players into top tennis shape. If they can do this drill using all of the variations for 1 hour and then walk without wobbling, they are tennis machines!

101. THREE-HIT CYCLE

Objective

To develop the combination of steps that players need to become proficient at the net. This drill develops good split stepping, the approach shot, and the feeling of skills for closing in on the net.

Description

This sweet combination of shots helps players develop footwork skills, confidence, finesse, and anticipation skills.

Execution

The server, positioned inside one of the service boxes, feeds three shots in from the opposite side of the net. All players should be standing 3 or 4 feet (about 1 meter) behind the service line, behind either the deuce- or advantage-court area. The first player in line hits a forehand approach shot down the line, closes in for a backhand volley crosscourt, and finishes with an attack forehand volley crosscourt. The player returns to the end of the line. The second player moves in for a backhand approach shot down the line, closes in for a forehand volley crosscourt, and finishes with an attack backhand volley crosscourt. Players should keep the three-hit cycle drill moving so that they don't become listless and lazy waiting in line.

Tip

Players should use the split step (ready hop) before hitting the approach and before hitting the volley.

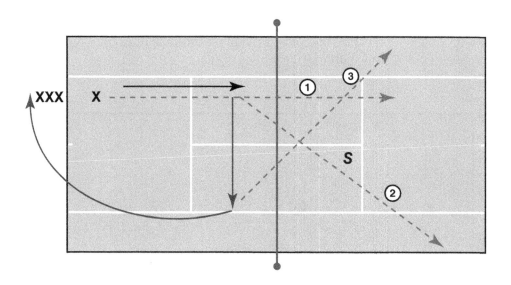

Objective

To teach players court and ball control.

Description

The drill puts players in the perfect position to pass the net person and shows the consequences for a failed attempt.

Execution

Player A stands behind the service line, and player B stands on the opposite baseline. Using only half the court and the alley, player A starts the point by hitting the ball deep to player B. Player A closes in to the net. Player B may not lob on the first return, but after that, anything goes. If player A wins the point, he or she starts the next point from the same position at the service line. If player A loses, he or she slides back to the baseline and player B slides up to the service line and starts the next point. They play to 15 or 21.

Variation

Players can try this drill crosscourt including the alley. In addition, both players can start on the baseline using only half the court (doubles alley is included). Player A starts the point by drop hitting a deep groundstroke. Play continues until one player hits short. The player who has to return the short shot must then come into the net and continue to play the point to completion. Play continues to 15 or 21, with serve exchange every five serves.

Tips

If players find that too many of their shots are landing short, they should check to see that they are completely following through to the target. If they tend to hit with excessive topspin, they may be pulling off the ball early, which will also cause shots to fall short.

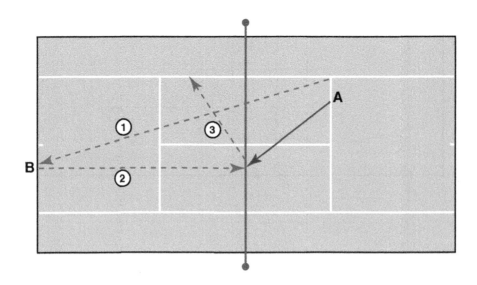

103. INSIDE INS

Objective

To help players create the proper amount of space between themselves and the ball when hitting an inside-in forehand and backhand.

Description

This drill is directly related to hitting a backhand return of serve off of a center (T) placed serve or hitting an inside-in forehand instead of the more often utilized inside-out forehand. The ball travels to the backhand side, but the player decides to hit a forehand instead. Players move or run around their backhand to hit a forehand in the direction one would normally hit a backhand crosscourt.

Execution

A player and ball feeder face each other, standing about 3 or 4 feet (1 meter) apart. The feeder tosses balls to the ad side about 3 feet (1 meter) to the side of the player and 1 foot (about 30 centimeters) in front, allowing enough room for the player to generate an excessive amount of racket-head speed. The player should generate topspin on the ball in a hooking manner inside in (down the line directly in front of the player) aiming for the ball to bounce on the far side of the service line area or deep in the court. The feeder should continue tossing balls alternating between forehands and backhands once the previous shot bounces on the far side.

Variation

This drill can be done using 4 to 12 balls. The player's ability and fitness level determine the number of balls chosen. This drill is excellent for helping players play their way into shape. If executed properly it can be strenuous, so it qualifies as a cardio tennis drill.

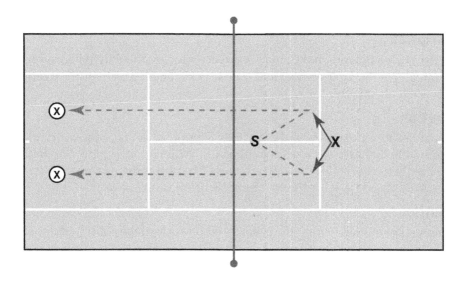

104. DEEP SHOT FOREHAND–BACKHAND

Objective
To help players learn how to hit deep, penetrating groundstrokes from the baseline with confidence.

Description
The drill forces players to keep the ball deep in the court or suffer the unforced error of hitting too short. Players need to learn how to place the ball deep in the backcourt area consistently and with aggressive confidence.

Execution
Positioned on the baseline, player A starts the rally with a deeply fed ball to player B, who is positioned at the opposite baseline. Play continues until a ball lands on or inside the service-court area. The player who hits short loses the point. Two or four players can perform this drill. They play 11-point games.

Variation
Players can use the service boxes or the full half court including the doubles alley. They can try going crosscourt short court first and then slowly slide back to the baseline. They can try playing an entire match within the service-court area, or they can try to keep the ball in play using only half of the court within the service-court area.

 105. UP AND BACK

Objective
To help develop backcourt players' experience in hitting deep defensive lobs and teach them how to play aggressively when returning a partner's overhead.

Description
This drill helps players make smart recovery choices and stay balanced when they have to move up to the net and then quickly back to recover the overhead and place it effectively.

Execution
Two players take positions on the baseline at opposite ends of the court. Player A alternately hits drives and lobs to player B. When returning the hit, player B alternates between volleys and overheads. Player B must move up to the net for the volley and back for the overhead. Scoring is optional.

Variation
Player A is positioned behind the baseline on one side of the court (either deuce- or advantage-court), and player B is up at the net diagonally from player A. Player A uses a combination of drives and lobs when hitting shots, and player B uses a combination of volleys and overheads. The first player to win 15 or 21 points is the winner.

106. FIVE-BALL OVERHEAD SEQUENCE

Objective

To help players learn how to set up to hit an effective overhead and how to recover in balanced position, ready to hit another.

Description

When attempting to hit overheads, many players allow the ball to drift behind their heads. This drill helps players learn to hit overheads when the ball is behind them and to close in on the net after hitting an overhead.

Execution

Player A takes a position up at the net. Player B is on the baseline opposite player A. Player B starts the sequence of shots to player A. Player B feeds a deep lob to player A. Player A hits an aggressive overhead, closes in, and taps the net. The instant player A taps the net, player B throws up another lob to player A. The sequence continues until player A hits five successful overheads.

107. SIX-BALL PATTERN SEQUENCE

Objective

To develop concentration and consistency and identify weaknesses in a player's game.

Description

Players must respond to a mix of shots, so they learn how to play all shots; get a feel for the next shot; and sharpen starts, stops, and the split step.

Execution

Player A takes a position behind the baseline, and player B is up at the net. Player A feeds six balls to player B in the following sequence: (1) a forehand volley, (2) a backhand volley, (3) a deep lob over player B's head, (4) a short ball to the forehand for an approach down the line, (5) one backhand volley, and finally (6) a lob for an overhead smash. The pattern may be altered.

108. QUICK VOLLEY

Objective

To develop quick reflexes, footwork, and hand–eye–ball control.

Description

Players can perform this practice tool before match play as a warm-up drill. The drill helps players improve footwork, quicken reflexes, and gain better ball and court sense.

Execution

Two or four players take positions at the net and volley straight ahead to each other or diagonally across to each other. If two players are drilling, both players are up at the net facing each other. If four players are drilling, two are on each side, facing each other. Players hit the ball using a forehand or backhand volley, keeping the ball in play without allowing it to bounce. As players improve, the speed of the balls can increase and players can alternate between forehand and backhand volley exchanges. Players should split step with every stroke of the ball, and after each hit they should split step before striking the ball.

Variation

Players A and B stand on opposite service lines. They volley back and forth, moving in with each shot to within 1 foot (about 30 centimeters) of the net. Once players have mastered closing in, they can back up with each volley and then close back in.

109. CROSSCOURT RALLY ATTACK

Objective

To increase players' knowledge of when and how to attack a short ball and where to hit it.

Description

Identifying and reacting to certain shots in tennis can sometimes be frustrating. This drill helps players develop the confidence they need to move in and continue moving up to the net to hit and put away the volley.

Execution

Player A and player B are positioned on opposite baselines and begin a crosscourt rally. When a short ball arises, the player who is receiving it must move in and hit the approach shot down the line. The backcourt player (player A) may try to pass player B, but player B will be ready to hop all over the volley. The players do this drill until both can identify the movements that opponents make just before they try to unleash a devastating passing shot.

Tip

Players should be reminded that anticipation is a learned response. So, the more they play, the more they learn to sense the kind of return the opponent may hit. Anticipation of the short ball definitely makes hitting the approach shots easier.

Objective

To develop good reaction time and a feel for identifying and hitting short balls.

Description

This drill helps players to identify the short ball, have the confidence to move in and attack, hit to a designated area, and follow up to the net to finish the point.

Execution

Player A takes a position at the service line and hits a deep ball to player B, who is positioned at the opposite baseline. Player B hits the deep ball back to a designated area on the court, which can be anywhere predetermined by the players. Player A then hits a short shot to player B, who attempts to retrieve the shot and place it aggressively away from player A. Player A should try to hit to a specified area of the court.

Variation

A server stands at the net post just off the court and feeds a short ball to one of the backcourt players, A or B, who are positioned on the baseline standing opposite each other. The receiving player hits an approach shot and closes in on the net. The opponent tries to pass or lob to win the point. They play 11-point games and then rotate positions.

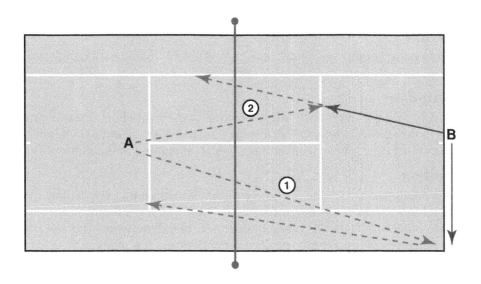

111. RISING STAR

Objective

To help players develop quick bursts of speed and intersperse them with the step-slide (the side gallop when moving across the baseline during recovery after hitting a shot) to recover to the proper position to hit the next shot. Stroking the incoming ball effectively requires the body, legs, and feet to be in the best position possible.

Description

This drill helps players learn to hit to a specific area, recover, get back into position, prepare to hit again to a specific area, recover, and get back into position again. The drill builds strong recovery skills.

Execution

Player A is on the right side of the baseline, and player B is at the center of the opposite baseline. Player A begins by hitting alternating crosscourt and down-the-line shots to player B. Player B must hit every ball back to player A using quick bursts of speed and the step slide to cover the course. After several minutes, they rotate sides.

112. HALF-COURT HUSTLE

Objective

To work on improving footwork, agility, and speed during match play simulation.

Description

This drill forces players to change direction and sprint short distances many times in the span of 1 minute. Short bursts of speed are essential in tennis, and players need dexterity to react and recover with balance and confidence.

Execution

Player A positions up at the net, and player B stands on the service line. Player A hits soft-angled volleys that force player B to run. Player B must tap each ball back to player A. If a ball is missed, player A immediately puts the next one in play. Player B shouldn't stop hustling until 1 minute has elapsed.

Tip

Players must keep their feet moving at all times while on court. If they stop moving, they're dead in the water.

113. APPROACH SHOT, PASSING SHOT

Objective

To help players develop strong passing shots while simulating match play.

Description

Approach shots are groundstrokes played with the intention of following them up to the net to gain control of the net and attempt to hit a winning volley. This drill helps players gain the fundamental knowledge of when and where to hit an approach shot.

Execution

Players A, B, and C are positioned behind one baseline, and player D is positioned behind the opposite baseline. Players A, B, and C take turns hitting down-the-line approach shots to player D, who attempts to pass the approaching player. Players should play out the point. After one player accumulates 11 points, players rotate. No lobbing is allowed.

114. NET APPROACH

Objective

To help players develop clear and concise check-pause, split-step, or stutter-step techniques as well as good team communication skills.

Description

In this drill, players must communicate and move in effectively to hit an approach shot as a team.

Execution

Two players begin just in front of the baseline. With a server feeding each shot in, both players move forward a few steps (remember to split step before each shot) after one of them hits the shot. By the third or fourth shot, both players should be up at the net engaged in a rapid volley exchange. They keep executing the drill and increasing the pace of play. Players try to get up to the net as fast as possible. The players do not play out the point; they perform the drill for consistency.

Tip

Players should be certain to use a split step, landing on the balls of the feet with each volley.

115. ATTACK AND SMACK

Objective

To help players develop their serve-and-volley technique.

Description

Serve-and-volley is an aggressive game plan for singles and doubles match play. The player or team that incorporates this method in its strategy will be a force to be reckoned with.

Execution

The server must use serve-and-volley style on both the first and second serve, or the player or team who is serving and volleying loses the point. They play a set using this method.

Tip

If the ball hits the net and drops onto the opponents' side of the court, the players should rush the net to cut off possible angles and force a low-percentage shot that the opponents may not be capable of making.

116. HOT-PEPPER DOUBLES

Objective

To help develop communication skills, teamwork, and the quick reflexes needed for outstanding net play.

Description

To develop quick reflexes for volleying and anticipating shot direction, this drill forces both players to stay in the frying pan without the option of backing out. Players work to build the confidence it takes to set up, attack, and win the point.

Execution

This drill is identical to the singles hot-pepper drill except that it involves four people and allows sharp-angled volleys. Players A and B play against players C and D. Teams are positioned behind the service line, each behind a service box facing each other. Player A starts the volley exchange by feeding the first ball underhanded to one of the players on the opposite side of the net. The fast-paced exchange continues until a player makes an error, hits a winning volley, or successfully hits a lob volley over an opponent. Players may hit around or through the middle of the opponents if they can find an opening. They play to 15 or 21 points and then rotate positions.

117. CRAZY-8 VOLLEY

Objective

To challenge players' ability to volley under stress and to develop quick hands and feet.

Description

Using a set pattern, players try to keep the ball going without missing.

Execution

Player A starts the action by hitting to player B, positioned directly in front of player A. Player B volleys diagonally across the net to player C. Player C volleys straight ahead across the net to player D, and player D volleys diagonally across the net back to player A. Players do not allow the ball to bounce. Scoring is optional.

Variation

This drill qualifies as a cardio tennis drill. Cardio tennis is a way of drilling that helps improve the conditioning of all players, no matter the level, through action-based tennis and on-court footwork drills. All players are positioned up at the net across from each other. Players A and B, who are partners, volley all balls down the line. Players C and D, who are partners, volley all balls cross-court. All play is up at the net. Scoring is optional.

Tip

Players who are afraid of the playing at the net should start by using QuickStart orange or green balls. They can then progress to volleying against a backboard. Remember, quick hands combined with quick feet make any player—no matter the level—hard to beat!

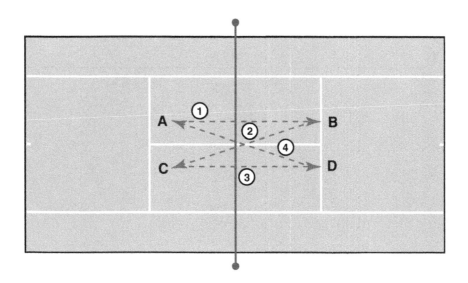

Objective

To help players learn how to pass on the run; recover quickly; and build total court coverage, confidence, agility, and speed.

Description

Running to hit any shot in tennis takes tremendous footwork, good timing, and good shot selection. Players must recover and set up for the return. This drill helps players isolate and practice running down groundstrokes, recovering, and deciding where to hit.

Execution

Two or three players start near the baseline on one side of the court. Two or three other players position themselves up at the net on the opposite side, facing the baseliners. A server feeds a groundstroke to the first baseliner in line, who hits the shot down the line to the volleyer. They move across the court together. The server feeds another ball to the baseliner, who hits another down-the-line shot to the same volleyer on the opposite side of the court. They proceed to the end of their respective lines, and the next two players move into position. They repeat this drill starting on the opposite side of the court.

Tip

This drill qualifies as a cardio tennis drill, because the quick movements and sprinting work the cardiovascular system. When players are at the net and a ball is coming straight at them at high speed, they should use the backhand volley for safety, because the backhand covers more area than the forehand or ducking will.

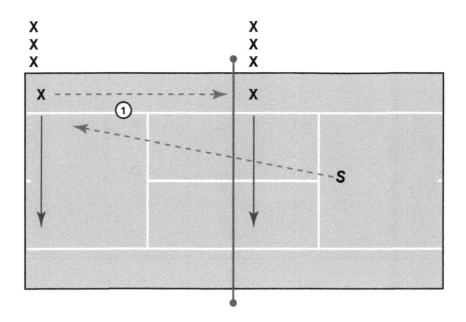

119. MONKEY IN THE MIDDLE

Objective

To help players learn how to keep shots away from the middle of the court and build net-playing skills.

Description

This entertaining and challenging drill can be performed with as few as three players or as many as six. By keeping their shots away from the net player (monkey in the middle), players develop sound crosscourt and down-the-line rallying skills. The drill forces players to move the ball around the center of the court or suffer the consequences.

Execution

Six players are on the court; two players are positioned at each baseline, and two are up at the net standing opposite each other. A server feeds the ball into play. The four backcourt players rally for points, trying to prevent the net players (monkeys) from snatching the volley away. When a net player steals or poaches on three balls and wins the point, that side of the net rotates so that one of the baseline players gets a chance to play up at the net.

Tip

Players should use the lob to open up the forecourt instead of trying to blast the ball through the net players.

120. DOUBLES HUSTLE

Objective

To help players learn how to move to various shots and areas of the court effectively with a partner while playing doubles.

Description

This exercise slows the pace of competitive play so that players learn when to take a shot, when to relinquish to the partner, and how to move together like well-oiled machinery.

Execution

The server stands in position up at the net with a large basket of balls. Team players A and B are positioned up at the net on the opposite side. The server gently feeds balls from side to side and down the middle of players A and B. When the ball is hit to the right, players A and B must move together to the right to hit the shot, trying to keep the same distance apart. Likewise, if the ball is hit to the left, both players should move together to try to hit the shot. If the ball goes up the middle, one player calls for it. Players must hit gently; this is not a drill for point playing. Whether the server lobs, drops, or something else, both players must move together. They play consistently for 2 minutes straight.

Objective

To teach players a key ingredient in doubles learning—to identify when to approach the net and how to recover after the opponent throws a lob over the team's heads.

Description

This drill helps a team learn how to take advantage of the short ball in doubles play, and in the event that one player is drawn back to the baseline, to return quickly to the offensive position.

Execution

Players A and B are positioned in standard doubles formation. The server or instructor is positioned on the opposite service line. The server feeds a short ball to player A, who hits an approach shot crosscourt and advances to the net with player B. The server returns the ball with a lob over player B's head. Player A recovers the ball and lobs it crosscourt. At the same time, player B moves over to cover the spot that player A vacated. Player A follows the high lob into the net again. The server returns the lob with a floater down the middle, which player B cuts off with an aggressive swinging volley. Play is continuous.

Variation

Have both players A and B start back on the baseline together. The server or instructor feeds a short ball to either player A or B. Both players should close in on the net. If player B hits the approach shot crosscourt, then the server hits the lob over player B's head and player A crosses over and covers player B's vacated spot. Player B should return the lob with a crosscourt, deeply placed lob and work back down to the net. Play is continuous.

Tips

On the backhand approach shot or volley, it is vitally important that players remember to keep their shoulders sideways throughout the stroke. Players should use the semi-Western or full Western grip so that they can put tremendous topspin on the swinging volley.

122. DOUBLES APPROACH-SHOT CHALLENGE

Objective

To help develop the doubles low-ball and short-ball attack and defense, the approach shot, and the strategies of attacking the net by closing in or staying back to work the point.

Description

This drill isolates the approach shot and helps players learn to complete the approach to the net after hitting the approach shot.

Execution

Two teams position themselves behind opposite baselines. The server feeds team A a soft, short shot at the service line. The server should give each team two chances to put the ball in play. Team A must execute an approach shot and then close into the net. The first team to win 21 points wins the match.

Variation

An extension of the approach-shot challenge, this drill helps players identify the best shots used for attacking and moving up to the net: Teams A and B are behind opposite baselines. To start, a server feeds a ball to team A. Both teams start rallying. When one team hits the ball into the service-court area of the opposite side of the court, the team receiving the short shot must approach the net together or automatically lose the point. Teams play out the point. The first team to win 21 points wins the match. Another variation is to have two teams a few feet behind the service line opposite each other. A server feeds a soft, low ball to team A, which will try to return it softly and low to team B. Both teams then close in toward the net and try to keep the ball low to close in behind and hit a winner.

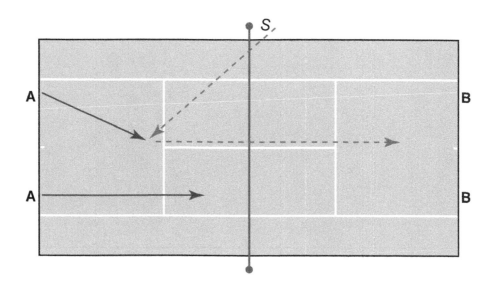

Objective

To help reinforce the fundamentals of approaching the net, attacking and defending the net, and countering the attack up at the net.

Description

This drill works to set up play so that a preplanned shot forces a team to move up, hit an approach shot, and then commit to attacking the net. The drill also helps players learn how to defend against the net attack.

Execution

Four players take position in standard doubles formation. The server hits a second serve and follows it to the net. The receiver returns and moves up to the net. Players try to use soft, low volleys to force the opponent to volley up to them so that they can move in and hit a winner. If the receiver can hit the return early from well within the playing court and keep the return wide out into the alley, he or she has an excellent chance at winning the point up at the net. A well-placed return helps set up the point for solid volley winners. Players play out all points to completion.

Variation

The server is allowed to serve and volley crosscourt only. The receiver defends by staying back after the return and works the point by mixing high, deep lobs and drives.

Tip

After hitting a high, deep, penetrating lob, players should not sit back and watch the action but attack the net.

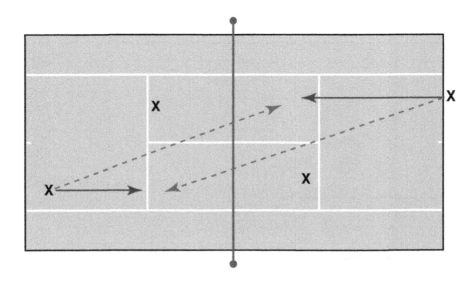

Objective

To practice closing in and attacking the net.

Description

This enjoyable drill helps players have fun hitting approach shots and volleys. The drill takes the pressure off having to decide who takes what shot and what the player does with it. This drill specifies who hits the approach shot, where the player hits it, and what happens after the player hits it.

Execution

Team A and team B start in standard doubles formation. Team A has been dubbed kings or queens of the hill. A server feeds an approach shot to one player of team A. The player hits the approach, and both players of team A move up to the net and play the point out against the opposing team. The challenging team (team B) must win 3 points in a row to knock the top team (team A) off the hill. If team B loses one of the points in the succession of points, then another waiting team rotates in. Team B must start from 0 points again. Only the points accumulated on the hill count. The team that accumulates 21 points wins.

Variations

Players can use all three doubles formations—monster, standard, and Australian doubles. In standard formation, the doubles players stagnate so that one player is on the baseline on one half of the court, and the other player stands in the service box closer to the net on the other half of the court. In the monster formation, the net player straddles the center service line at the net. In the Australian formation, the server's partner stands on the same side of the court as the server.

Tip

Players should always hit their approach shots and volleys with slice or backspin. This tactic helps keep the ball low and forces the opponents to hit up on the ball, allowing players to move in and attack.

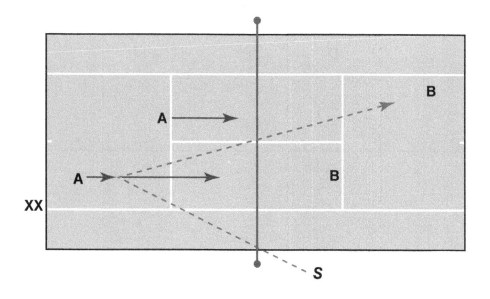

Objective

To develop poaching, serving, and volleying skills.

Description

The idea of using various formations in doubles is to take advantage of a weakness in the opposition, to block their strengths, to cover up a team's own weaknesses, or to use the team's strengths to their fullest. In the Australian formation, the server's partner stands in the same court as the server instead of standing in the opposite service-court area.

Execution

Players can play this aggressive form of doubles in three ways: The server's partner crosses on a sortie; the server's partner makes a sortie if possible, but the server crosses; or the server takes whichever side his or her partner doesn't take. *Sortie* is a French term that means to "strike out" or "exit" or "going out." In tennis, *sortie* means "to poach." Whichever method they decide to use, players should play it aggressively.

In the first style (the most popular one), the server (who is positioned behind the baseline) serves the ball either into the opponent's body or down the center (T). The server moves straight up to the net, while the partner poaches or crosses to the other side. This style gives the server the shortest route to the net, and the poacher distracts the receiver. Now both players are up at the net looking to end the point with a volley or overhead. They continue to use this formation until the server's game ends.

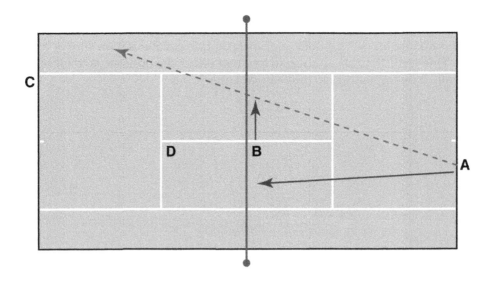

Objective

To help a team keep the opposition off balance and improve serving, volleying, and poaching skills.

Description

This style of doubles play is a variation of the Australian doubles formation. The difference is the positioning of the serving team's net player. The net player of the serving team straddles the center service line up at the net. Now the net player of the serving team is in the perfect position for poaching directional signaling. Because the net player is positioned in the middle of the court up at the net, he or she must create directional signals to alert the partner about which direction he or she will attempt to poach. If the player poaches to the right, the server should cover the net or court to the net player's left. Players can invent their own method of signaling. This formation throws off the concentration of the opposing team. And it's fun!

Execution

The server's partner straddles the centerline, squatting and positioned approximately 3 feet (about 1 meter) from the net. Good communication is essential for this poaching style of play. The net player must poach to one side or the other at the sound of the partner's serve. By signaling the partner beforehand, the net player lets the server know which side to switch to after serving. By anticipating the direction of the service return, the net player can intercept or sortie the shot and volley it through the hole or at the opposing players' feet. Players play to 20 points or a regular set of doubles using this method.

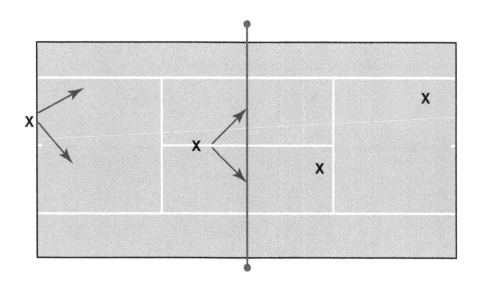

Objective

To help develop quick hands and feet, stamina, ball sense, and control.

Description

By restricting play to the service-court area and not allowing the ball to drop, players develop the split-step method needed for sound volleying, quick hands, shot anticipation, and the confidence to stay in the mix when things heat up during competition.

Execution

Players A and C are positioned up at the net standing opposite players B and D. Any additional players wait off court ready to jump in when any player flubs a shot. To get the action started, the server feeds a ball to player A. Player A hits to either player B or player D. Play continues until a player lets the ball hit the ground. The point ends when a player lets the ball drop or misses outright. The next player in line takes a place. This is an individual exercise; players A and C are not partners, nor are players B and D.

Variation

This variation qualifies as a cardio tennis drill and should be performed not to improve volleying technique as in the former execution, but for cardio exercise with a class as small as 3 or as large as 10. Remember a player's feet must never rest during this drill; the player is constantly moving forward, jumping up, bending down, and moving side to side. After only 3 minutes of performing this drill properly, the legs will feel a burn. Players can be on teams. Players can use the nondominant hand to build strength and control on both sides of the body.

Tip

When hitting crisp, penetrating volleys, players should not take the racket head back past the shoulder. Volleying against a backboard is a perfect way to develop the punching or blocking motion needed to hit volleys.

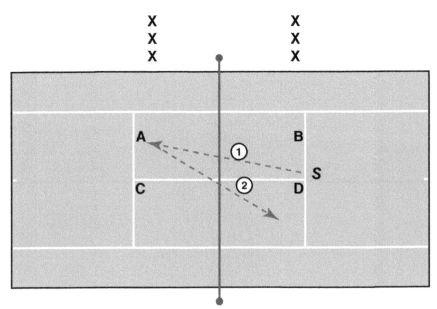

128. SHORT COURT

Objective

To help players learn to control the pace of the ball in a restricted area of the court while developing the building blocks needed to execute finesse shots.

Description

This drill isolates finesse shots by permitting players to use only touch shots and touch volleys.

Execution

Two or more players can perform this drill. They must stay within the service-court area, one on either side of the net. Players attempt to use touch and angle shots to keep the ball in play. They must hit 10 to 15 consecutive shots before using the shot in a game.

Chapter 10

Court Surface Tactics

Hard, soft, grass, or carpet, the game of tennis is played on a multitude of court surfaces around the globe. Each surface has its own characteristics that affect the playing style of the game. Playing on each of these court surfaces can be fun, scary, and complex, but each commands a player's full attention to the type of ball he or she can hit or receive. Each will dictate what kind of spin and power a player should use, and each will expose what kind of physical and mental condition the player is in. The experience can be utterly maddening to players who don't change their tactics and strategy to accommodate each surface.

In general, two types of court surfaces exist: hard and soft. To perform and play the best on hard courts, players must expect a fast-paced, powerful game in which first serves are vitally important and aggressive returns are the name of the game. To play on softer courts such as clay and grass, players must get ready for bad bounces and slippery footing. Players have described grass as a tricky surface to play on. Players who have dreamed of playing on grass must be ready for some fast-paced, quick-footed drilling to prepare for this unforgiving surface. In contrast, clay or Har-Tru court players must possess an endless supply of patience and oxygen. They must become human backboards and never miss.

Whatever the court surface, players must be ready to adapt and adjust their game plan. This chapter deals with how to adapt playing styles to compete successfully on all tennis court surfaces.

Objective

To focus on quick change of direction and recovery while playing on clay.

Description

Hitting behind the opponent is a wonderful tactic for players to have in their repertoire. The idea is to get the opponent running in one direction and then hit to the area just vacated. On clay the player will have a hard time getting enough traction to reverse direction quickly.

Execution

Players should be on a clay court. Player A is positioned behind the baseline near the center (T). Player B is positioned behind the service line on the opposite side. Player B feeds a sequence of four shots, moving player A from corner to corner hitting forehands and backhands. On the fifth feed, player B sends the ball back to the place that player A just left. This method is called *hitting behind a player*. Players repeat the drill until they gain a firm grasp on how to perform a quick change of direction and recover with good balance. Scoring is optional.

Tip

Sliding into shots is not only fun, it's smart. An important tip is to keep the front foot pointed somewhat into the direction of the slide. The back foot can be sideways because it will skip over any catches in the clay instead of being jammed into them.

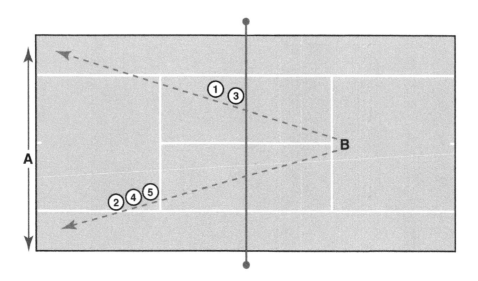

Objective

To focus on serving with added spin to keep the ball lower and hitting low, controlled approach shots while playing on clay.

Description

Players should expect to need better serves and approach shots for success at the net while playing on clay. Opponents will have more time to set up on passing shots or lobs, and players will have less traction to make sudden cuts toward the ball. Serve-and-volley style players typically have a tough time on clay.

Execution

Player A is positioned behind the baseline near the center (T), and player B receives the serve from the deuce-court on the opposite side of the net. Player A hits a predetermined slice serve to player B. Player B returns the serve cross-court, and the players play out the point. When a short ball arises, the player who receives it should move in and hit an approach shot down the middle or down the line with lots of slice or backspin, trying to keep the ball low. Players should play out the point. They play games of 11 points and switch positions after each game.

Tip

Clay courts are great equalizers. Big servers sometimes find themselves neutralized by the slow surface, so they should work on placement rather than power.

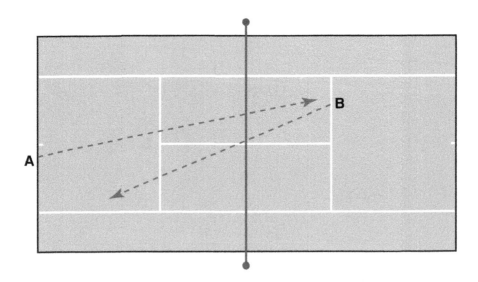

Objective

To help players develop better traction and balance for playing on clay.

Description

This simple but vitally important drill helps players learn how to run down the ball on clay, slide into the ball, and recover to hit the return shot. By having to respond to quick feeds in all directions on the court, players develop the muscles they need to dig into the clay court, hold their balance, and change direction as fast as they can on hard courts.

Execution

Player A takes a position at the baseline near the center (T). Player B is up at the net on the opposite side armed with a basket of balls. Player B hits a series of random shots to player A. Player A must run to return the shots to player B and then return to the center (T) after each shot. Player B can hit a predetermined number of shots or continue until player A can't run anymore.

Tips

Because opponents will be able to retrieve shots more easily, hitting with pace and accuracy is important to hitting winners on clay. Slice helps keep the ball low to the ground and determines whether or not an opponent is physically fit enough to play on clay. Players should exploit the drop shot and the lob and watch the opponent slip, slide, and hustle to recover their strategically placed shots.

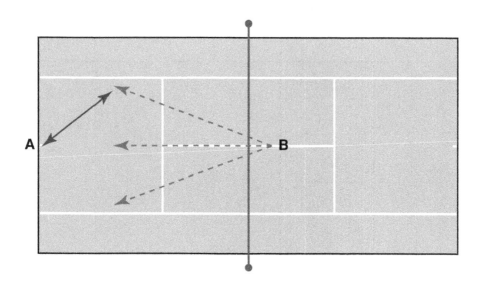

Objective

To help players work on serve and return placement, quick reaction to the ball, rapid change of direction, footwork, and recovery skills.

Description

The serve and return of serve are a player's bread-and-butter shots on grass. The better the ball placement, the better the chance of winning the point. Most players play with placement, depth, and pace (speed and spin); they just don't think about it until after the fact. The goal is to keep the opponent guessing. On the return, players seek to keep the incoming attacker off balance.

Execution

Player A takes a position behind the baseline near the center (T) in the service ready position. Player B takes a position behind the deuce service court. Player A starts the point by serving and approaching the net to hit a volley away from player B. Player B tries to hit the return at player A's feet or pass down the line. Players play out the point. The first to win 21 points wins the match. Players should rotate after the first set of 21 points.

Variation

Players can play an entire match trying to serve and volley.

Tip

The returner should focus most of the returns down at the feet of the serve-and-volleyer. This approach will cause the server to volley the shot up and gives the returner prime opportunity to move in and smack a winner.

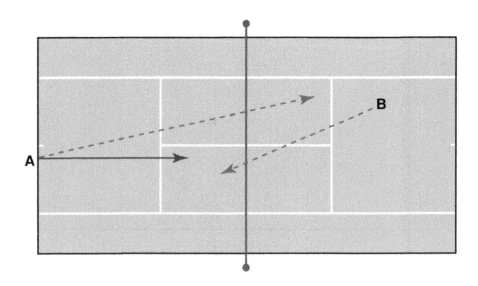

133. FOUR-HIT SERVE-AND-VOLLEY

Objective

To develop a strong, reliable, rhythmic serve-and-volley, split step, and movement diagonally forward to the volley.

Description

The serve-and-volley is a key strategy for playing hard-court and grass-court tennis. Practicing this drill will help players create new dimensions in their game and develop sound offensive singles tactics.

Execution

Player A serves into the deuce-court, the court to the right of the receiver. Player B, positioned on the opposite side of the court, returns the ball so that player A can follow his or her serve up to the net and volley into the advantage-court, the court to the left. Player B shifts over to cover the shot and attempts the passing shot. The players repeat the sequence; player A serves into the advantage-court. Players should rotate after several minutes.

Variation

After players have rotated and practiced in both positions, they play out the points. After one of the players hits the fourth ball in the sequence of shots, the point starts. If the players miss any of the balls during the four-ball sequence, play must start over until the players execute all four patterned balls. They play 11- or 21-point matches, rotating service after every 2 points.

Tip

Players should think of attacking the net more often when the court surface is fast, the wind is at their back, and they feel their presence at the net may put tremendous pressure on their opponent and cause an error.

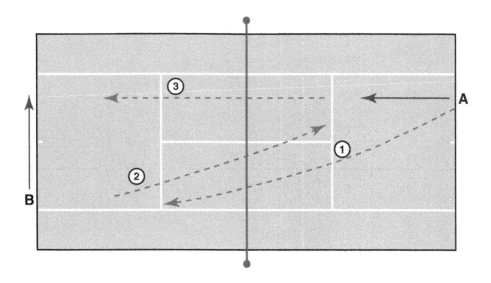

134. THREE-HIT BASELINE

Objective

To build groundstroke consistency, placement of shots, footwork, and recovery skills.

Description

The drill calls for two players at opposite ends of the court. The challenge is to keep many balls in play to build groundstroking consistency and confidence in placing various types of shots.

Execution

This baseline drill begins with a drop-hit groundstroke serve. Player A feeds a drop-hit serve deep in the backcourt to player B. The ball must pass over the net three times before the point starts. Players do not volley within the first three hits. They play 11 or 15 points.

Variation

The drill can be done as a doubles drill, and players can adjust the number of times the ball must pass over the net before the point starts.

Tip

Hard-court tennis is quick, powerful, and exciting. Players should work on their consistency, depth, spin, and speed. Their reflexes must be on, and they must have timing and confidence.

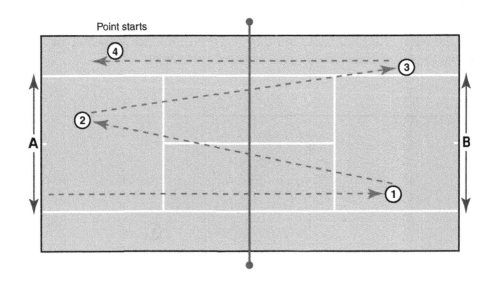

135. HURRICANE

Objective

To build stamina for playing on clay and help clay-court players learn how to change directions quickly, keep good balance, and place shots effectively.

Description

This drill works to improve players' stamina through running short distances with quick bursts of speed to recover shots hit randomly around the court. During most clay-court matches, points take a long time to complete. Outright winners are virtually nonexistent, so players can expect at least a 10- to 15-ball exchange.

Execution

Player A is positioned on the baseline at the center (T). Player B or a server is up at the net on the opposite side. Player B hits a series of random shots to player A around the singles court. Player A may hit anywhere within the singles-court area but must hit each ball on the first bounce. If player A misses a shot or lets the ball bounce more than once, he or she must keep attempting to hit the same shot until a successful shot results. Player B or the server should make the balls challenging but not out of reach of player A. Player A must stay on the court until he or she completes all shots.

Variation

The baseliner can attempt to hit 10 balls in a row. For every ball missed, a point is deducted. For example, player A hits balls 1, 2, 3, and 4 over but mishits ball 5; the player must then start from ball 4. If the player mishits ball 4, he or she starts from ball 3, and so on.

Tip

Slice is the most effective spin players can use on clay.

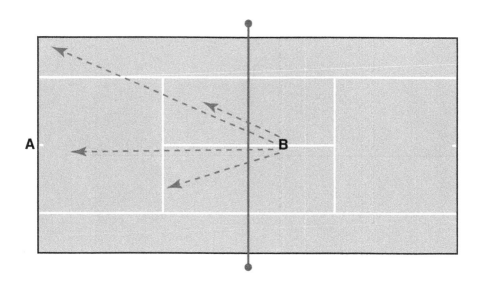

136. MAD BATTER

Objective

To develop quick feet and quick hands for clay-court tennis.

Description

In this his tough conditioning drill, players are required to hit drop shots and recover in time to hit another shot before it bounces twice. Traction and stamina are important with this killer drill. Players who can complete 2 minutes of this drill will not only be able to handle clay but also will be in phenomenal shape.

Execution

Player A is positioned on the service line, and player B is positioned up at the net on the opposite side. Player B feeds player A a soft ball that drops just in front of the net on player A's side. Player A must run up and hit a drop shot anywhere on the opposite side of the net and then backpedal and touch the service line (T) with the racket. Player B feeds a sequence of soft shots for a 2-minute period. Player A continues to run up, hit a drop shot, and backpedal to the service line (T), touching it with the racket each time until he or she completes 2 minutes. Players should switch positions after each 2-minute period.

Tip

If players are still learning how to hit the drop shot, they aren't yet able to disguise it fully. They should limit their use of the drop shot during competition until they have mastered it and opponents can't read when it's coming.

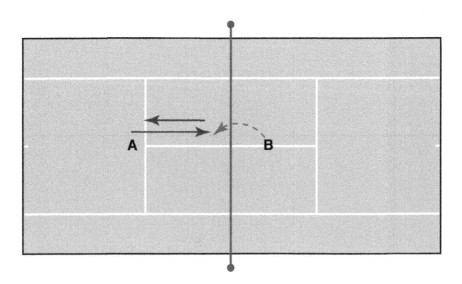

137. FAST GRASS

Objective

To help players develop a sound serve-and-attack game for fast surfaces.

Description

A grass surface forces players to play perfect tennis. Players must place their serves, hit stinging, meaningful returns, and keep their minds focused two strokes ahead of the present. On this surface, rallies are scarce but incredibly exciting when they occur.

Execution

Players A and B are positioned at opposite baselines. Player A begins the rally with a serve to player B. The players rally until one player hits a shot inside one of the service boxes. The player who received the short shot must attack the shot and close in on the net. Both players can be up at the net at the same time. The goal of this drill is to keep the ball deep in the opponent's court so that he or she will never have the chance to come to the net to hit a winning shot.

Tip

A dry court is radically different from a damp one. The footing will change, as will the strokes. For that reason, players at Wimbledon must adapt their strategies as they get closer to the final rounds. The courts are drier and harder, so players must come up with strokes that shorten the rallies.

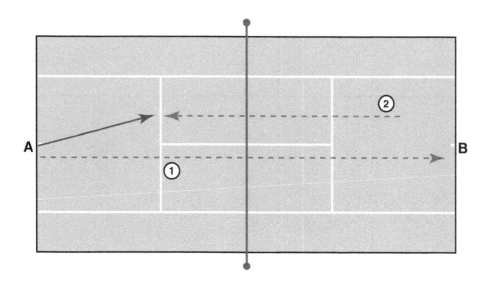

Objective

To develop quick reactions to fast serves, quick feet, a compact backswing, and a pronounced forward attack.

Description

This unique drill can be intimidating at first, but with continuous effort the player who returns will start to develop better footwork, quicker reflexes, and confidence in returning powerful serves.

Execution

Player A, positioned up at the service line, serves to player B. Player B, positioned at the baseline behind one of the service boxes, must try to react quickly enough to handle the serve. Player B should try to return using all four stances and work on returning the ball with topspin or slice. All returns should hit a targeted area either crosscourt deep or down the line deep in the corner.

Variation

After the returner starts to attack every serve using all the hitting stances, the server should start backing up 2 feet (about 60 centimeters) at a time until reaching the baseline, while continuing to serve. The server should alternate sides of the court from the deuce-court to the advantage-court and practice the same techniques. Players rotate positions after several minutes.

Tip

Split stepping is essential to reacting quickly and catching the ball out in front of the body.

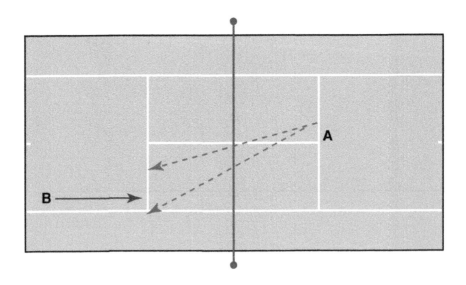

139. HOT-PEPPER SINGLES

Objective

To help players develop stamina, net-coverage ability, reflexes, footwork, and confidence when facing fiery action up at the net.

Description

To be effective at the net, players must have excellent reflexes and volleying skills. This entertaining drill forces players to stay in the frying pan without backing out. Players will build the confidence they need to keep attacking. Players whose reflexes are quick enough can ultimately rule the net.

Execution

Players A and B face each other standing within the service boxes and strad-dling the center service line. Player A begins a volley exchange by hitting the ball underhand to player B. The exchange continues until a player makes an error, hits a winning volley, or successfully hits a lob volley over the opponent. Players may not hit outright hard winners at the opponent, and play must start inside the service-court area. They play to 15 or 21 points.

Variation

The point starts after players execute a three-ball exchange. They play forehand-to-forehand volleys only or backhand-to-backhand volleys only.

140. ADVANCED SINGLES HUSTLE

Objective

To help players learn how to hustle for a variety of shots on the court, develop staying ability on the court, and improve confidence.

Description

This drill builds stamina for long points and teaches players how to run down and cover a variety of shots while playing singles.

Execution

Players position themselves behind the baseline standing in single file with their feet moving (jogging in place). The first player steps up to the center (T) of the baseline. The waiting players move back against the fence or curtain while still moving their feet. A server feeds balls to the first player, making the player hustle for each shot. The server feeds 20 shots—forehands, backhands, drop shots, lobs, short shots, and so on. The level of difficulty should increase for each shot. No scoring is involved.

Variation

Two players hustle to hit and recover all kinds of shots as a team.

Objective

To help players develop quick thinking skills while hitting passing shots on the run.

Description

To play good hard-court tennis, players must improve their overall conditioning, quicken their footwork, and develop consistency, agility, and anticipation skills. This drill helps players stay steady while running down shots by improving their placement and footwork and while hitting on the run and recovering.

Execution

Player A, at the net on one side of the court with a basket of balls, puts the first ball into play by hitting it down the line. Player B returns the ball to player A, who then volleys the ball crosscourt to a target (a prepositioned cone or marker). Player B runs and attempts to hit a passing shot down the line past player A. Player A then slides over to the other side of the court and repeats the steps. Players switch positions after every few points.

Variation

Players rotate to different positions after playing three to five points.

Tip

Players should angle their volleys 99 percent of the time. Volleys hit down the middle of the court tend to come back as winners for the opposing player.

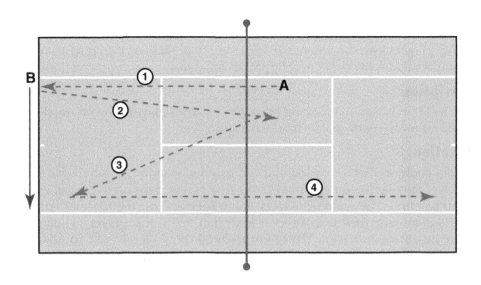

Objective

To help players improve their serve-and-volley tactics, finish off points on hard or grass courts in less time, improve footwork, and develop quick reaction to the ball and rapid advancement to the net.

Description

The drill works the techniques needed to execute the serve-and-volley effectively, and it gives players the opportunity to work on the serve-and-volley game while playing out points.

Execution

Players A and B, who are both positioned behind the baseline, alternate serves to player C. Player C, positioned behind either the deuce or advantage service box, returns the serves. The servers should use only second serves; second serves tend to have more spin and are slower, so the returner can more easily return the ball. Player C can use either the chip and charge or the drive when returning the ball. The first player to accumulate 11 points wins. Players should rotate positions.

Tip

Hard-court tennis is difficult to master and extremely hard on the body. The surface doesn't allow players unlimited years of comfortable, injury-free play. Players should have an alternative game plan that allows them to end points in fewer than six shots.

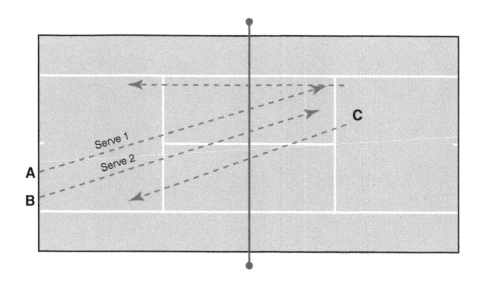

Chapter 11

Mental Mechanics

I have been playing and coaching tennis for more than 40 years. At every decade in my tennis playing life, I learn another lesson about not only the game of tennis but about how the inner game of tennis works. I had the pleasure of meeting and working with Joshua Warren, an MS Sport Psychology Consultant, a PTR Professional Tennis Instructor, the creator of http://integratedtennis.com/, and one of the best up-and-coming tennis instructors who now coaches for Colby College in Waterville, Maine. He has always had his finger on the pulse of what it means to play out of your head or be the ball. Warren mentioned that he would often hear players remark, "I should have won that match, but I beat myself" or "I play better when I drill than in a match." I asked him what he thought about those familiar words.

He said that he first asks players to think of an approximate percentage of how much the mental game influences their tennis play. Next, think of the percentage of time that they practice working on mental toughness. Then he asks if they understand how the difference between the importance of the mental game and the amount of time they practice the mental game affects their play. Warren also makes sure his players understand and learn what it means to be mentally tough and how to improve this skill. *Mentally tough* means nothing can distract a player from what they are trying to accomplish—not a bird, plane, or heckler. They are focused completely on their game, game plan, and ball. Practicing mental mechanics can help players learn how to get out of their own way in order to play their best tennis even under pressure situations.

He also believes in his players being able to play with total mental freedom (*getting in the zone*), and he believes that players who maintain focus and presence on the relevant task during key points will end up successful. He stresses that working on the mental game will take any player's game to the next level just by committing to practice on mental mechanics, an area of the game that is incredibly important yet often underpracticed. Players should cross-train to train the mind, body, and technique. Placing tennis athletes in an entirely new area of competition, such as running track or speedskating, helps to develop flexibility, resilience of thought, and the courage to reach deep inside and perform at their peak performance level.

At least 90 percent of the process of playing well is the result of mental conditioning and mental attitude. To get past lost points, lost matches, or just ordinary off days, players must find a way to purge their minds of negative thoughts so that they can stay in the game, stay in the moment. This chapter focuses on conditioning mental attitude, which should begin from day one of training and continue throughout each player's tennis experience.

143. CHANGEOVER

Objective

To help players develop a private set of crucial techniques to keep on court during match play. They can think of it as their secret pocket tennis coach.

Description

When playing tournaments or club matches, players are entitled to take 90 seconds to rest between games. They should spend this time wisely by focusing on the game plan and preparing for the next move.

Execution

Players should never rush to get back into the fire just because the opponent is standing ready to serve. The opponent's action is a tactical maneuver to throw off the player's rhythm. If things aren't going well, players should take this time to think back over the last game. Is the serve working? Are returns going deep and to the targeted areas? Players should check the game plan. Are they sticking to what works for them? They should avoid thinking too much about missed points and concentrate only on the last game and the game plan. Incorporating yoga and meditation will help any player learn how to keep focused during long matches and easy matches. Sometimes just keeping a simple mantra or song in the back of the mind can help a player find focus. They should stick with the game plan but be flexible at the same time. Perhaps a player goes into a match knowing that the opponent has a weak forehand but quickly finds that the opponent is winning big with it. The opponent's forehand has become an effective weapon, and the player must change the pregame plan. During your off-court practice sessions, a player should work on every kind of match scenario possible, including playing against a hulk (power player with little control) or a sloth (slow-moving player who seems to take forever to put a serve into play), so that when faced with an unpredictable player, he or she can reach into the bag of tricks and play with full confidence.

Variation

When nerves and or anxiety creep into players' psyche, they should use breathing techniques, such as breathing in deeply, holding for 10 seconds, and exhaling. Do this 3 times, regroup, and move into the next point. They should take all of the allotted time in between points, games, and changeovers to regroup, recoup, and regain composure.

Tip

Advanced planning can really pay off in doubles, so players should plan. When they sit down during changeovers, players should talk quietly with their partners about strategy. Two heads are often better than one.

144. TICK-TOCK

Objective

To use rhythmic patterns to teach players how to set up strategic patterns for placement of shots in singles play and to help players concentrate on their game.

Description

Good athletes make performing their particular sport look like a dance. To make shots look as smooth as silk, players must use rhythmic patterns to develop rallying strategies.

Execution

Player A is positioned on the baseline at the center (T), and player B is positioned on the opposite baseline. Player A begins the rally with a drop-hit serve. Player A hits one shot crosscourt and the next down the line. Player B does the same. The players use each pattern of hitting for at least 10 minutes before trying the next. Player A hits three shots crosscourt and the next one down the line. Player B does the same. *Tick-tock-tick-tock* stands for a crosscourt, down-the-line, crosscourt, down-the-line pattern. *Tick-tick-tick-tock* stands for three shots crosscourt and then one shot down the line. Pattern development will help players concentrate more on the game plan than on the opponent.

Variation

Players can mix up tick-tock rhythmic patterns. Using cue words such as *bounce-hit* when drilling or playing can help develop concentration skills. A cue word is one that players say to themselves or one that the coach says repeatedly to players while they are working to achieve a certain task. It may sound silly, but it really works.

Tip

Players should remember to keep the head steady and still through contact the way golfers do. One overlooked leading cause of a mishit groundstroke is a slight lifting of the chin or head (sneaking a peek at their shots) before the shot is fully executed. This tiny movement changes the angle of the racket face, thereby changing the hitting zone. It can also throw a player off balance. In order for players to drive shots the full length of the court with increased accuracy, they need to learn to trust themselves and keep the head down and eyes focused on the ball through contact.

Objective

To teach players how and when to hit approach shots and to build their confidence in hitting solid passing shots.

Description

By isolating strokes and patterns, players can practice them so that they become second nature. When players are in match play, patterns of performance should click right in without their having to think about it.

Execution

Player A is positioned behind the service line, and player D is positioned on the baseline. Players C and B wait in line to rotate in after one point is played. Player A hits a ball to player D's backhand and approaches the net. Player D hits the passing-shot ball, and player A volleys the ball to the other side of the court. Players C and B repeat the pattern several times to the same side of the court. Player D rotates with player A after the players have had a chance to play. Scoring is optional, because this is a practice drill.

Variation

Players can rotate to all positions. Players can hit forehands.

Tips

Players should train for good endurance, strength, flexibility, and speed. They should enhance their repertoire of shots and add topspin, slice, lobs, and drop shots and remember that their physical fitness determines their mental toughness.

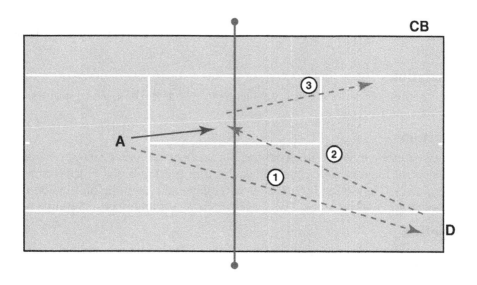

146. TWO BACK–ONE UP

Objective

To teach players quick recovery skills, liability of short volleys, passing-shot coverage, quick feet and hands, and anticipation skills.

Description

This drill challenges a net player's game. By having two players positioned on the baseline to challenge the net player, the drill forces the net player to work hard and think clearly in order to move quickly enough to cover every shot.

Execution

Two players position themselves behind the baseline, one on the deuce-side (the service court to the player's right when facing the service-court area), and the other on the advantage-side (the service court to the left). One player is up at the net on the opposite side of the net. The baseliners hit shots at the net player and try to move him or her around as much as possible. The backcourt players should hit lobs and mix in some passing shots. All balls should be within reach of the net player. Scoring is optional.

Tip

The backcourt players should use a variety of lobs, topspin, and backspin and hit high and deep or with bullet trajectory. They can mix in some soft passing shots as well.

147. SHADOW VOLLEY

Objective

To teach players proper footwork while volleying in a simulated point-playing situation.

Description

This entertaining drill helps players learn to watch the ball, set up points, and anticipate shots.

Execution

Players separate into two lines behind the service line center on opposite sides of the court. Players volley against each other until one player misses or the ball bounces. They must hit all shots as volleys and keep the ball inside their respective service box areas. The first team to accumulate 11 or 15 points wins.

Variation

Players can be limited to using only their forehand volleys or only their backhand volleys. If players are restricted to the use of the forehand volley, a shot hit with the backhand volley ends the point. This rule forces players to use their feet and strategically figure out how to hit to the opposing team's wrong side.

148. EVERLASTING SERVICE

Objective
To help players develop good concentration skills while trying to hold or break service games.

Description
This drill eliminates the second serve to force players to concentrate on executing good ball tosses, spin serves, and excellent placement of serve while under pressure.

Execution
Player A serves game after game until player B breaks serve. If player A loses serve on the first attempt, player B takes over the service game. Players can execute this method while playing an entire match.

Tip
Players should work on consistency and be patient while building the point.

149. CAPTAIN HOOK SERVICE

Objective
To help players develop consistency and effectiveness of second serves; the second serve must be as reliable as the rising of the sun.

Description
This drill helps players develop a reliable second serve by allowing only one serve per point.

Execution
In a set or match of singles or doubles, players are allowed only one serve per point. If they miss the serve, they lose the point.

Variation
Players should incorporate the one-serve-only rule while playing a 15-point game or a 12-point tiebreaker. These mental tactics should really challenge players' service fortitude while under pressure.

Tip
Servers should concentrate on using second serves and placement. The second serve should have a lot more spin and less pace.

Objective

To help players build confidence for match play situations by playing with preplanned formulas of shot combinations to isolate a specific area of the game.

Description

Players play an entire set aiming the serve and return to a specific area. Players practice one predetermined pattern of shots to help make the sequence of strokes second nature.

Execution

Player A serves every ball to player B's backhand, and player B returns every ball to player A's backhand volley. Only serves and returns are predetermined; all other shots are up to the players. After the return, players play out the point as usual using regular scoring. Players may use this method to play an entire match or just to practice a few points. As players run this pattern, they start to imprint it in their minds for future match play.

Variation

Players can use any preplanned configuration of serve and return of serve.

Tip

Anticipation, like the killer instinct, is an art learned through many hours of practice and playing hundreds or thousands of points, games, and matches. One can't simply buy it or find it.

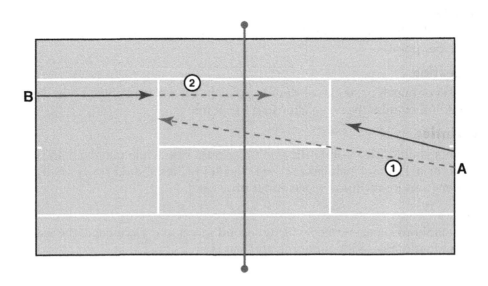

Roger Federer
Icy Coolness

Roger Federer is considered one of the world's greatest tennis players with 17 Grand Slam wins—7 at Wimbledon, 4 at the Australian Open, and 5 at the US Open as of March of 2013. His success has come from his development of mental toughness. As a juniors player, he wore his emotions on his sleeve for everyone, including his opponents, to see. However, as he entered the frying pan of men's professional tennis and began performing in front of millions of people, he developed the ability to reign in his emotions.

Federer has said that he doesn't get nervous during a match anymore, and he doesn't feel the need to throw rackets or balls out of the court or scream. He laughs on the inside about it a little bit when an opponent does it. Even though he did enjoy watching Goran Ivanisevic and John McEnroe throw their rackets and scream at the chair umpires, while on the court, Roger thinks to himself about respect for the fans sitting there and not embarrassing himself in front of millions of people.

Today, Roger is one of the coolest tennis players on the pro tennis tour. He can fall 2 sets behind and you would never know that he was losing; no matter the score, he plays like a winner. Perhaps that is why he has a way of coming back from 2 sets down, 5-0 in the third set, 40-love and winning the match!

Objective

To develop players' control and accuracy in a groundstroke-to-volley game situation.

Description

This drill keeps players on their toes while teaching them to control the ball, recover quickly after hitting, and maintain a solid hitting pattern while under some stress. The drill helps singles players build the confidence they need to run down any shot and get to any volley hit wide or down the line.

Execution

Player A starts at the baseline, and player B is up at the net. Player A hits every ball down the line, and player B hits every ball crosscourt. After 5 or 10 minutes they switch directions.

Variation

Player A must hit every third ball with a specific stroke and to a specific area on the court. For example, player B hits every volley down the line and player A hits every shot crosscourt, but on the third ball player A hits a crosscourt topspin lob.

Tip

Players can improve their ball control if they learn to obey their on-court "speed limit." Players' speed limit on the tennis court is the maximum pace they can put on the ball without losing control of it. By limiting the speed, players will improve placement and consistency and will become better, stronger players.

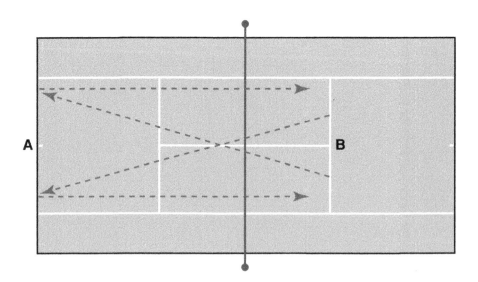

152. BALL-MACHINE STRETCH VOLLEY

Objective

To improve volleying or groundstroking skills, footwork, athletic proficiency, quick reaction to the incoming ball, and placement of shots under stress.

Description

Working with a ball machine is challenging both mentally and physically. The ball machine never misses! Because players can set up the ball machine to send balls anywhere on the court, they can isolate and work on a specific stroke or series of strokes as long as they desire without having to stop and start because of a partner's rallying mistakes. Ball-machine drilling helps make any practiced stroke better. Setting the ball machine to oscillate in order to practice certain patterns of play can help players find ways to dig out of defensive situations and get back in the game.

Execution

Players set up the ball machine to feed shots down the line. They position themselves up at the net so that they are ready to hit. The balls coming across the net should simulate the shots of a baseliner trying to pass his or her opponent. After having some success with this drill, players will be able to reach anything that even the best opponents will throw at them.

Variation

Players can use the ball machine to drill any stroke—volleys, overheads, short shots, lobs, forehands, and backhands—from the net to the baseline. They can set the ball to work on groundstroke patterns such as the two-to-one pattern. Players will hit two forehands crosscourt and one backhand crosscourt. Or, try this three-to-one pattern: Players hit three forehands crosscourt and one backhand crosscourt.

The ball machine can also be set to help players learn how to retrieve drop shots and lobs. Set the ball machine to shoot one soft ball, which should land inside of the service-court area, and one hard high shot, which should drive a player back to the baseline to retrieve the lob.

Tip

When using ball machines, keep the playing court clear of loose balls so that players can focus on the oncoming ball. Obviously, the ball machine will continue to shoot balls out and in the players' direction whether they look for them or not, so players must be reminded to keep their eyes peeled and focused on the action at hand.

Objective

To develop players' confidence in hitting passing shots when on the run and when tired.

Description

The drill helps players learn to hit to a certain area of the court when tired or on the run. Players will learn how to perform and carry out the game plan even when they would rather be lying on the ground.

Execution

Player A is positioned up at the net on one side of the court, and player B is positioned behind the baseline on the opposite side of the net. Player B must return all balls to player A's side of the court. Player A volleys them back to just barely within reach of player B. The intention is to get player B to run as much as possible for each ball but at the same time keep the ball in play for as long as possible. Scoring is optional, because this is a practice drill. Players rotate positions after several minutes.

Tip

When hitting a ball and running at full speed, players must keep the eyes focused on the incoming shot and keep the head steady. If they try to peek at the shot, they will mishit the ball or the shot won't make it past the service line on their side of the court.

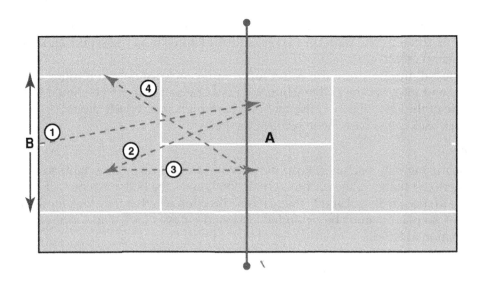

154. VOLLEY LUNGE

Objective

To develop stamina, quick evasive movements, quick recovery, and anticipation skills.

Description

This challenging drill develops sound volleying technique, helps players avoid swinging up at the net, forces players to keep the racket out in front, and allows players to let the racket do most of the work.

Execution

Player A stands to the right of the center (T) at the baseline. Player B stands up at the net inside of one of the service boxes, either deuce or advantage. Player A hits a ball wide to player B down the alley sideline. Player B returns the shot with a volley back to player A. Player A hits the ball wide crosscourt back to player B. Player B returns the shot with a volley back to player A. They repeat this sequence a few times, then they switch positions.

Tips

Players must remember to split step before every volley. If players have a tendency to hit volleys into the net, they may be stopping the forward movement of the racket. This action causes the racket head to dump over slightly, which sends the ball down into the net. Another problem is releasing the tension in the wrist and allowing the racket head to drop out sideways below the wrist. Players should try to keep moving as they approach the volley to ensure a solid hit. When stretched out wide to hit a passing-shot volley, they should always keep the wrist cocked high.

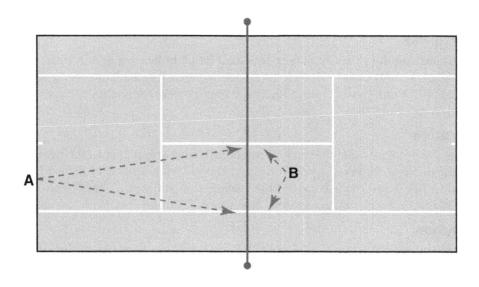

155. SERVE-AND-VOLLEY

Objective

To isolate the serve-and-volley to develop quick feet and hands, anticipation skills, and ability to close in on the net.

Description

By practicing only the serve-and-volley tactic, players can work specifically on the footwork, reflexes, and confidence they need to use this aggressive plan during match play.

Execution

Player A is behind one of the service boxes and hits returns, while players B, C, and D serve and volley from behind the opposite baseline. Servers alternate playing out points against the receiver. The first player who wins 10 points, either the receiver or one of the serve-and-volleyers, wins the drill.

Variation

Servers are allowed only one serve and must close in and volley or forfeit the point and turn. The receiver must hit returns to a designated area of the court (down the line, down the middle of the court, or a chip low at the server's feet).

156. RAZZLE DAZZLE AT THE NET

Objective

To help players learn how to move out wide for volleys and recover quickly with control; and to help players build agility, speed, and confidence in total court coverage.

Description

By exhausting the primary player, this drill helps in becoming a more physically and mentally balanced player. After performing this drill numerous times, players will think that running down shots or leaping for shots during match play is a piece of cake.

Execution

Players A and B position themselves on the baseline, and player C, the primary player in this drill, takes a position up at the net. Players A and B feed balls from the backcourt in such a way that player C must lunge from alley to alley to make the volleys. Players switch after several minutes.

Variation

Players set up the same way except that player C starts at the center of the opposite baseline. Players A and B are positioned up at the net and feed balls so that player C is forced to run but the balls are within reach. The purpose is to run player C from side to side and up and back. Player C must return the ball.

157. PATTERNED NET RUSH

Objective

To isolate a game plan for attack and recovery at the net, enhancing midcourt and net coverage, quick footwork, development of net confidence, and anticipation; and to help players build overall knowledge of what to do in common situations in singles match play.

Description

During match play, players must perform extremely fast-paced exchanges of volleys at the net. The purpose of this drill is for players to practice those fast volleys in a programmed fashion to solidify the techniques they need in order to perform effectively under stress.

Execution

After announcing where the serve will land, player A serves to player B. Player B returns the serve to player A. Player A makes a first volley back to player B. Player B lobs the ball over player A, and player A hits an overhead. For both players to benefit, at least five shots must go over the net and in the court within reach of the opponent. Players must keep the first five balls in play. From the sixth ball on, both players may try to win points.

Variation

The server should serve to different areas of the court, and the receiver should return to both sides to vary the pattern.

158. SCRAMBLED EGG

Objective

To improve confidence, speed, conditioning, and agility at the net.

Description

The drill helps players develop the speed, agility, confidence, and fundamental technique they need to hit any shot they may encounter up at the net during competition.

Execution

Player A serves and attacks the net. Player B, who is on the opposite side of the court, disregards the served ball and proceeds to hit a sequence of 20 different shots from a nearby basket of balls. Player B should watch for loose balls rolling around under player A's feet. The object is to make player A hit the first volley and move quickly from side to side and up and back for difficult drives, lobs, and fluff balls. After completing a sequence of 20, players switch positions or rotate. No scoring is involved.

Competition and Match Play

This part of the book is dedicated to all tennis players who love to play and want desperately to improve their skills, but despise drilling. Drilling is hard work. Players spend grueling hours repeating drills such as hitting forehands crosscourt over and over until their legs feel like jelly. During drills they sweat, they huff and puff and, quite frankly, they get bored. This part offers many creative ways to make drilling fun, which in turn helps players welcome a good volley or groundstroke drill.

Cardio tennis drilling is just one exciting method tennis instructors are using to enhance the same drills their students have been doing for years. It may seem sneaky to hide the drill behind the thrill of a game, but players will get similar practice without the urge to complain about it because of the added element of fun. Players can truly accomplish huge changes because drilling while playing competitive tennis games is more fun, more inclusive, pressureless, and easier to grasp. Instant results is what all tennis players want when they take a lesson, but the reality is that it takes countless hours and balls in order to make a technique stick. So if a player must hit 5,000 serves in order to finally learn and feel how to hit a kick serve, what's better than learning how to hit that pesky serve than through fun, game-based learning?

The introduction of QuickStart Tennis red, orange, and green balls allows for a great way to help not only very young tennis players who are new at hitting but also adults who may want to start playing tennis later in life. Using QuickStart balls helps to slow the game down to a speed and level that is height appropriate, age appropriate and friendly to all levels of ability.

The next few chapters offer an array of competitive singles, doubles, and multiplayer competitive tennis games. Competitive tennis games are a combination of strategic drills and entertaining games. So while players are having fun laughing, playing, and huffing and puffing, they are also learning how to move, focus, and think like competitive tennis players. Reinforcing tennis fundamentals doesn't always require constant drilling, nor should it. A much better approach is playing challenging, fun, competitive singles, doubles, and multiplayer games.

Chapter 12

Singles Games

Fun, challenging competitive singles games can greatly accelerate the learning and understanding of all tennis strokes, tactics, and strategies. Playing competitive games is the best way to reinforce what players have learned through drilling. The games in this chapter give beginners through tournament-level players a chance to see the fruits of their tennis labor. Playing singles games helps to solidify all of the fundamentals of playing and competing in the game of tennis but in a pressure-free environment. Players can start to put basic match tactics and strategies into play while building confidence in using all that has been learned. Competitive game playing allows identification of any small progression in players' game development; players will be able to see if they really understand the fundamentals of tennis.

A key ingredient in becoming a successful player is confidence in one's strokes. Confidence helps create champions on and off of the tennis court. Playing the creative competitive games in this chapter will guide players in keeping a positive attitude—whether winning or losing—and competing at all levels of match play. The games in this chapter will also help players master the art of competing mentally and physically under matchlike conditions while still enjoying the competition.

159. KING OR QUEEN OF THE COURT

Objective

To help players of any level improve their singles skills in a fun, mildly pressured game situation.

Description

This game allows players to test their consistency, ball-placement skills, and singles strategy while competing in a singles match play situation.

Execution

One player, dubbed the *king* or *queen*, takes the top position on the opposite side of the court from the challengers. The challengers are positioned off the court and take turns playing out points against the king or queen to try to take over the top position. After accumulating a certain number of points (perhaps 10), the challenger dethrones the king or queen and takes over the top position of the court. Only the challenger collects points. The king or queen works only to play out the points to prevent the challenger from dethroning him or her. All the other players lose their points and must start from zero once the king or queen wins the desired number of points.

Variation

Players can play this game in the minicourt area using QuickStart red, orange, and green balls. Players can play king or queen doubles, by playing two people (Kings or Queens) on one side of the court against two other players on the opposite side of the court.

160. TENNIS BLACKJACK

Objective

To develop ball-placement skills, footwork, and groundstroking skills.

Description

This game challenges players to use their weaker strokes. Forcing players to choose only a weaker stroke isolates that stroke, which helps to improve it.

Execution

During the game, players may choose to use any stroke that they think they need to work on, such as running forehands, backhands, overheads, or something else. All players are positioned single file behind the baseline center (T). A server is on the opposite side of the court up at the net. The first player in line comes up to the baseline center (T) and attempts to hit the specific stroke. If the player hits the shot into the singles-court area between the net and the service line, 1 point is earned. Placing the ball between the service line and the baseline earns 2 points. Players rotate after every shot. If a player accumulates 13 points, a turn is lost, all points are forfeited, and play starts again from 0. The first player to reach 21 points wins.

Objective

To help develop good footwork, strategy, groundstroking fundamentals, and gamesmanship.

Description

This game encourages singles strategizing. Playing two against one is hard enough, but incorporating the *anything goes* rule (there are no restrictions on the types of shots a player may hit) helps the singles player and doubles players think of creative ways to build and set up shots to win the point or game. This game is important because it is the beginning stage of learning how to think strategically on the tennis court. Singles players must decide how to set up the shot so that they can close in on the net and finish the point fast, or they will literally run out of steam trying to out-rally two players on the opposite side of the net.

Execution

Player A takes a position at the opposite side of the court behind the baseline center (T). Player A is king or queen of the court. Other players take positions in teams of two behind the other baseline. The singles player hits into the doubles alleys, but the challenging teams use only the singles-court area. A server feeds the ball to player A, the king or queen, to start. Player A plays out the point against the first team up on the baseline. If the team wins the point, they keep it and continue to play until they either accumulate 15 points and win the match or lose a point. Teams rotate whenever a point is lost. The first team to reach 15 points against the king or queen wins the match.

Variation

Including an additional player to compete against the king or queen adds a level of difficulty for the singles player.

Tips

Players can use QuickStart orange and green balls to slow the pace of the ball and the game. Players should remember that depth and control are more important than pace. Singles players have quite a bit of court to cover, so playing smarter instead of trying to hit every ball harder is the way to go. Players should be definite about shot selection and court positioning, and they should work to build up points before unleashing every weapon in their arsenal.

162. MINI-ME TENNIS

Objective

To help develop finesse skills, footwork, and court movement.

Description

This game helps players develop a feel for the ball by isolating the playing area. Players can hit any type of shot and spin with pace or use a little finesse to win points.

Execution

Players are positioned up at the service line opposite each other. Player A starts the game with either a drop feed or by using a regular serve. Players can use any combination of shots. They should try playing an entire match using the service-court area.

Variations

Players can use QuickStart red, orange or green balls. Players can also work on their serving and volleying; they can use the rule that the server can score points only by serving and then volleying.

163. SINGLES MINING FOR GOLD

Objective

To teach players how to control the ball, direct the ball, and use various strokes to hit to designated targets during match play.

Description

In this entertaining gaming method, players play out a regular game of tennis, scoring in the usual manner until one player hits a designated target, for which he or she will be rewarded with extra points or games. This game can be played either full court, half court, or minicourt.

Execution

Players A and B are positioned behind opposite baselines. Players play out a regular tennis match with standard scoring. Three small hoops or targets are placed on each side of the net. Both players try to hit a ball into one of the targets while rallying and playing out a point. A player who hits a target automatically wins the point. Scoring is by the regular scoring method—15, 30, 40, game.

Variations

Players under 10 years of age can use QuickStart orange and green balls to slow down the game. Target hoops are placed only in service boxes, and players can win points by serving into the target hoops. Another variation is to require players to use only one stroke (perhaps backhand groundstrokes or backhand volleys or overheads) to hit targets and score a point or game.

164. CHEESEBURGER AND FRIES

Objective

To promote good footwork and teach players how to play defensive and offensive singles.

Description

This game is King of the Court with a twist. By taking positions next to the doubles sideline at the service line, players learn good footwork, realize the value of early racket preparation, and have fun while learning to keep the ball in play.

Execution

One player takes a position on the opposite side of the court on the baseline and is dubbed the *cheeseburger*. The other players (*fries*) line up one behind another next to the doubles sideline at the service line on the opposite side of the court. The server gives the "Go" command, and the first player in line sidesteps out to the center service line (T) and then backpedals to the baseline. At this point the server feeds a forehand ball to the challenger (fries). The players begin rallying until one misses. If the challenger wins the point, he or she has 5 seconds to run from the baseline over to the other baseline, while the next player standing in line sidesteps out to the service line (T) and backpedals to the baseline. If the cheeseburger wins the point, he or she keeps the point and remains the cheeseburger. The challenger goes to the end of the line. The first player to win 15 points wins the game.

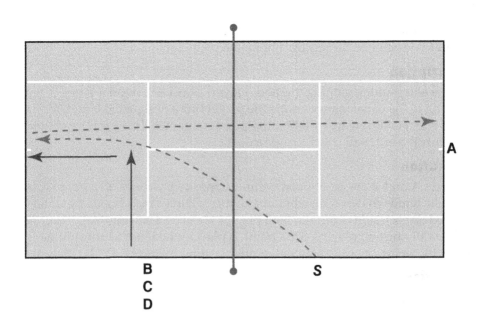

165. ROTATING SINGLES

Objective

To reinforce groundstroking skills, footwork, and ball placement.

Description

Players learn how to build up points and to move in and attack to win the point.

Execution

Rotating Singles is like O-U-T (see chapter 13, drill 172) except that after hitting the first ball, players rotate to the end of the line on their side of the court only. Players A and B take positions behind one baseline center (T), and players C and D take positions behind the opposite baseline center (T). The doubles alleys are out. The server feeds the first ball to player A, who hits a groundstroke to player C. Player A rotates to the end of the line, and player B steps in to receive the shot coming back from player C. Player C hits player A's shot and rotates to the end of the line, and player D steps up to receive the shot that player B will hit. Players hit and rotate until the point ends. The first team to win 21 points wins the match.

Variation

To turn this game into a great conditioning tool, players can jog in place between hitting the shots and use QuickStart orange and green balls because they slow the pace of the game down and really force players to stroke through various shots.

166. SINGLES ATTACK

Objective

To reinforce groundstroking fundamentals, singles strategy, ball placement, and footwork skills.

Description

This game requires players to use all their groundstroking skills to set up points to attack when the opportunity arises.

Execution

Players A and B are positioned behind opposite baselines. Player A starts the point with either a serve or a drop-hit serve to player B. Both players rally for the point until player B yells, "Attack!" Player A must then rush the net, no matter where the ball is or where player A is. The players try to finish the point. They play to 21 points.

Objective

To help players develop ball-control skills, footwork skills, ball placement, and direction.

Description

This game requires players to learn how to control where they hit the ball. Isolating strokes and the boundaries of the playing court forces players to really concentrate on improving technique. It helps players to forget about all of the other areas within their game that may need work. Adding a little competitive point play also helps players use the troubled area while under the pressure of match play.

Execution

Players A and B are on opposite baselines. Both players are restricted to using only half the court, including the doubles alley. Players can use the deuce half or the advantage half of the court. Player A serves the ball with a drop-hit serve to player B. The serve should fall behind the service line. Both players play out the point using every stroke they know to win the point; anything goes. The first player to accumulate 21 points wins the game. Serves rotate every 2 points. Players should play with only three balls to keep loose balls away from the playing area.

Variations

Players can play this game using only the alley, or they can play crosscourt and include the doubles alleys. Another variation is to require the receiver of a short shot to move in, play the approach, and then attack the net. The attacking player can retreat from the net only if lobbed. He or she may then stay back and work the point.

Tip

A simple rule to help players achieve the desired direction of many shots is to know that the racket face controls the direction of the ball. The ball will go in the direction the strings are facing, because the ball bounces off the racket at right angles. When the racket face is looking diagonally across the net, the ball will go crosscourt. When the racket face is looking squarely at the net with the strings parallel to the net, the ball will go down the line. If players are having trouble controlling where they hit the ball, they should remember this rule.

168. SINGLES GO

Objective

To help players work on singles strategy, countering overhead smashes, and retrieving lobs.

Description

This fast-paced, exciting game really gets players moving. The game emphasizes lob recovery, overhead placement, and strong baseline recovery skills.

Execution

Players line up behind the baseline. A player dubbed the *king* or *queen* is at the net standing on the opposite side. A challenger steps up to the baseline. A server feeds a difficult overhead to the king or queen, who tries to put away the overhead against the first challenger. If the king or queen is successful, he or she stays up at the net, receives one point, and faces another challenger. If the king or queen loses the point, the server yells, "Go!" and the challenger runs from his or her side of the court to the other while the server hits a high lob that is difficult for the challenger to put into play against the new challenger. If the new king or queen wins the point, he or she starts up at the net. The king or queen who lost goes to the end of the line but keeps the points.

Variation

Players can play a doubles version of this game using the preceding rules.

Chapter 13

Doubles and Multiplayer Games

Doubles is truly the sport of a lifetime. Doubles by definition suggests shared responsibilities on the court, which translates into less energy output by each player. Doubles isn't as taxing on the body as the game of singles is. Players have less court to cover and the focus is on the placement of shots and strategy instead of power and sprinting from side to side and up and back. There are some players who reach the age of 70 and pick up tennis again or start playing for the first time. They have a wonderful time playing as well as getting a great low impact workout. Many doubles players play for 3 or 4 hours a day, some of them up to 7 days a week. Some of these tennis diehards are over the age of 60, and they love playing doubles.

It's also a wonderful idea for younger players to learn how to play doubles because it teaches patience, court strategy, placement of shots, and consequences of shot selection and is an alternative to solely playing singles.

Doubles players are smart players. They know that teamwork, strategy, and communication are keys to success in the doubles game. The best way to prepare for a long and happy lifetime of playing doubles is to learn the doubles game, drill to work on weaknesses, and practice what experience has taught during competitive doubles games or multiplayer games (games with many players participating in it). Playing competitive doubles games helps players discover their specific jobs and responsibilities during a doubles match. A player who knows the specific responsibility at each position can perform with elevated confidence during actual doubles competition. Playing the games in this chapter will help players develop the fundamentals for playing doubles matches effectively and competitively.

169. KNOCKER TENNIS

Objective

To help players determine their skill level and give them a sense of what it's like to play in a tournament.

Description

Six or more players can participate in this method of match playing. Players of different abilities can compete against each other. The rotation of match playing gives each team and player an opportunity to play a variety of match-playing game styles.

Execution

Players should partner up into doubles teams. Teams A, B, C, and D compete against one another. When a team wins a match, they collect 1 point. The team that wins 15 points wins the competition. Each team plays the best of four regular scoring games. The winning team rotates one court up toward the first court, the highest court.

Variation

Players can play singles and minicourt singles or doubles using this game.

Tip

Players should work on building the points slowly and steadily. This approach builds confidence and success on the court. Players should remember the C + A = S equation: Confidence + Aggressiveness = Success.

170. TENNIS BASEBALL

Objective

To reinforce the value of directing the ball to different areas of the court.

Description

This great game teaches players how to direct and control shots. By using baseball terminology for placement of shots, players get a sense of team participation while practicing groundstrokes.

Execution

As few as 2 or as many as 20 players can play tennis baseball. With fewer than 4 players on the court, all players begin on the same side of the court positioned behind the center (T), one behind the other. A server is positioned up at the net and is the pitcher. The first player in line comes up to the baseline (T) or the service line (T), depending on ability level. Each player gets two strikes and then must give up the turn for the next player to step up and hit. Strikes are balls hit into the net, out of the court area, or missed outright. Any ball hit between the net and the service line, which extends into the doubles alley, counts as a single, for which the player receives one point. A ball landing inside no-man's-land (the area of the tennis court which lays 2 feet inside of the baseline and 2 feet behind the service line) is a double and earns two points. A ball hit into the doubles alley but behind the service line on either side of the court is a triple, worth three points. A ball that hits the baseline on the first bounce is a home run and earns four points. Players keep their own scores. This version of baseball tennis includes no base running, catching, or tagging.

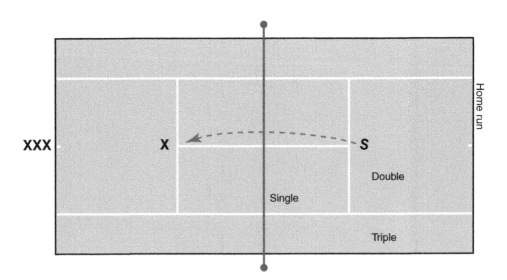

Variation

When six or more are playing, the players split up into two teams, team A and team B. Team A takes a position behind the baseline as the hitting team. Team B is in the outfield on the other side of the net scattered around the court. The net post on the right side of the tennis court is first base, the center (T) is second base, the left net post is third base, and the baseline center (T) on the hitting team's side is home plate. When a hitter hits a ball in a designated area of the court and a fielding player catches the shot out of the air with his or her hands, the hitter is out. Balls that bounce are safe shots, and the hitter takes the base that coincides with the placement of the shot. For example, a ball hit into no-man's-land is a double, and the hitter takes second base. Runs are forced in, and tagging and running from base to base are not allowed. The placement of the balls hit by the hitter determines the scoring of the runs. After three outs, teams rotate. They play nine innings and eat lots of hot dogs!

Tip

Learning to play against and work with different types of players enhances a player's ability to identify and compete against different styles of games and players.

171. STICKY SITUATION

Objective

To develop volleying and lobbing skills.

Description

This game improves confidence during attack and defense in doubles play.

Execution

Team A is positioned on the baseline facing team B, positioned up at the net. A server feeds the first ball to team A to start the point. Team A tries to hit a deep lob over team B. Team B tries to knock off the lob with an overhead to win the point. If the lob is successful, team B must retrieve the lob and hustle back up to the net. Team A is allowed to lob only; no groundstroke passing shots are allowed. The first team to win 21 points wins the game.

Tip

Players must remember that doubles is a team game. As a team, players should exploit the lob over their opponents' heads and then attack the net. Many teams fail to attack when the opportunity arises. That failure can prove costly because it's easier to win a point at the net than it is at the baseline. Players can use the lob to open up the forecourt rather than try to blast the ball through their opponents at the net.

172. O-U-T

Objective

To help players develop consistency, ball placement, and strategy.

Description

In this entertaining game, players split up and take positions behind opposite baselines. Only one ball is in play, and players must keep the ball going back and forth across the net in the singles court only. The action is almost like juggling one ball among a large group of players.

Execution

O-U-T. can be played with six or more players—the more the better. Players split up and take positions opposite each other, standing in a single-file line behind the baseline center (T). A server feeds a ball to the first player in line on either side of the net. That player hits the ball and runs to the end of the line on the opposite side of the court. The first player in the opposite line returns the ball and runs to the end of the line on the opposite side of the court. Play continues until a player misses. That player receives the letter O. Play resumes. Players who accumulate all letters of the word *OUT* are out of the game and sit in a designated area until the game ends. The last player left wins.

Objective

To help players develop lobbing and overhead skills.

Description

Six or more players can play this game. The game teaches players how to lob over their opponents' heads. By isolating the lob and the overhead stroke, players can work out any jitters they have about hitting them during competition.

Execution

Players A, B, and C are a team; and players D, E, and F are a team. Players A and B are on the baseline, and player C is up at the net on the same side. Players D and E are on the opposite baseline, and player F is up at the net on the same side. A server feeds the first ball to player A. The four players at the baseline can hit only lobs. Their goal is to lob over the players at the net so that players C and F can't hit an overhead. Players C and F may not go behind the service line to hit a shot. The players play out the points up to 21 and then rotate so that each team member has a chance to play the net position.

Tips

Weak lobs allow the opposition to move up and smash an overhead for a winner. Players should focus on hitting forward through the ball, apply a little topspin with a low-to-high motion, and complete the follow-through as they would when hitting groundstrokes. Players should also try to hit high defensive or offensive lobs with backspin.

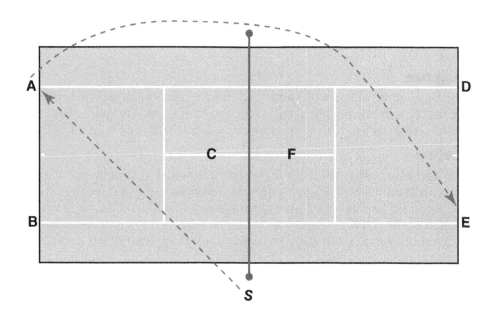

174. STAYING ALIVE

Objective

To reinforce good stroke production, footwork, shot selection, and ball placement.

Description

This game promotes teamwork and teaches players to think before they hit to avoid setting up themselves or their partners to be killed off.

Execution

This game can be played with four or more players—the more the better. Players split up into two groups. There are no teams; players keep their own scores. Players start with 10 lives; each time they lose a point, they lose a life. One group of players is behind one baseline (T), and the other group is behind the other baseline (T). A server starts the point by feeding a ball to the first player in one of the lines, who hits the ball and rotates to the end of the same line. The first player in the opposite line hits the return and then rotates to the end of that line. The second player in the first line hits this return and rotates. This sequence continues until a player misses and loses a life. Players who lose 10 lives sit on the side of the court until the game is over. Play continues until one player remains.

175. FLUB OR SCRUB

Objective

To develop consistency and concentration skills during a heated ball exchange up at the net.

Description

This game is about quick hands and quick feet. When playing doubles, players must be able to react quickly to balls hit straight at them. This game livens up net play so that players will be ready for any ball hit at them or away from them.

Execution

Four players are positioned on the baseline, two on each side of the net. Players begin with 21 points each. Player A puts the ball in play with a serve to player B. Player B returns to player C. Player C returns to player D, and player D returns the ball to player A. Players must not break the sequence of shots. A player who misses a shot loses a point. The player who loses the fewest points wins.

176. RUSH AND CRUSH

Objective

To practice in a situation that forces players to use their serve-and-volley, passing-shot, and return-of-serve skills.

Description

Players must use their serve-and-volley technique to start the point or they lose the point. The receiving team must use passing shots without lobbing on the first ball.

Execution

Players take standard doubles positions. Team A plays against team B. Team A must serve and volley on both the first and second serves. Team B must return using a passing shot only. After teams use this beginning method they can play out the point in any manner they choose. They play a set using regular scoring methods.

Tip

The receiving team should hit to the feet of the serve-and-volleyer.

177. SINK OR SWIM

Objective

To help players build doubles-playing techniques and communication.

Description

This game helps players learn how to work as a team. By rewarding one team with a point advantage over the other to start, the players on the defensive team are motivated to fight hard and take advantage of any opportunity to attack.

Execution

Two teams position themselves behind opposite baselines. A server feeds a deep shot to team A to start the point. Teams play out the point using doubles strategy. If team A wins the point, they move up to the service line to start the next point. Team B is on the baseline to start. The server feeds another ball to team A to start the point. Teams play out the point. If team B wins this point, team A must backpedal quickly to the baseline and team B starts up on the service line. The server feeds another ball to team A to start the point. If team B wins this point, they move up to the net for their last starting position, and team A starts on the baseline. If team B wins this point, they collect the first game of a 10-game match. The server feeds another ball to team A. If team A wins the point, they move up to the service line, team B backpedals all the way back to the baseline, and the game continues. The players switch sides to start another game. The server should feed the first ball to team B.

178. QUICK CHANGE

Objective

To use a game method that forces players to use all three types of doubles formations—Australian, monster or I formation, and standard.

Description

Players are required to use all three doubles formations during all service games of their match.

Execution

Team A, the serving team, must serve using a different doubles formation to start each point of their service game, or they must forfeit the game. Team B plays in the standard doubles receiving manner. After team A completes the game, the serve shifts to team B. Team B must serve each point using a different doubles formation, or they must forfeit the game. The teams play an entire match using this method.

Tip

Players should be encouraged to communicate with each other; communication between partners is the key to a strong doubles team.

Chapter 14

Match Simulation Games

Tennis players know that pressure is a part of competing. Many players wonder why they are nervous about competing every time they step on the court to play a match, and they want to get over the prematch jitters. Some players are nervous before, during, and even after the match ends. Some are so nervous that after a match is over, they barely remember playing it. The best way for players to get used to performing under pressure is to do it over and over and over until playing points, games, and matches are as common as putting one foot in front of the other.

When faced with a competitive situation in a match, it is important for a player to know how to best select tactics and shots to play the next point or game. The key to being successful in a competitive situation is to practice by playing match simulation games. Nothing can substitute for the pressure of actual match play competition, but specific drills and match simulation games work as excellent physical and psychological grooving devices. This chapter contains some of these situations for players to practice and use during competition. Using the following match simulation drills and games will help players learn how to deal with frustration and setbacks and to win gracefully.

179. DINGLES MULTIPLAYER GAME

Objective

To help players improve their awareness, anticipatory skills, and ability to rally crosscourt.

Description

Players will improve their ability to hold a crosscourt rally in doubles formation, improve their awareness of other players' positioning, learn to work with their partner, and improve anticipatory skills for poaching. Dingles is that little bell that goes off in a players head when they finally understand what's happening on the court and with the opponent.

Execution

Two teams of two players start at the baseline on opposite sides of the court. Two simultaneous crosscourt rallies begin. An outside feeder or two of the players can start the rallies. When one of the balls is missed (hit outside of the doubles lines or anywhere out of the playing area including not being hit crosscourt), the other ball that has been in play begins the point and is the *live* ball. If each team alternately misses both balls, then a let is called and the point is replayed. If both players on one team miss their crosscourt shots, the other team is awarded 1 point. Otherwise, the team who wins the *live* ball rally wins the point. The game can be played to 11 points, then players or teams rotate.

Variations

Try awarding teams or players 2 points if they win a point with one or both players having hit a volley and successfully winning the point. Another variation is with all four players starting at the service line and working their way into the net after the first balls are fed in. It also adds a little flare if players call out "Dingles!" once the point becomes *live*.

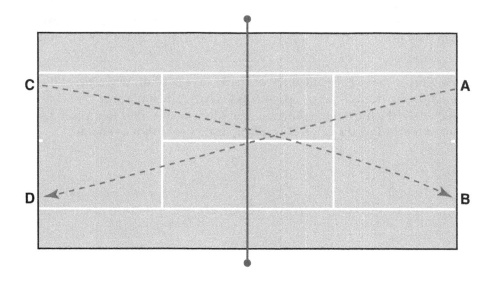

Objective

To help players improve specific team serving strategy and technique by learning why and when to use specific strategies and what should happen during match play when they use them.

Description

Players should not only practice drilling specific shots or combinations of shots, they should also practice them in gamelike situations. Playing in gamelike situations helps players adopt the strategies they need to succeed under certain conditions and in certain matches. They play the following situations as the serving team only.

Execution

Players play an eight-game pro set (the player or players must reach eight games and win by a margin of two games). The server must serve and volley on the first and second serves. They practice using signals and poaching on volleys. They should play a 12-point tiebreaker and poach on at least two of every three first serves and on half of the second serves. They play a 12-point tiebreaker using the monster (I) formation on every first serve and on half of the second serves.

Variations

In playing Australian doubles, each player serves four points in the ad-court. If the serving team is having a hard time serving and volleying because the receiving team's returns are too difficult, players should try using the Australian service formation. This formation eliminates the receiving team's crosscourt return. In playing monster doubles, the net player should poach on at least one of the four points. This service formation is a variation of the Australian formation. Players should remind their partner to assume the ready position below the level of the net tape to avoid the risk of getting hit in the back of the head by the serve. Players should also discuss signaling before the start of the match. This aggressive formation really confuses the opposing team, so players can use it when they need a little extra psychological boost to help control the match.

Tip

The net player should execute a visible body fake (a bluff) when up at the net and not moving. A bluff causes opponents to change their original plan of attack when they see the movement. The returner often mishits the attempted change of shot or hits it directly to the player who used the bluff movement.

181. CHIP-LOB RETURN

Objective

To help players counter against teams that use the monster (I) doubles formation or just like to poach a lot.

Description

Players can use this method of defense against a team that likes to poach and on second serves. They can use the chip-lob return as a way to get to the net early and force the opposing team to change their game plan.

Execution

Team A is positioned in the monster (I) doubles formation or standard doubles formation. Team B players start back on the baseline. Team A starts the first point of the first game by serving and volleying. Team B must chip lob the return over the net player's head and stay back to work the point. Once team A retreats and scurries back to retrieve the lob, team B should look to attack the net. Both teams continue to play out the point. The teams start each point of each game using this method. Scoring is by the regular system. To reinforce the chip-lob return, teams should play at least three or four sets using this method.

Tip

Players should try to keep the ball in play as long as possible and use high defensive lobs with topspin or backspin.

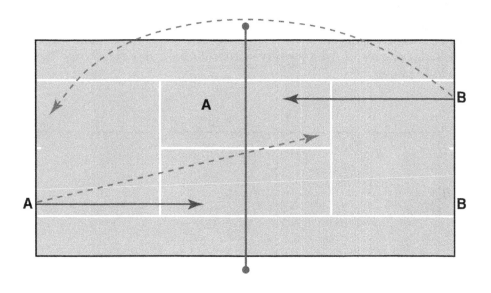

182. ROTATING DOUBLES

Objective

To reinforce all aspects of doubles play.

Description

This game helps develop players' various responsibilities during match play.

Execution

Players on team A are at the net as the kings or queens of the court. If five players are playing, two are a team on the opposite baseline. This team must acquire three points consecutively to take over team A's position. A server positioned at the net post feeds the first ball to the player of the challenging team standing behind the deuce court, who has two chances to put the ball in play. If the player misses, he or she rotates over to the advantage side, the player standing behind the advantage-court rotates out, and the waiting player moves up to the baseline behind the deuce court. The new challenging team starts with zero points, and a new point begins.

Variation

With an even number of players, teams rotate. Teams must win three consecutive points to become the kings or queens. If the challenging team loses a point, a new team rotates in, and the losing team drops all points. When a challenging team accumulates three points, they move to the other side and take the net position. The dethroned kings or queens retain the points they accumulated together and build on that total when they partner up again as kings or queens. Challengers do not keep the three points they win to dethrone the kings or queens. This new team starts with zero points and accumulates points together as the kings or queens. After the server feeds the ball, the point starts. The first team to 15 points wins.

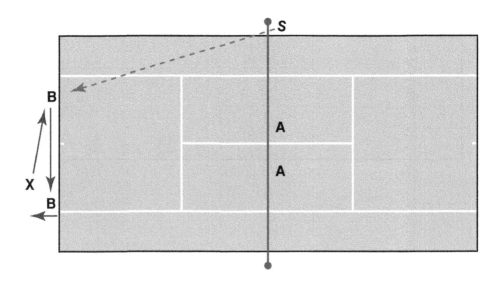

Objective

To help players work on service placement, approach volleys, and finishing volleys.

Description

This game emphasizes serving down the center (T) of the service court, working on the approach, and finishing volleys during match play.

Execution

Team A and team B should position themselves in the standard doubles position. Only one serve is allowed in this game per team and per player. Team A serves the first ball down the center (T) of the deuce service court to team B and closes in to hit the approach volley back to the same place the server served it. The receiver on the deuce side of the court of team B must return the serve, trying to hit it low to the feet of team A's server. Team A's server, after hitting the approach volley back to the same place he or she hit the serve, should close in and try to hit a second volley winner. After this three-hit combination, play continues until one team wins the point. Each server serves a 15-point game and then rotates.

Tip

When trying to hit an approach volley, players must stutter step or split step before hitting, hit the ball out in front, and move forward to the ball. They should not wait for the ball to come to them.

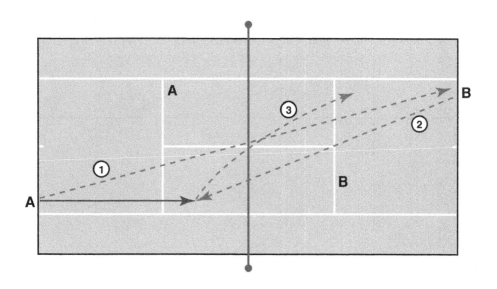

184. PASSING-SHOT MEDUSA

Objective

To help players work on approach shots and passing shots.

Description

This is a great game to play with four or more players. Players attempt to win points by hitting passing shots against the player dubbed *Medusa, queen of a million arms and hands,* up at the net.

Execution

A server feeds balls from a position to the side and off the court. Challenging players B, C, D, and E are lined up at the center (T) behind the baseline. Player A is positioned behind the baseline on the opposite side of the court. The server feeds a ball into the midcourt section of the court to player B. Player B moves forward to hit an approach shot and then closes in on the net. Player A (Medusa) attempts to hit a passing shot past player B. Both players play out the point. When the point is over, player B returns to the end of the line, and it's player C's turn. Lobs are not allowed on the first passing shot. A challenger who wins three points becomes the passing-shot queen (Medusa).

Variation

When playing with eight or more players, players should team up and play with the same rules except that the doubles alleys are good.

Tip

One of the most important principles in the use of passing shots is keeping the ball low at the net player's feet. This action forces the volleyer to hit up, decreasing the opportunity to make an aggressive half volley or approach volley. Topspin balls drop faster than flat or underspin balls do, so players should try to use substantial topspin when hitting the blistering passing shot.

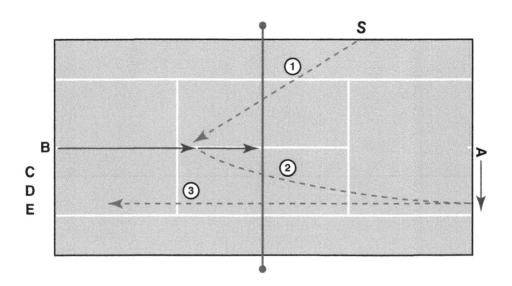

185. HALF-VOLLEY PASSING-SHOT CHALLENGE

Objective

To help players work their half-volleying skills, passing shot, and point-finishing strategy.

Description

This game helps players develop the touch needed for half volleying.

Execution

Team A is 3 feet (about a meter) behind the service line. Team B is behind the opposite baseline. A server behind the net post on team A's side of the court feeds a baseline shot to team B to start the point. Team B attempts to hit a passing shot, which they may not lob. Team A moves up to catch the shot as a half volley and then closes in to finish the point. After team A hits the half volley, both teams try to win the point. They play 21-point games and then rotate players.

Tip

Players having problems hitting half volleys may be trying to shovel the ball over the net with the hips above the ball. They should keep the hips and knees lower than the ball by using the thigh muscles to maintain a strong foundation. Players should keep the hitting arm firm and the wrist and grip tight so that the head of the racket is solid as they come through the shot.

186. GRIP-AND-RIP OVERHEAD

Objective

To emphasize hitting the overhead to win the point.

Description

This game helps players shorten the backswing so that they can catch the ball farther in front, quicken their reaction time, quicken their footwork by emphasizing the ready hop, and work the point from a defensive position.

Execution

Two players (team A) are at the net, and two players (team B) are behind the opposite baseline. A server stands behind the players on the baseline and feeds a somewhat difficult lob to team A. Team A attempts to hit and put away the overhead, which team B tries to retrieve. Team B then tries to hit passing shots or lobs to win the point. When a team loses a point, another team of players, team C or D, rotates in. The first team to 21 points wins.

Tip

Players should let the racket head lead as they would in serving and make sure that they get underneath the ball. The ball will bounce in front of them when they are in the correct position.

Objective

To focus on improving team communication, overheads, lobs, groundstrokes, doubles strategy, and volley placement.

Description

Six or more players can play this action-packed game. Players learn how to identify and react to different shots, place shots, and hustle to cover and recover from hitting and winning points.

Execution

Team A (the kings or queens of the court) is in standard doubles formation on one side of the court. Challenging teams—B, C, and D—are on the opposite side, one behind another next to the doubles sideline and service line. A server stands to the side of the court on team A's (kings or queens) side. On the server's cue, the first challenging team (team B) sidesteps along the service line, sprints forward toward the net, taps it with their rackets, and shuffles backward in preparation for an overhead. The server feeds a deep lob over challenging team B. Team B must react, recover the lob, and play out the point. If team A wins the point, they remain the kings or queens and keep that point. If team B wins the point, team A runs to the end of the line of challenging teams. Team B has 5 seconds (counted down by the server) to run the net posts (team members run around opposite net posts to cover both sides) and get into standard doubles position before team C completes the lob recovery. Teams play out the point. The first team to 21 wins the game.

Variation

The server can use overheads, drop shots, or a combination of shots instead of just lobs. Teams rotate only on their side of the court instead of running from one side to the other. If six or more teams are involved, this game can be very exciting for all involved, because teams must really concentrate on hitting, moving, and placement of shots so as not to set up their teammate or the team moving in and playing just behind them to get crushed. Instructors or players can experiment with the original execution and use virtually any shot or combination of shots to keep the action exhilarating and educational.

Tip

Players should return a lob with a lob hit diagonally to use the additional 5 feet of extra court.

188. PEG-LEG DOUBLES

Objective

To help players play more accurately by emphasizing consistency and placement of shots.

Description

Players use only half of the doubles court, playing out points and games crosscourt. Players must work to keep the ball in play and away from the volleyer. Players must use all types of shots to keep the net player from stealing the ball out of the air.

Execution

Teams are positioned in standard doubles formation. Team A serves into the deuce-court. Team B returns crosscourt. Teams play crosscourt only, including use of the doubles alley. Net players may try to poach once the serve is in play. Net players from both teams may hit only crosscourt shots such as volleys, drop volleys, or overheads. Teams play an entire set, switching serves and positions after every game and using regular scoring.

Variations

The serving team uses the serve-and-volley tactic on every first serve. Alternatively, the serving team may be restricted to one serve per point per game.

Tip

Players having trouble stroking solid service returns should be sure that they aren't standing flatfooted, a stance that slows reaction to the ball. Players should keep their feet moving while the server is setting up, split step as the server strikes the ball, and move forward when stroking.

Court Movement and Conditioning

The demands of playing tennis for fun or in tournaments can appear to be a continuous series of emergencies—sprinting to the ball, quickly changing direction, stretching, lunging, stopping, starting—on all types of surfaces and in all types of weather. Being able to perform these actions while also maintaining proper balance and technique throughout a match is critical for optimal performance on the court.

To keep up with the physical demands of tennis, today's players need three ingredients: speed, stamina, and agility. Performing exercises both on and off the court will help players improve all three. To increase speed and stamina, players can perform sprint training drills. To improve agility, players can include proper stretching before and after training to enhance the body's flexibility and balance.

To be successful and to compete at all levels of tennis including club player, junior tournament competitor, and professional tour athlete, players must be in better shape today than they were 10 years ago. The technology in equipment has improved to the point of bringing the game to incredible speeds, strengths, and physical demands on the body. Players have to get to the ball quicker and have the footwork to set up, stay balanced, be upright, keep their eyes on the ball, stay steady when striking the ball, transfer body weight, and recover back to an offensive position in a matter of seconds. The drills in the following chapters will help players build a program for moving better forward and backward, side to side, and forward and backward at an angle; and jumping and landing like a cat without injury—all while keeping their balance and focus. On- and off-court training will help improve stamina, lessen the effect of fatigue, and build strength for long and short matches.

Tennis takes years of practice, so players' bodies must be able to sustain the grueling hours, months, and years of training. Players should remember that the mind, body, and spirit are the greatest assets they have for any sport. They must treasure them and keep them in shape.

Chapter 15

Endurance Training

Endurance is staying power for athletes of any sport. Tennis players need endurance to stay strong and to feel fresh throughout a 1- or 2-hour match. With endurance, players can not only avoid feeling sluggish during long matches, they may even feel better than they did when they first stepped onto the court. Without endurance, players not only lose focus, they are more likely to lose the match. Endurance training for tennis is dramatically different from endurance training for long-distance running. Long-distance runners need to maintain a constant speed for long periods of time; tennis players need the endurance to sprint over and over again for as long as the match lasts without falling one step behind the opponent. Sprinting, changing direction quickly, stretching, lunging, stopping, bending, leaping, and making explosive starts and stops are all characteristics of the fitness demands of tennis today; it's hard work. Players must embrace the hard work it takes to become fit for tennis, mixing in flexibility, strength, endurance, power, agility, speed, and aerobic and anaerobic fitness. Doing this hard work consistently can improve tennis players' games tremendously.

This chapter is filled with wonderful on-court speed and agility drills, which can be done outdoors during in-season training. Players who practice them with discipline and respect will reach their tennis fitness goals.

189. POINT AND GO

Objective
To teach players the skills necessary for quick changes of direction.

Description
This drill helps players build the dexterity they need for changing direction quickly, sprinting forward, backpedaling, leaping, and lunging. The drill can have a player sprinting from side to side, up and back, or diagonally forward and backward.

Execution
Players spread out in the backcourt area and stand in the ready position facing the net. A leader, standing directly in front of the group, extends either arm and points to the side, forward, backward, or forward or backward at an angle. Players respond to the pointing movement by sprinting in the direction in which the leader points. The leader lets the players sprint a few steps and then points in another direction. Players should sprint in all directions, forced to change direction quickly. A good routine is 2- or 3-minute periods of sprinting followed by 30-second rest periods. The length and number of sprinting periods should increase as players build endurance.

190. DARK SHADOW

Objective
To help players develop quick reflexes, explosive starts, and sudden stops while executing tennis strokes and encouraging good communication.

Description
This drill is a fantastic way for players to learn how to move quickly to the ball and change direction with the explosive burst of speed needed to recover drop shots or returns of serve.

Execution
Players pair off, and each holds a racket in the hitting hand. One member of each pair is the leader; the other is the dark shadow. The leader assumes the ready position facing the net in the backcourt area. The shadow, also in the ready position, stands approximately 3 feet behind the leader. The leader then simulates a movement—any movement that players must make in actual tennis play. The leader can pivot and swing for a forehand and backhand or run forward to play a short ball either forehand or backhand. The shadow imitates the leader's movements. The drill continues with the leader trying to lose or confuse the shadow. After 3 or 4 minutes of action, players rest for 30 seconds. They reverse roles and resume the drill.

191. RUN, HIT, AND RECOVER

Objective

To help players improve court movement and build leg strength.

Description

Players not only need to be quick in moving along the baseline, they also need to be agile enough to move explosively to short balls, sharp-angled shots, and drop shots. This drill works on those skills.

Execution

Player A stands on the baseline, and player B is up at the net. Player B, armed with a basket of balls, alternately feeds player A short balls, drop shots, sharp-angled balls, and deep groundstrokes. Player A's goal is to hit every ball and return it crosscourt deep without missing. Players should try this drill first with 20 balls and work up to 100.

Variation

To improve their weak shots, players can hit balls to any area on the court.

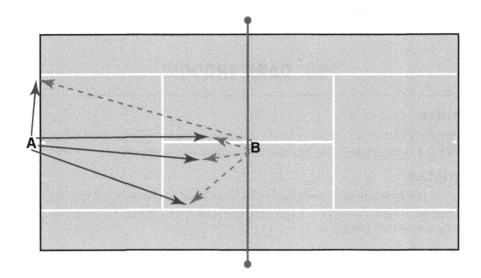

192. STEP-OUT VOLLEY

Objective

To help players develop the footwork technique and agility needed to hit volleys or groundstrokes using the open stance.

Description

The step-out technique facilitates preparation for using the open stance and recovering quickly.

Execution

Players position themselves around the court facing the net, each with enough room to move 5 or 6 feet (about 1.5 to 2 meters) in all directions. On a leader's cue, players step out to the side with the left foot. The hips should face the net. Players do not close the hips with a crossover first step. Together, players perform a split step, step out with the left foot, and then perform a crossover movement into the ball, keeping the back knee bent low to the ground to simulate proper volley footwork. They then split step to recovery. Players perform this movement without the racket 20 times for the forehand volley and 20 times for the backhand volley, all at maximum speed. They repeat the drill with the racket in hand, resting for 1 minute after each set.

Tip

Players must maintain correct posture while performing this drill. Good posture helps players develop strong, confident, sound volleys.

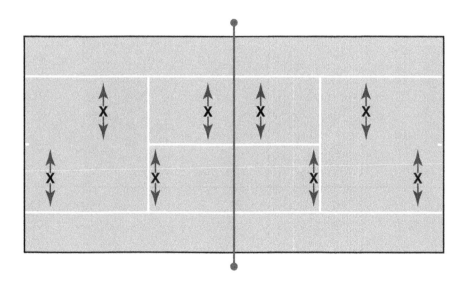

Objective

To improve players' agility and speed needed for good court movement.

Description

Players use the alley to quicken and tighten the compact movement needed for strong, controlled volleys.

Execution

Players position themselves one behind another in one of the doubles alleys, 4 or 5 feet (about 1 to 1.5 meters) apart. Players should be in the standard ready position without rackets. On a leader's cue, players explode into quick running-in-place steps for 15 seconds. On the second cue, players split step, step out with the left foot, crossover step with the right foot, keep the back knee low for a low volley, and hold for 10 seconds. On the third cue, players recover with a split step. On the fourth cue, players run in place for 15 seconds. They repeat the cycle for the backhand low volley, rest for 1 minute, and repeat the cycle for the high forehand volley and high backhand volley. They rest for 1 minute and repeat the cycle for the waist-high volley. They do the complete cycle two or three times.

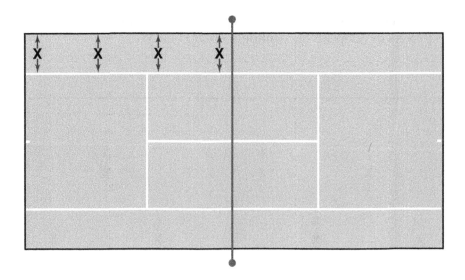

194. DEXTERITY BALL

Objective

To teach players better communication, movement, ball tracking skills, and agility and to quicken reflexes.

Description

Two or more players can perform this drill. Players do not need rackets, only a dexterity ball—a ball with knots all over it so when it hits the ground it bounces in wacky directions. Players are forced to move quickly and to focus on catching the ball as it bounces in unpredictable ways.

Execution

Players pair up. Player A holds two balls and takes the leader position. Player B performs the catching and rolling action. Player A kneels approximately 4 feet (about a meter) in front of player B. Player B stands in the standard ready position in front of player A. Player A starts the drill by rolling one ball wide to player B's forehand side. Player B split steps and performs the stepping-out footwork, recovers the ball, and rolls it back quickly to player A's hands. Player A rolls the second ball wide to player B's backhand side. Player B split steps, performs the stepping-out footwork, recovers the ball, and rolls it back quickly to player A's hands. Players should perform this drill at maximum speed for 2 minutes and then switch positions. Players work up to doing five solid sets in each position.

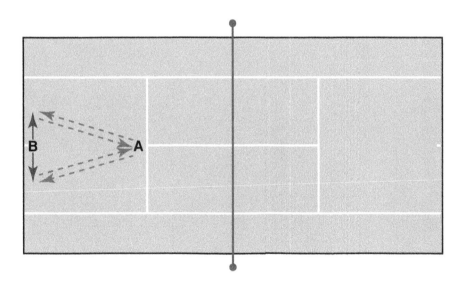

Objective

To help players improve balance and lateral movement on court.

Description

Starting behind the doubles alley and balancing a ball on the strings of a racket, players weave through markers set out along the baseline, racing against time.

Execution

Six or more flat markers or cones should be placed 3 feet (about 1 meter) apart along the length of the baseline. Players stand off the court behind one of the side alleys. On cue, the first player steps up to the first marker, balancing a ball on the racket strings. The goal is to shuffle laterally, weaving through markers without dropping the ball off the racket, to the end of the baseline and back in 20 seconds. Players who drop the ball start over from the beginning, and they should keep trying until they successfully complete the drill within 20 seconds. Players get three times to complete the drill within 20 seconds.

Variation

Players can bounce the ball down to the ground (downs) or up on the racket (ups) or do the combination of one up and one down (ups and downs). This is what tennis instructors mean when they ask a player to practice their ups and downs.

196. FAN

Objective

To help players to improve speed and quick change of direction.

Description

This drill simulates the footwork and direction players will be moving to cover the backcourt area during match play. Moving in sequential patterns, players develop certain footwork so that it becomes second nature. The drill also emphasizes the explosive, fast movements needed to hit certain shots on the court.

Execution

Players begin behind the baseline at the center (T), holding a racket. They sprint to base 1, touch the junction between the baseline and sideline with one foot, and touch the ground in front of them with the racket. Players then return to position X. They repeat the movement to all the other bases (2, 3, 4, and 5; see diagram), except that they run backward to and from base 3. They repeat the sequence three times and time themselves. Players should try to beat their times in the next training session.

Tip

Players should never start a sprinting drill with cold muscles. To warm up, players should jog around the tennis court six times—the first lap forward, the second lap sidestepping facing the court, the third lap reverse sidestepping by turning away from the court, the fourth lap backpedaling, the fifth lap sprinting, and the sixth lap walking it off. They can use this warm-up routine before conditioning or hitting drills.

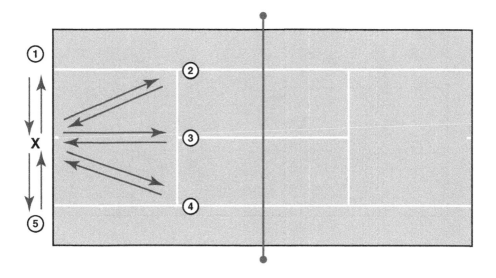

197. SHUTTLE RUN

Objective

To improve players' speed, endurance, quick changes of direction, and recovery; and to build and strengthen the muscles of the upper thighs.

Description

This drill, often known as the suicide drill, is one of the most hated but simplest on-court exercises to improve overall speed and fitness on the court. In this drill, players can impart explosive starts and stops to the ball.

Execution

Players (A) sprint from the baseline to the service line and back five times, changing direction as quickly as possible. They repeat the same routine from the baseline to the net. This isn't a race.

Variation

Players (B) start on the outside doubles sideline, sprint to touch each line on the court with a racket in hand, and return to the doubles sideline. They do this three times in a row.

Tip

Anyone who plays tennis must be in good physical condition. This particular drill is used in many different sports to help athletes attain optimum physical conditioning, quick feet and hands, and the never-quit attitude when competing. Exercise and proper nutrition are keys to success on the court.

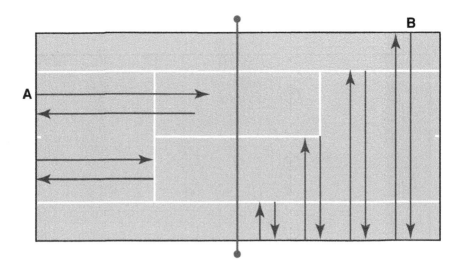

198. COURT CIRCUIT

Objective

To improve players' speed, stamina, and proficiency on the court.

Description

This drill helps build footwork, speed, agility, and dexterity for hitting and recovering easy and hard-to-reach shots during competition. The drill helps players become comfortable with all areas of the court and be aware of where they are on the court during heated competition.

Execution

The following diagram shows where to set up flat sprinting markers. Players follow the route from 1 to 14, sprinting as fast as they can. They run backward from 5 to 1, 7 to 1, 6 to 1, and side shuffle 12 to 1 and 13 to 1, full on sprint 1 to 3, 2, 4, 9, 8, and 14 (for deep shot) recovery. They touch the ground with a hand at each point, and at the front of the court they touch the net. This is a random setup chosen to mimic point play.

Variation

Players can leap up and over cones placed on the designated stop points.

Tip

Some players may feel as though they have the speed of Superman, the agility and dexterity of Spider-Man, and the gracefulness of a prima ballerina, but they still can't figure out how to run down certain shots. These players are prime candidates for spending more time on their on-court footwork. Players should practice any kind of fancy, speedy footwork routine possible and watch the level of their on-court readiness soar!

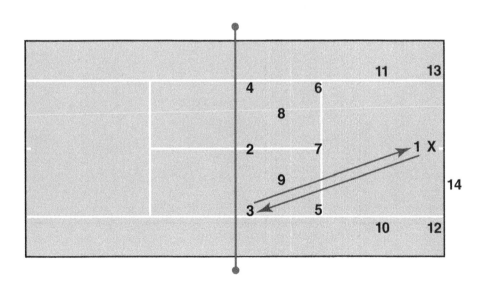

Objective

To help players' footwork and hitting become more fluid and to keep stamina training interesting by having them hit balls at the same time.

Description

This drill allows players to train on court for superior court stamina and at the same time practice tennis by working on consistency, direction, and control.

Execution

Players A and B rally crosscourt to each other trying to hit a specific target (X) placed in the corner where the doubles alley and baseline meet. After each shot, players return to the center (T), hitting groundstrokes on the run. They perform this drill for 5 minutes, change sides of the court, and repeat. If they can maintain a continuous rally and push hard to return to the center (T) after each shot, they will find this a top conditioning drill and lots of fun as well.

Variation

Players can hit down-the-line forehands and backhands, or any combination of shots, such as two forehands crosscourt then one backhand crosscourt.

Tip

Tennis players need to be in top physical condition to keep the progression process flowing smoothly. Conditioning drills combined with hitting balls creates a "light at the end of the tunnel" effect for many players who hate just drilling or working out to stay in tennis shape.

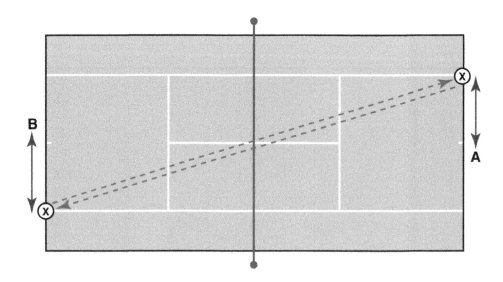

200. SPIDER

Objective

To promote short explosive movements, deceleration, and quick change of direction in a controlled manner.

Description

During this drill players work on short explosive sprints, immediate deceleration and change of direction, and the use of the hands in a controlled manner. This exercise is great for players who are preparing to play on clay to work on their sliding to a certain point as they would in sliding into a shot.

Execution

Three balls are placed along each singles sideline: one where the baseline meets the sideline, one at the service line, and one at the net. Another ball is placed at the center (T) on the baseline and another on the service line at the net. This ball layout is to be the same on both sidelines of the court, amounting to a total of eight balls on each side of the court. A player is positioned in the center of the court on the service line (T). The player sprints to each ball individually, sprints back to the starting point, and places each ball down on the service line one at a time. The player decides the order in which to collect the balls; the order is not set.

Variation

This exercise has several modifications. Two players can race against each other with balls set up on both sides of the court (8 on each side). To make the exercise more strenuous, players can also return balls back to their original spots immediately after all eight have been placed in the center. On the eighth ball, players do not put it down; they must sprint through the center of the court to the original starting spot where they intend to place the ball and then proceed in returning all of the other balls individually. On clay, players should slide to each spot where they are picking up the ball; the lead sliding foot stops at the ball. Players should work on using both legs as the lead leg.

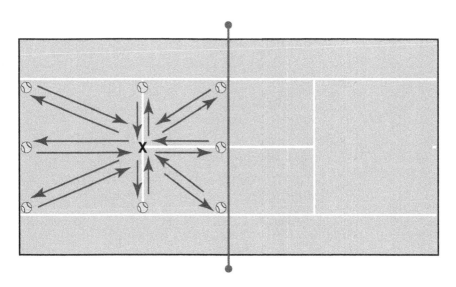

Chapter 16

In-Season Maintenance

The purpose of in-season maintenance training is to maintain the strength, speed, power, and agility players have built up over the season and to continue to improve on their overall physical conditioning. Over the course of a season, tennis makes tremendous demands on the body and mind. If players neglect any part of their workout regimen, it will show in their on-court performance, their mental ability to close out matches and finish tough practices, or their strength and physical health. Players need to use their workout time wisely and choose a routine that includes all of the following: building strength in the lower and upper body, training balance and coordination, training aerobic and anaerobic endurance, improving hip and pelvic rotation for striking power and flexibility, exercising rotation for uncoiling the trunk, improving timing for footwork and shots, and exercising body rhythm.

Players must not neglect in-season, off-season, and preseason nutritional maintenance as well. All athletes must maintain healthy body weight to be able to continue to improve without hindering endurance. Rest, eating the correct combination of foods, and drinking the correct combination of liquids all contribute to players staying in sound tennis shape for the many years they look to compete on the courts.

A specific, comprehensive physical conditioning program will improve players' confidence, improve their technique and power, reduce the number and severity of tennis-related injuries, delay fatigue, promote faster recovery after competition, reduce the number of down hours after training, and enable the development of better athletes. The exercises in this section provide an on- and off-court training program for total body conditioning of tennis players.

201. CALF STRETCH

Objective

To stretch the calf muscles, Achilles tendon, and lower hamstrings, which are prone to injury in tennis.

Description

The calf muscle is the fleshy, muscular back part of the leg between the knee and ankle.

Execution

Players stand in front of a wall or bench with one foot 2 or 3 feet (about a meter) behind the other and the toes pointed forward. Keeping the back knee straight and heels on the floor, players bend the front knee and lean forward until they feel the stretch. After 30 seconds they switch legs and repeat. Next, they stand erect with feet together and both heels on the ground. They lean forward until they feel tightness in the calves and Achilles tendons. After holding the position for 30 seconds, they release the stretch and return to standing position.

202. HAMSTRING STRETCH

Objective

To stretch the hamstrings, lower-back muscles, and upper calf.

Description

This stretch focuses on two tendons at the rear hollow of the knee.

Execution

From a seated position, players bend the left knee and place the sole of the left foot against the inside of the right knee. Keeping the back and right knee as straight as possible, they reach toward the foot with both hands. They hold each stretch for 30 seconds, switch legs, and repeat.

Variations

For the standing hamstring stretch, players stand in an upright position with knees locked. They bend forward slowly, moving the hands down the backs of the legs toward the ankles until they feel tightness in the hamstrings. For the hurdler's hamstring stretch, players sit on the floor with one leg turned backward and the other extended forward (high hurdler's position). They bend the torso and head down toward the knee until they feel tightness. Players hold each position for 30 seconds and then relax and return to the original position.

203. STORK QUADRICEPS STRETCH

Objective

To stretch the quadriceps and shin muscles.

Description

This exercise stretches the quadriceps muscles, which are located in the front of the thigh.

Execution

Players stand on one leg and grasp the other foot or ankle. Keeping the back straight, they pull the foot up behind the buttocks so that the knee points to the ground (without twisting the knee). For balance, they extend the arm in front of them or hold onto a wall, pole, or the net. They hold for 30 seconds, switch legs, and repeat.

Variations

For the hurdler's quadriceps stretch, players lie on the back with both legs together. They grasp the left ankle with the left hand and slowly pull the ankle toward the waist until they feel tightness in the quadriceps. For the prone quadriceps stretch, players lie on the stomach with both legs stretched out behind them. They bend the left knee toward the buttocks, grasp the foot with the left hand, and pull it directly toward the buttocks. They hold for 30 seconds, relax, and repeat using the right leg.

Tip

Players must be patient, work within their limits, and stay relaxed.

204. POSTERIOR SHOULDER STRETCH

Objective

To perform preventive shoulder conditioning to combat common overuse problems from hitting overheads, serves, high backhand and high forehand volleys.

Description

When repetitive movements are required in sports like tennis, the shoulder and upper back muscles can get overworked. Players need exercises to help keep these areas loose, strong, and stretched in order to prevent injury to the neck and shoulder areas.

Execution

Players stand and hold the left arm out in front. Bend the arm 90 degrees across the body. Use the opposite hand and grasp the elbow of the bent arm and gently pull the arm across the body and hold for a count of 10. Release and switch arms, repeating the same movements using the other arm. Next, lift your arm overhead with your elbow bent and pointed up toward the ceiling and the hand hanging down the center of the back holding the grip of a tennis racquet with the head of the racquet facing down toward the floor. With the opposite hand, grasp the head of the racquet and pull the racquet gently down towards the floor, hold for 10 seconds, release, and switch arms. Repeat this stretch 3 to 5 times.

Tip

Players should never stretch a muscle during any exercise to the level of discomfort or pain, or they run the risk of tearing it.

205. CRUNCHES

Objective
To strengthen the abdominal muscles that protect the lower back and add power to all strokes.

Description
This exercise helps to develop a strong rectus abdominis (trunk), which is the source of many movements in tennis and allows the upper body to stay synchronized with the lower body.

Execution
Players lie on their backs with the knees bent, feet flat on the floor, and hands behind the head. As they slowly lift the head and shoulders toward the knees, they contract the stomach muscles, breathing out as they rise up and breathing in as they lower down. The head should be in line with the neck, and the eyes should focus on the ceiling. They hold this position while exhaling for 5 seconds and then slowly lower themselves to the floor while inhaling. Repeat 10 times.

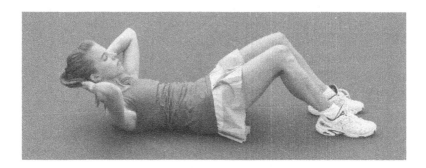

206. LEG EXTENSION

Objective
To exercise the quadriceps for strength, prevention of knee injury, and rehabilitation.

Description
Players extend the legs upward against the resistance of added weight, straightening the knees fully but not hyperextending them. They slowly lower the weight to the starting position.

Execution
Sitting in a leg extension machine, players should adjust the backrest so that the knees bend at the edge of the seat. The lower pad should be just above the ankles. Players put the feet behind the pad and lift until both legs are almost fully extended. They pause, slowly lower the feet to the starting position, switch legs, and repeat. Repeat 10 times for each leg, rotating legs between sets.

Objective

To strengthen the internal and external obliques, the abdominal muscles responsible for rotating the torso.

Description

This excellent exercise develops the rotational strength required on groundstrokes and serves, and it helps protect the lower back from the twisting and turning movements that are essential in tennis.

Execution

Players begin in a standing position. Hold a bar behind the neck with both hands, keeping the back straight and the hips facing forward. Keeping the rest of the body steady, they twist from the waist, first to the right and then to the left, as far as they can.

Variation

To make the exercise more challenging and improve specific strengths needed for tennis, players can try trunk rotations using a medicine ball, which adds weight resistance. Standing in the position as above, two players face each other, one holding a medicine ball. Players start by gently tossing the medicine ball. The other player catches the ball and twists to the right. Twisting back to the front, the player tosses the ball back. They toss and twist to the right then toss and twist to the left. Repeat 10 times, rest and repeat for a set of 3.

Tip

In order to increase power on groundstrokes players must strengthen their core. The core is the power transfer station, which includes the abdominal muscles, lower and upper back, and gluteal muscles. Players who work to strengthen these muscles will notice increased power when hitting using the open stance on groundstrokes and swinging volleys.

208. LEG CURL

Objective

To work the often ignored hamstrings, which are key muscles for sprinting, backpedaling, and stability when playing low balls.

Description

Players will either use a leg curl machine that puts them in a standing position or laying on their stomach. Players should slowly curl the feet toward the buttocks and then slowly return the weight to the starting position. The knees should never hyperextend when performing this exercise.

Execution

Players lie facedown on a leg curl machine, letting the leg pads touch just above the ankles. Starting with the knees bent slightly, players slowly bring both feet up toward the buttocks, trying to achieve at least a 90-degree angle. They hold this position for a moment and then slowly let the weight down. Complete 3 sets of 10 repetitions on each leg. Start by using 5 pounds and slowly build up.

209. LEG PRESS

Objective

To strengthen the buttocks, quadriceps, hamstrings, and calves.

Description

This multijoint exercise is great for developing overall leg strength, which helps build stamina and the ability to stop and start.

Execution

Players position themselves in the leg press machine with the back flat against the backrest and the feet on the platform shoulder-width apart. They bend the legs at a 90-degree angle and slowly push the feet against the platform until the legs are extended. They hold for a moment and then slowly return to the starting position. To target the inner and outer thigh muscles and the gluteal muscles (used for side shuffling, up-and-back movements, low-ball hitting stances, and open-stance strokes), they place the feet farther apart with the toes pointing outward. Complete 3 sets of 10 repetitions. Start with 5 to 10 pounds and build once that weight becomes easy.

Tip

Explosive starts, stops, leaping, lunging, bending, or sprinting can't happen without the strength of the lower body. Even to be able to execute fundamental groundstrokes, players must be physically able to move out of the ready position.

210. SPEEDY INTERVAL TRAINING

Objective

To improve heart rate recovery time and raise the anaerobic threshold.

Description

By incorporating intervals (periodic bursts of speed followed by resting cycles) into an off-court training program, players accomplish two things. First, they improve their heart rate recovery time so that they won't be gasping for air after a long rally. Second, they raise their anaerobic threshold (the point at which the muscles go into oxygen debt and become exhausted) so that they stay fresher longer.

Execution

Players should find a track or smooth straightaway for their training. They sprint 60 meters 10 or 12 times with a rest of 90 seconds or 2 minutes after each sprint. Then they sprint 100 meters 8 or 10 times with a rest of 2 or 2 1/2 minutes after each sprint. They sprint 200 meters 10 or 12 times with a 6- to 8- minute rest after each sprint. Finally, they sprint 400 meters four to six times with a 5- or 7-minute rest after each sprint.

211. BASIC INTERVAL TRAINING

Objective

To develop the capacity for high-intensity sessions with adequate rest intervals.

Description

Players rated at 2.5 and above probably find themselves rushing the net one minute and rallying along the baseline the next. Their interval training should follow a similar mix-and-match approach. Varying the length and intensity of each cycle will mimic their on-court actions and challenge their muscles.

Execution

- Sprint for 10 seconds, and walk for 5.
- Sprint for 15 seconds, and walk for 10.
- Sprint for 30 seconds, and walk for 15.
- Sprint for 5 seconds, and walk for 5.

Variation

Players can continue to mix up the length of the sprints and recovery periods, but no sprint should last longer than 90 seconds.

Tip

To improve explosive speed on the court, players can also try running up stairs or spinning.

212. CROSS-TRAINING

Objective

To add variety to keep players fresh and on top of their fitness development.

Description

Developing an effective cross-training program is as simple as swapping the stair climber for the treadmill or taking a step-aerobics class. Players should remember that they need activities that involve the energy systems and movement patterns of tennis. Repeating the same cardiovascular activities gets the body in a rut and lowers benefits, so mixing it up is key (hence the name *cross-training*).

Execution

The following is a suggested cross-training schedule:

Monday, Wednesday, Friday

- Weight training
- Cardiovascular training in cycling classes, on a ski machine, an elliptical trainer, or other such machine or class

Tuesday, Thursday

Track training using the basic or speedy interval training schedule:

- Sprint for 10 seconds, and walk for 5.
- Sprint for 15 seconds, and walk for 10.
- Sprint for 30 seconds, and walk for 15.
- Sprint for 45 seconds, and walk for 20.
- Jump rope in 2-minute intervals for 10 sets.

Variation

To improve coordination and balance, players can try yoga, Pilates, or kickboxing. These disciplines help keep stress levels under control, build total body strength, increase balance, and loosen up the body so that players can put more power behind each shot.

Tip

Players should warm up with a light 3- to 5-minute jog to prepare the muscles for exercise. Players should know that tennis isn't solely aerobic; in fact, it's primarily anaerobic. So, incorporating aerobic exercise such as jogging, spinning, and swimming combined with anaerobic exercise such as interval training that includes short bursts of sprinting speed helps players of any level reach the optimal physical condition needed to play good tennis.

213. SPINAL TWIST

Objective

To stretch the core area of a players body, which consists of the lower back and abs.

Description

The lower back is the region of the vertebrae nearest the lower end of the spine. It is an area of the body that most tennis players over time tend to incur some sort of injury. Strengthening the lower abs helps to strengthen the lower back. These two components are essential in the development of a player's center of power and stability.

Execution

From a seated position, players bend the right leg and place the right ankle on the outside of the left knee. They take the left arm over the right knee, and while looking over the right shoulder, they slowly turn the shoulders and torso to the right. They hold for 30 seconds, switch legs, and repeat for 5 sets on each side.

Variation

For a knees-to-chest stretch, players lie flat on the ground with the legs stretched out in front of them. They bring the knees together toward the chest by grasping the lower legs just below the knees and guiding them up and flat against the chest. After holding for 30 seconds, they relax and straighten out the legs. They perform at least three sets of 30-second holds.

214. DEEP-CHAIR PUSH-UPS

Objective
To increase the range of motion of all joints in the body and to aid in agility.

Description
A good basic stretching and strengthening program keeps limbs and joints functioning through a full range of motion. Benefits of stretching include reduction of muscle tension and correction of postural imbalances that often develop in tennis, which stresses the joints and muscles unequally on opposite sides of the body.

Execution
Adult and junior players perform different versions of deep-chair push-ups. Adults place their feet on a chair or bench placed behind them and place each hand on a chair positioned beside them. They do regular push-ups, lowering the chest close to the ground between the two chairs and never letting the torso dip below the hands or feet. Juniors use the same method except that they keep the feet on the ground instead of using a chair positioned behind them. All players try to do three sets of 12, resting 45 seconds between sets.

Tip
Players should warm up their muscles with a low-intensity activities such as jumping jacks, jumping rope, or jogging in place.

215. COMPOUND ROW

Objective

To develop the rhomboid, trapezius, posterior deltoid, and biceps muscles.

Description

Rowing is a great back developer and is useful for the prevention of injury and rehabilitation of the rotator cuff. Rowing also builds power on the backhand, especially for hitting high balls with the one-handed stroke.

Execution

Players sit with the back straight, feet braced against the crossbar, and legs slightly bent. With a neutral grip (palms facing each other), they pull their arms toward them and then slowly extend their arms to a straight position. The elbows should be close to the body and near the waistline.

216. LAT PULL-DOWN

Objective

To develop the latissimus dorsi and biceps muscles, which help absorb shock during forward arm movements.

Description

This all-purpose back exercise targets the lats, (latissimus dorsi), the muscles used for the serve and overhead smash.

Execution

Players sit facing a lat pull-down machine with the feet flat on the floor. They grasp the bar with the hands shoulder-width apart and palms toward them. They pull the bar down slowly to the upper chest, keeping the head and back straight and the elbows close to the sides. The release should be slow to prevent the machine from overstretching the shoulders. If the grip is wider than shoulder width or if players lower the bar behind the neck, the rotator cuff muscles can be strained.

Tip

Players must know that it takes more than a killer desire to nail a service ace or a blistering overhead smash. It takes many hours of training and building the muscles associated with hitting serves and overheads. Learning how to properly train the lats will increase service and overhead strength and will help keep players free of shoulder injuries.

217. OVERHEAD PRESS

Objective

To work the front and sides of the shoulders.

Description

This is a general upper-body conditioning and strengthening exercise.

Execution

Players should adjust the seat height on an overhead press machine so that the handles are about even with the shoulders. They sit in the machine and hold the handles with the palms facing up. They slowly push the arms up to full extension but don't lock them. After holding for 2 or 3 seconds, they slowly bring the weight down.

Variation

Players can perform the exercise without a machine. For push-ups from the floor, players place the hands shoulder-width apart with the body in a straight line from the toes to the head. They slowly lower themselves until the upper arm is parallel to the ground. They push themselves upward until the elbows are completely straight, and they round the back outward as a cat would. This rounding motion at the end of the push-up is significant and increases the work done by the muscles that stabilize the shoulder blade.

218. CHEST PRESS

Objective

To develop the pectoralis major and minor, serratus anterior, triceps, and anterior deltoid muscles.

Description

This movement primarily targets the chest muscles but also works the front of the shoulders and the triceps muscles.

Execution

Players sit with the feet flat on the floor and the hands shoulder-width apart on the handles. Keeping the back straight against the backrest, they push out from the chest until both arms are fully extended but not locked. They hold for 2 seconds and then return to the starting position.

Tip

Players should remember to warm up before performing any strength- or endurance-training program. Players should exhale during the pressing part of the routine and inhale as they return the weight to its starting or resting position. Players should get into the habit of continuous breathing; it can be too easy to hold their breath while weightlifting. Inhaling delivers oxygen to the muscles and exhaling helps an athlete relax, thereby limiting strain and stress on the muscles.

219. LATERAL DELTOID RAISE

Objective

To develop the sides of the shoulders, which are used for hitting strong one-handed backhands.

Description

This exercise targets the usually underdeveloped sides of the shoulder muscles. Development of these muscles is vital in protecting the rotator cuff and strengthens the backhand, especially the one-handed topspin backhand.

Execution

Players sit at the machine with the back straight and the chest up. The roller pads should rest just above the elbows. Players grip the handles loosely and slowly push up with the elbows until the arms are at a 90-degree angle to the body. They hold for 1 second and then slowly return the elbows to the sides. Use minimal weight and start with 5 pounds and then slowly build. Try 3 sets of 10 second intervals.

220. SURFACE CROSS-TRAINING

Objective

To help players practice playing on various court surfaces such as clay, hard, and grass.

Description

Pros who compete on a variety of surfaces often change the length of intervals based on the type of court they're competing on.

Execution

Playing on clay usually means playing longer points, so players training to play on a surface like that at the French Open should train at longer intervals. For training to play on a surface like Wimbledon's or on any fast indoor surface, the intervals should be shorter. Those who play most of their matches on clay or other slow surfaces should concentrate on 200- to 400-meter sprints with a 1- to 2-minute rest between sprints. For hard-court and grass play, they should incorporate shorter intervals of 50 to 100 meters with a 30- to 60-second breather after each set.

Tip

The most important aspect of any cross-training program is rest for the body and mind. Players must set aside time to recuperate from training on and off of the courts. The muscles and mind undergo tremendous pounding throughout years of training. To make sure players are able to compete and enjoy the game 10 to 50 years later, all athletes must rest their performance instruments—both body and mind.

221. BURPEES

Objective

To help players develop all of the major muscles needed for explosive and well-coordinated reflexes, stamina, and flexibility.

Description

This drill works the cardiovascular system, legs, shoulders, core, chest, and arms.

Execution

From a standing position, players sink down into a deep squat with the gluteal muscles on the calves and put their hands on the ground in front of the body. They transfer the body weight onto the arms and jump back with both feet simultaneously. If this is too hard, players can step the legs back one at a time. The body should stay perfectly straight in a plank position, holding the core tight and not letting the hips sink. Players perform one deep push-up and jump with both feet forward close to the hands, keeping the glutes low, almost touching the heels. The more flexible players become, the easier the body folds into this position. Players jump or leap up as high as possible and land into the squat position again, softly and quietly, resisting with the thigh muscles in a controlled movement. Players must be smooth and light on their feet. They should strive for a maximum height in each jump and the lowest possible position in the push-up while keeping the core extremely tight. Players work up to performing 15 to 20 repetitions.

Tip

This exercise is used in military and martial arts training and is a dynamite cardio workout, but if players' knees hurt, they should not jump; they can walk in place instead.

PART

Competitive Group Games

Teaching game-based tennis lessons is growing and fast becoming the number one way to keep children and adults interested in the sport. Now that QuickStart balls and modified rackets are available, children are catching the tennis bug at younger and younger ages, and adults are enjoying jumping into the tennis game at older ages. The combination of player-friendly equipment coupled with player- and age-appropriate playing tools such as rackets for all ages, weights, heights, and ability levels, has brought more people to tennis. In addition, lessons that are more engaging, entertaining, and educational will keep them coming back for more.

Playing competitive group games is a wonderful way for players to learn the fundamentals of the game, practice what they've learned while exercising, and have a lot of fun at the same time. Instructors understand that giving effective lessons to a group of children or adults is a constant challenge to their teaching ability. In teaching the fundamentals of the game, they must deal with players of varying age, physical ability, learning skills, athletic background, and personality. Instructors have to work harder when giving group lessons, especially if their aim is to give some undivided attention to each student. They have to keep the balls coming to players, keep them moving so that boredom won't set in, and keep the lessons interesting, educational, and enjoyable while providing a stream of encouragement and advice. The key is proper balance between game-based teaching and skill-based teaching: in other words, *edutainment*. Balance between the two styles for teaching group lessons to children and adults is essential to keeping students wanting to play and learn. Instructors should remember that tennis is a game first and should be fun, but that offering a dollop of learning opportunities must be part of the equation.

As an instructor, I have experienced many teaching challenges throughout my years. One very special memory happened last summer. While working late one night in my pro shop, a man came up the stairs and started walking toward me. He stopped and looked at me, and as I looked at him I thought he looked familiar. His face and mouth dropped as did mine when we both realized at the same moment that he was one of my favorite students that I had when he was 7 years old. Now, 20 years later, slightly balding and in a business suit, he was coming in to see me. That was a moment I will never forget. And yes, he is still hitting the ball!

This part of the book delves into games for children and adults that reinforce the drills that players have worked on in the other parts. Whether players prefer to enjoy tennis games in a structured class or with a group of players practicing against the backboard, they will find plenty of exciting ways to keep their game on.

Chapter 17

Teaching Group Games

Teaching tennis to children is a rewarding and fantastically fun way to make a living. Instructors laugh, cry, console, give advice, and play tennis all day with eager students who look at you like you are a tennis master. When an instructor is faced with a group of junior tennis players of all ages, abilities, and learning styles, you must come up with inventive ways to teach the technical side of tennis without boring your students to death. The term *edutainment* says it all; it fuses game-based tennis with stressing the fundamentals of tennis at the same time. An example of edutainment would be teaching students how to hit a forehand crosscourt while trying to stay out of tennis jail. I haven't seen students so interested in serving practice, which usually means serving a cart of 350 balls to be exact, as they are when I suggest we play Nail It.

In 2013 the United States Tennis Association (USTA) introduced 10 and Under Tennis. Also known as QuickStart Tennis, it is a new and unique way to get future tennis players not only involved in playing tennis at an earlier age, but playing and seeing results from day one. Using softer, lighter, bigger, color-coded balls; smaller tennis nets; smaller courts; and shorter, lighter tennis rackets, tennis is growing at a rate that harkens back to the 1980s and '90s.

Most people learn tennis through group or multiplayer lessons. A well-organized group lesson keeps all players busy, learning, and having loads of fun. Children 3 through 10 years of age learn the fundamentals of playing tennis through game-based tactics that reinforce tennis techniques such as groundstroking, moving to the ball, hitting the ball, keeping score, and developing a mature approach to competition.

Through game-based tactics, adults and juniors ages 11 and older develop not only the fundamentals of the game but also the physical and emotional maturity required of athletes. With the aid of entertaining and exciting tennis-related games collected in this chapter, parents and professional instructors can introduce a new and exciting way to teach tennis to children, juniors, and adults. In a nutshell, games are used primarily to teach developing players in an enjoyable way how to become physically and emotionally mature as skilled competitive tennis players. What better way to educate the mind, body, and spirit than through fun and games? Students will never forget the instructor or what they have learned and the fun they had while doing it. The following pages contain a plethora of activities, games, and instructional tips to keep all players of all ages interested, excited, and enthusiastic—and keep lesson plans and instructors' imaginations fresh.

222. BALL PICKUP

Objective

To create an interesting and enjoyable way to encourage ball pickup time on court—the greatest challenge of teaching group lessons.

Description

Clearing balls from the court and returning them to the teaching cart is never the highlight of a student's tennis lesson. If this boring task can be made into a challenging, entertaining game, the students will find it enjoyable and will request to do it.

Execution

Instructors ask players to build a castle, teepee, or pyramid when they stack the balls on top of their rackets. Or they can ask players to make a pizza with the balls. Before the students put the pizza into the oven (ball cart), they tell the instructor what kind of pizza it is.

Tip

Instructors should always reward ball pickup. For example, the student who picks up the most balls gets to choose which game will be played.

223. ME AND MY SHADOW

Objective

To develop hand–eye coordination, footwork, and the ability to follow directions.

Description

This game helps young players use their imagination and choose the type of stroke they want to hit. It also keeps the other students involved while one student is hitting.

Execution

To ensure safety, students should be in a single-file line, not too close to each other. Poly spots (flat, colored place mats) can designate where students will stand so that they won't run into each other with their rackets. The first student in line hits a series of shots—forehands, backhands, volleys, and so on—and the other students pretend to be his or her shadow. The students mimic every movement; that is, the strokes and the footwork.

Tip

To limit any accidents with rackets, young players should use their hands to mimic the movements or be placed very far apart from each other. Think safety first!

224. OOPS! I FORGOT MY RACKET

Objective

To develop hand–eye coordination, ball tracking, ball sense, and general motor ability.

Description

Before young players or even beginning players can master hitting a small tennis ball, the instructor should help them become familiar with the feel and dexterity of catching and throwing the ball.

Execution

Students are positioned 3 feet (about 1 meter) away from the tennis net. The instructor stands across the net opposite the students and tosses balls to them. Students must catch the ball on the first bounce and then toss it back over the net to the instructor or into a bucket. The instructor can vary the difficulty of the tosses.

Tips

To slow the pace, players can use QuickStart red, orange, or green balls. The instructor should establish a simple reward system on the first day of lessons to motivate young players to follow directions, focus, and give their best when participating.

225. BLAST THE TARGET

Objective

To develop hand–eye coordination, dexterity, general motor skills, and athletic agility.

Description

This game helps players learn how to direct tennis balls to specific targets.

Execution

The instructor should position the players across the service line, standing next to each other. Cones, buckets, or tennis rackets standing butt down should be placed on the opposite side of the tennis net. Players enjoy throwing or hitting balls at targets. When a player hits a target, a reward is earned. The first player to hit a target gets to pick the next game for the day. This approach saves on ball pickup time, because now all of the balls are on one side of the net!

Tip

This little game is a great way to teach young players how to score in tennis. For every target hit, that player should yell out a score, such as "Fifteen!" or "Thirty!" until four targets are hit. Then the player would yell "Game!" Six games win the set; 12 win the match.

226. POP-UP VOLLEY

Objective

To develop confidence up at the net, hand–eye coordination, fast reaction to the ball, and ball-tracking skills.

Description

This interesting twist on volleying helps young players develop a sense of volley eagerness. It makes them really hungry to "bop" or block the ball. Creating a fun environment for volleying also keeps young players from shying away from the net.

Execution

Players take positions standing one next to the other approximately 3 feet (1 meter) from the net. Players should be in squatting positions with rackets up in the volley position. The instructor stands on the other side of the net and tosses balls one at a time to the players. On cue from the instructor, the players pop up, hit a volley, and then squat again like a jack-in-the-box. If the player hits the volley, he or she gets to stand up and hit the next volley. If the player hits this volley, he or she may try to hit an overhead. If the player misses any one of the shots, he or she starts over from the squatting position. All players who successfully hit all three shots over the net win.

Variation

The instructor can turn this game into storybook volley land by assigning the name of a character to each student. On hearing his or their character mentioned in the story, students pop up and hit a volley. For example, the frog (the player with the frog character pops up to hit a volley) telephones the turtle (the turtle pops up to hit a volley) and asks if the turtle wants to come over and share some pizza with rabbit (the rabbit pops up to hit a volley), and so on. Letting children choose their characters keeps them interested and can result in an interesting story line. The first few times you try this drill, you may want to come up with a few rounds so you're not left with pauses in the middle of the game while you try to think of what to say next.

Tips

Use QuickStart red, orange, or green balls with this drill for both adults and children until the players become more confident and comfortable with volleying. If an oncoming tennis ball has ever hit you in the face or neck or even the back of your head while attempting to volley, then you realize how scary it can be. Multiply those feelings by a factor of 10, and you will understand why children and some adults are reluctant to jump into the volleying frying pan. Don't rush children or timid adults into volleying; let them show you by their willingness, excitement, and eagerness to "bop" the ball.

227. TEE TIME TENNIS

Objective

To develop racket and ball control.

Description

Players use some of the techniques of golf to aim the ball into the net as if they are putting the ball. They follow it up by hitting a serve toward a target. This game takes the pressure out of learning how to serve over the net, a difficult task for players who may not even be as tall as the net.

Execution

Players form two lines behind the baseline or service line, depending on ability. A target and stack of balls on a racket are placed in front of each team. The first two players run forward and place a ball on top of a cone with the top cut off. Players hit the ball with their rackets using a golf swing (forehand) into the net. They retrieve the ball and serve it toward a target on the other side of the net. Players run back to their teams and tag the next player. The first team to hit the target or hit all balls over the net wins.

Variation

Players can use their backhand or their nondominant hand.

228. TENNIS FOR TIGERS

Objective

To develop hand–eye coordination, balance, and ball sense.

Description

When tossing involves a bounce, it is best to match the word with the action. This exercise could involve the vocalization of three words (*toss, bounce,* and *catch*). Teaching a child to balance a ball on the racket demands body coordination and balance, and ups and downs are excellent for developing hand–eye coordination. Ups consist of bouncing the ball in the air with the racket. Downs involve consecutive bounces and hits off the court. A self-drop hit calls for the ball to be dropped close enough to the body to be hit after one bounce.

Execution

Players take positions across the baseline with rackets and balls. On the instructor's cue, each player places a ball on the strings of the racket and tries to balance the ball for 10 to 15 seconds without dropping it. Next, players try to hit as many ups as they can in 15 or 20 seconds without letting the ball drop. Next, players try to hit as many downs as they can in 15 or 20 seconds without losing control of the ball. Last, players try a combination of ups and downs.

Variation

Players can walk, run, skip, hop, or spin around during the game.

229. DUCK, DUCK, GOOSE

Objective

To develop footwork, fast reaction to the ball, speed, athletic agility, and ball control.

Description

This game really gets players to concentrate on keeping the ball in play. If a player misses a shot into the net or hits it out of the court, then he or she must rely on speed and agility to outrun the other players trying to hit three consecutive balls over and in play before the player makes it back to home base. All players must focus.

Execution

Players position themselves in a single-file line behind the baseline or service line. The instructor feeds a ball to the first player in line, requiring the player to hit either forehand or backhand. If a player hits the ball over the net and in play, the instructor says, "Duck," and the player runs to the end of the line and is considered safe. If the player misses the shot, the instructor yells, "Goose!" and the player must run completely around the markers set up on the opposite side of the court and get back to the end of the line before the student standing in line hits two shots in a row over the net and in play. If the *goose* makes it back to home base in time, he or she doesn't receive a goose egg. But the goose that doesn't make it back in time receives a goose egg. Play a certain number of minutes or rounds, or until players start to lose focus. The player with the fewest goose eggs at the end of the game wins. Try not to make the focus of the game on scoring, though. Encourage players to do their best each time it's their turn, regardless of the number of goose eggs he or she may have.

Variations

Players can use groundstrokes, volleys, and overheads. The rules of the game can also be slightly adjusted. For example, line students one behind the other behind the center (T) of the service line or baseline. The instructor starts by feeding one ball to the first player in line. If the player hits the shot over the net and onto the court, the player is safe and can proceed to the end of the line. If the player misses the shot after two attempts, the instructor yells, "Goose!" The player, with racket in hand, must spring from his or her side of the court, around the markers on the opposite side of the court, and back to the end of the line on the original side of the net before each student standing in line hits three balls in a row each over the net. If the runner (goose) makes it back before each student accomplishes this task, the goose doesn't receive a goose egg. If not, the player receives one goose egg.

230. WATTLE, WATTLE, QUACK, ATTACK

Objective

To promote agility, dexterity, focus, and lots of laughs.

Description

This game helps players learn how to serve in a no-pressure game situation. Having players squat and walk like ducks up to the service line with a ball balancing on their rackets keeps the fun involved in learning how to hit up on the serve.

Execution

Players line up across the baseline with 10 balls next to each of them. On cue, each player squats like a duck, puts one ball on his or her racket, waddles up to the service line, pops up, and attempts to hit the serve over the net. If the ball goes over the net, they give a loud quacking sound, then they squat and waddle back to the baseline and continue until all of the balls are served over. The first player who serves all balls over the net and is squatting like a duck comfortably on the baseline wins.

Variation

For younger groups, use QuickStart red, orange, or green balls.

231. NAIL IT

Objective

To increase accuracy, depth, and control of the serve.

Description

This game promotes accuracy with serving in a noncompetitive, fun atmosphere.

Execution

The instructor places targets in both of the service boxes. Students line up across the service line or baseline and attempt to *nail* (hit dead on) the target with a serve. If the target is nailed, then the instructor does a predetermined number of push-ups.

Tip

Make sure students use the correct service motion to hit the target, or the serve doesn't count toward a push-up. That's your out!

232. MESSY CHEESEBURGER

Objective

To develop hand–eye coordination, concentration, and balance.

Description

Players learn how to keep their eyes on the ball, focus, and balance. This game also emphasizes team spirit and teamwork.

Execution

Players form teams behind the baseline. Each team has two players; if more players are involved, teams can be bigger. Each player will help to build the *cheeseburger* by placing a tennis ball on the team's racket face. On cue from the instructor, the first player in line starts to build the burger by racing from the baseline to the first designated area called out by the instructor, placing the ingredient (a ball) on the racket face, and racing back to the baseline balancing the ingredient on the racket. They hand off the racket to the next player in line who races to the next designated area to add to the cheeseburger. Players cannot use their hands to keep the ingredients on the racket. They must hold the racket at the grip and balance all of the ingredients. If a player who is racing to place another ingredient on the racket drops a piece of the burger, the player must race back to the baseline and hand the racket to the next player. The next player will race (on cue from the instructor) to place another ingredient on the racket. Play continues until one team has placed all of the ingredients on the racket and successfully returned to the baseline with a fully built cheeseburger, and all teammates are standing on the baseline. Use as many balls as necessary.

Tip

This is a game of balance, concentration and teamwork, so encourage each player to slow down and focus.

233. CHICKEN TENNIS

Objective

To help players practice footwork, teamwork, dexterity, speed, and agility.

Description

This game is a great way for players to get some extra cardiovascular exercise.

Execution

All of the players are on one side of the tennis net lined up in one of the doubles alleys. The instructor chooses one player to be the fox, who will take a position in the middle of the tennis court on the same side of the net as all players. Without warning, the instructor will yell, "Chicken!" The players who are lined up in the doubles alley will try to run across the court to reach the other alley before the fox player tags them. If the fox tags (with hands only) one of the chickens, then that player joins the fox and is now a fox chasing the chickens as well. When all of the chickens except one are tagged, the game is over; the last chicken standing is the winner.

234. FAMOUS CASTLE

Objective

To promote racket and ball control, footwork, and fun.

Description

This outrageously fun fairytale game helps students learn how to hit ground-strokes, move around the court, and aim while playing.

Execution

The instructor is the dragon, and a basket of tennis balls (called *fire balls*) is the dragon's *fire pit*. The instructor will be on one side of the net, and the royal family will be on the other side of the net. Players line up off of the court next to the doubles sideline one behind the other. Rackets are in the down position for safety. The instructor assigns jobs in the castle such as royal dog, cat, princess, prince, court jester, or king—whatever the players want to be. Next, the instructor places poly spots or space holders, which are flat and brightly colored in the three designated hitting areas of the court (castle). The first spot is the royal living room placed on the junction of the service line and singles sideline (T). The next stop is the royal kitchen up at the net. The last spot is the royal bedroom. Place the poly spot on the junction of the service line and the singles sideline (T) on the far side of the court so that players can hit backhands. As the players move forward, the instructor hits fire balls to each player until the player reaches the net (the kitchen). The instructor can hit as many fire balls to the players as they like. When all three areas are full with royal subjects (the king in the living room, princess in the kitchen, and queen in the bedroom), the instructor can feed all three areas and then rotate players until one of the royal subjects hits a fire ball into the fire pit. This game can go on and on until all fire balls have been used.

235. GO TO JAIL!

Objective

To encourage good groundstrokes, footwork, and teamwork.

Description

This game helps to promote the use of all groundstrokes, footwork, hitting, catching, and running in a fun, noncompetitive situation.

Execution

Players line up behind the service line center (T). The instructor is on the opposite side of the net. Players aim to hit their shots into a designated area on the opposite side of the court. For example, have all students aim for the area known as no-mans-land. If the students hit their shot into this area, they are safe and run to the end of the line. If they miss and hit their shot any other place on the court, they go straight to jail. Jail is the other side of the court. Players get out of jail when they catch a ball that another player hit. The game is over when one student is left hitting and he or she hits a shot into no-mans-land.

236. SHARKS AND MINNOWS

Objective

To promote quick, evasive reactions on the court and develop agility, speed, and coordination.

Description

This game is wonderful as a warm-up or cool-down.

Execution

Players divide into two groups and stand in both doubles alleys facing each other. One team is the *sharks,* and the other team is the *minnows.* The instructor calls out, "Minnows!" All the sharks must then try to catch and tag the escaping minnows before they make it successfully across the court and into the sharks' cave (the opposite doubles alley). Each minnow caught becomes a shark. The last lonely little minnow left wins the game.

237. SPINNING OUT OF CONTROL

Objective

To teach players how to hit various types of spin.

Description

This game encourages players to move their feet and watch the ball connect with their rackets. Players learn what various types of spin do to the ball and therefore will want to learn the grips and technique needed to hit them. For grip changes see chapter 1.

Execution

The instructor splits players up into two teams, positioning them behind the baseline or service line. The instructor hits shots with various types of spin to the first player in each line. That player attempts to hit the shot back over the net and onto the court. The team that hits the most balls over the net and in the court wins. Alternatively, the first team to hit 25 shots over the net and onto the court wins.

Variation

Players can practice catching with their hands, a hat, or a bucket. For example, position all players single file behind the center (T) on either the baseline or service line. Each player has a hat or bucket to attempt to catch the shot that the instructor hits. This game is an excellent way to teach on-court foot movement coupled with the agility and speed needed in order to catch a tennis ball with topspin in a hat or bucket.

Tips

Players should avoid diving to catch the ball with their hands, hats, or buckets. If the game becomes too competitive, instructors may want to set boundary lines, such as circles or squares, around each player. Instructors should try to emphasize the positioning of the racket head when connecting with the ball. Players should strike the ball at the precise vertical angle to impart the desired spin on the incoming ball.

238. RED LIGHT! GREEN LIGHT!

Objective

To teach players how to manipulate the ball and racket to develop balance and coordination, and to help develop the *steady head, eyes down* position through impact technique (a vital tactic that helps players consistently nail the ball with the sweet spot of the racket). See chapter 2 for proper footwork and body positioning.

Description

This is a great game for a class warm-up or cool-down. The game can also be performed using tennis ups and downs. The instructor should encourage players to watch their own balls and rackets, because young players tend to watch everyone else and end up dropping their balls off their rackets. Tell players to "Keep your eagle eyes peeled and focused on the ball."

Execution

The instructor lines up players next to each other on the baseline. Each player places a ball on the strings of his or her racket and tries to balance it on the strings. The instructor yells, "Green light!" While balancing balls on their rackets, the students can run, walk, or skip up toward the net until the instructor yells, "Red light!" Then all activity stops. The first student to reach the net without dropping the ball off his or her racket is the winner.

Variation

Instructors can add another colored light (for example, *purple light* means that students must spin around while balancing a ball on their rackets). When the instructor yells, "Red light," students should stop, bend down, and touch their toes while continuing to balance the ball on their racket. If the students drop the ball, they should start over from their original starting position.

Tips

Instructors should be flexible with their lesson plans, varying the activities depending on skills and attentiveness. Players appreciate the enthusiasm of an instructor who demonstrates and participates, so instructors should join in on most of the games. They should show players that they too can make mistakes or that they can run, skip, jump, or dance. Instructors should show students by example that if they practice hard enough, they too can perform well. When instructors set a good example, students learn more, play more, and will never forget who taught them how.

Objective

To reinforce the fundamentals of groundstroking, footwork, directing the ball, and racket and ball control.

Description

Having players combine hitting, thinking, and running adds tremendous fun to learning fundamentals. Players have a chance to hit a groundstroke in play (on the opposite side of the net) or when sprinting a race to win games.

Execution

Players line up across the baseline. Each player gets a number (any number between 1 and 30). All leftover numbers are ghost numbers. The instructor calls out a number. The student with that number runs up to a designated spot and hits a forehand or backhand groundstroke over the net and onto the court. If the student misses the shot, he or she receives the letter *S*. The student receives a letter for each subsequent miss until *SPUD* is spelled out. But that's not the only way students gain letters. Remember the ghost numbers? When the instructor calls out a ghost number, all players must run as fast as they can up to the net, touch it, and then run back to the baseline. The first player to cross the baseline loses a letter, and the last one gains a letter.

Variation

ABC SPUD is played exactly like regular spud. Instead of using numbers, the game uses the 26 letters of the alphabet. When the instructor calls out a letter, the student whose letter has been called runs up to hit either a forehand or backhand and has 7 seconds to think of a word that begins with that letter. All other rules stand.

Tip

Playing fun tennis games helps players young or old, beginner or veteran, incorporate all of the fundamental stroke techniques for good match play learned and solidified through drilling. Players will get a good sense of competitive play while participating in a stress-free tennis environment.

240. FLY CATCHER

Objective

To develop the fundamentals of groundstrokes, footwork, tracking, and hitting an incoming ball.

Description

Having players use their imagination to create a magical kingdom surrounding the tennis court takes the pressure off performance. The players cast themselves in various roles and try to act as their characters while learning the fundamentals of tennis.

Execution

Players line up behind either the baseline or the service line. The instructor informs them that they are now the kings and queens of their castles. Their tennis rackets are fly swatters, and the balls are flies. As long as the kings and queens swat the flies back over the net, they remain royalty. But if they miss the flies, they turn into frogs! The frogs must run over to the instructor's side of the court, which is a big lily pad where all the hungry frogs live. The only way for frogs to turn back into royalty is to catch one of the flies hit by a king or queen before the fly rolls off the lily pad into the murky pond surrounding them (anywhere outside the tennis court). The winner is the last remaining king or queen who can successfully swat flies back over the tennis net.

Variation

Once players progress to controlling a sustained rally, let the frogs battle it out against the royalty. For example, if a king swats his fly (ball) over the net and a frog swats it back, let the two players continue until one player wins the rally.

Tip

Instructors and parents should work to develop positive attitudes about competition so that players enjoy the game beyond winning or losing. Helping players learn how to let go of the need-to-win or the desire-and-fear attitude will help them concentrate solely on playing and hitting the ball. This causes them to have a sense of tennis integrity, a pride in their own game-playing ability as well as respect for their opponents. Playing the *game* of tennis takes priority over the desire to win and the fear of losing.

241. BUG CATCHER

Objective

To develop hand–eye coordination, groundstroking technique, and ball-tracking skills.

Description

Players at the beginning and advanced beginning stages enjoy trying to hit the ball past their opponents. This game introduces mild competition. This is the jump-off point for instructors or parents to teach the beginning player the rules of tennis. Try to incorporate the official tennis scoring, game, and match playing system.

Execution

Players line up behind the center (T) of the service line or baseline. The instructor feeds a forehand or backhand ball for the first player to hit. If the player misses, he or she runs to the other side of the court. In this position the only way the student can get back into the game is to use his or her racket to trap a ball that was tossed by the instructor or hit over the net by a hitter. A player who accomplishes this task switches places with the hitter. The winner is the last player who hits a ball over the net and escapes being trapped.

Variation

The Catch a Fly variation is like Bug Catcher, except the instructor mixes up the balls fed, and the students are restricted to a specific part of the court. When a student misses a shot, he or she must run over to the instructor's side of the court. The only way for the player to get back into the game is to catch a ball out of the air that was hit by a student who is still a hitter. If the player succeeds in catching a ball, he or she takes the place of the hitter. The last player who hits a ball over the net into the correct part of the court without the ball being caught wins.

Tip

Instructors and parents should praise attempts to catch and throw, especially with very young players who are still working on their general motor skills. Any encouragement from the instructor or parent will help young players progress in their emotional and physical development as athletes. When giving feedback—even corrections—using positive, encouraging statements such as "That's great; now let's try it this way" or "Wow, what an arm you have! Now let's see if you can hit the ball into the basket" leads to greater success than using negative statements such as "Don't hit that way" or "Stop swinging so fast." Even if the statement begins as negative in the mind, turning it into a positive when giving feedback will ensure positive responses from all players at all ages.

242. BASKETBALL TENNIS

Objective

To promote good racket and ball control for hitting balls out in front, hand–eye coordination, and competitive emotional development.

Description

Adding the elements of a basketball game helps players identify with a sport they may be familiar with. This method adds lots of fun, competition, and stimulation for the learning process. This game also helps to develop the basic stroke concepts of *hitting out in front,* which means all balls should be hit out in front of the player's torso in whatever direction the player's torso is facing.

Execution

The instructor divides players into two or more teams. Team A and team B are positioned behind the baseline at the center (T). When the instructor gives the cue, the first player in each line bounces a ball down with the racket to the net and attempts to hit a groundstroke to a specific area (which the instructor has marked beforehand) on the opposite court. The instructor can set points for shots that land in specific parts of the court. Balls that hit the baseline are worth three points, balls that land in no-man's land are worth two points, and so on. The team with the most points wins the game.

Variations

Players hit balls from various areas on the court and use various types of shots. The teaching cart can be the basketball net, and a shot hit directly into the basket can count as a slam dunk. Another variation is to place several buckets around the interior of the singles court or doubles court area, and assign a point value to each bucket. The first player to accumulate 21 points wins the game.

Tip

The instructor should remind players to keep their heads steady and eyes down through impact. This practice promotes consistent contact on or near the center of the strings. It is also a great way to get students to pick up the balls and return them to the teaching cart. Young players get bored with simply collecting the balls to put them back in the cart, but if it turns into a game, they will never realize they're simply picking up and putting away the balls.

243. CREEPY CRAWLY

Objective

To develop racket and ball control, dexterity, ball sense, footwork skills, hand–eye coordination, and concentration skills.

Description

Players form a tightly connected line and attempt to pass a tennis ball from one person to the next. When the ball reaches the last person in line, the leader of the line should have sprinted to the end of the line to keep the line progressing forward and the ball passing continuous.

Execution

Players split into two or more teams. Teams are positioned on the baseline, each with a stack of balls beside them. The first player in each line balances a ball on his or her strings and passes it to the next player in line. When the last player gets the ball, the first player in line should sprint back to the end of the line to keep the ball passes moving. Each team creeps and crawls (walks using tiny steps) their way up to the net. When a team reaches the net, a player hits the ball over the net using a service motion and the team runs back to the baseline to start all over. The first team to hit all their balls over the net and take seats on the baseline wins the game.

Variation

Players use various strokes to hit the ball over the net. Players can also use only their hands and continuously flip the ball up and back over their heads to the player behind them, who catches the ball. They continue the flipping pattern until one player flubs either a catch or flip.

Tips

Have players flip or hit (pop up) soft, low, controllable passes so that the player who is receiving the ball can catch and pass with control. Have players bunched together so as to encourage short stepping. Precision footwork is the key to balance and timing when attempting to hit effortlessly, consistently, and with fluidity and tremendous power. A player who bounces quickly on the balls of the feet will be mentally prepared for successful play.

244. LIZARDS HAVE TWO SKINS

Objective

To develop hand–eye coordination, physical skill, and good racket and ball control; and to help players learn good teamwork and communication skills.

Description

This mildly competitive game encourages players to work on strengthening their forearms and hand–eye coordination in an entertaining way. Beginning players discover the fun of hitting the ball with their racket using their own style and strategy. Players will ultimately gain confidence in the use of their feet, hands, eyes, and their everchanging bodies.

Execution

Team A and team B take the court and flip a coin to decide which team is the stationary team and which team gets to move while bouncing their balls. Players from the team that wins the toss (in this case team A) each have a racket and two balls and are scattered randomly around the court. On the instructor's cue, players from team A move around the court, bouncing the ball in the prescribed manner (ups or downs). Team B waits patiently in place, bouncing their balls, waiting for just one mistake. When a player (from either team) loses control over the first ball, the second ball is used. Players who lose control of their second ball lose their *skin* (turn). A player can restore his or her skin if a teammate opts to give the player one of his or her two balls. The team that has the fewest skinless players wins.

Variation

Players can bounce the ball in the air or alternate ups and downs. Have players attempt bouncing the ball on the edge of their racket head or even the butt of the racket.

Tip

To help players focus on watching the ball and not the other players, the instructor should ask them to try to read the number printed on the ball while bouncing it down or up on the racket. How many ball numbers can a player read correctly while practicing tennis ups and downs? Or, how many times can each player bounce the ball down or up or a combination in a row? Instructors can also join in the competition. When players see instructors performing the task, it encourages them to try harder.

Objective

To promote quick bursts of speed, good footwork, and hand–eye coordination.

Description

This game encourages patience when trying to hit under pressure. Players can run, walk fast, or hop up on the their team's pile of balls and attempt a serve into the correct service box. Players who miss, keep trying until they get the ball into the service court.

Execution

Players split up into two teams and take positions on the baseline next to each other. On the service line directly in front of each team is a big pile of balls. On the instructor's cue, the first player in line from each team runs up to their pile of balls. The player picks up a ball, spins around the pile, and then hits a serve over the net. If the player succeeds in hitting the ball over the net and into the correct service box, he or she runs to the end of the line while the next player takes off. If the player misses the ball into the net, he or she retrieves the ball, runs back to the service line, and keeps trying until successful. The first team to serve all their balls over the net wins the game.

Variation

Players can hit balls to various areas on the court or use a variety strokes. There are many ways to get players who may be having some coordination issues to really feel and connect with the ball. For example, the players can pretend that the ball they will be tossing is a baby bird; they gently toss the baby bird up to help it fly away. Players are then asked to catch the bird up high with their tennis racket. Or, players can pretend the ball is a planet that they are responsible for placing high into the sky. Then they can land their rocket ship (racket) on that planet. The point is to be creative with teaching. Soon all players will be serving on their own.

Tip

The instructor should encourage students to support a teammate who is having trouble focusing and can't serve or hit the ball over the net. Instructors should remind players that it's perfectly normal to make mistakes during practice. That's what practice is for—to make mistakes and learn how to correct them. If players are attempting to learn a new stroke or shot, throw major support and encouragement their way so that they will be eager to keep trying.

246. FREEZE-TAG TENNIS

Objective

To develop racket and ball control, athletic proficiency, and teamwork skills.

Description

This game is played a lot like freeze tag except that tennis players are required to practice a tennis task while attempting to tag other players from the opposing team.

Execution

Players of two opposing teams are scattered randomly around the court, each with a racket and ball in hand. Both teams should designate two or more players as taggers. On cue, all players start moving and bouncing the ball all around the court trying to avoid the other team's taggers. If the ball gets away from a member of team A, that player retrieves it, freezes in place, and bounces the ball while stationary. The frozen player of team A may resume moving if tagged by an unfrozen teammate. The winner is the last unfrozen player left bouncing the ball around the court.

Variation

Players can try this game applying the same rules, but using a tennis dexterity ball. A dexterity ball has bumps all over it, so when it is dropped, the ball does wacky unpredictable bounces. Using the dexterity ball helps young players develop quick hands and feet and coordination, and it increases their tracking skills.

247. TOTALLY TOUGH TENNIS

Objective

To develop footwork, fast reaction to the ball, quick reflexes, evasive action to move away from the ball, speed, agility, and rapid change of direction.

Description

This game introduces the skill needed to keep the ball in play on the court. Players learn how to move, hit, and direct the ball to various areas of the court.

Execution

Players form two teams in front of a wall with rackets in hand. Each team has one ball. On cue, the first player in each line drop hits the ball against the wall. The next player in line moves forward and hits the ball, then the next, and so on until someone misses. Rotation is continuous.

Variation

Teams can try to hit as many shots as possible in a timed session, use only the hands or feet, or use volleys or overheads.

248. AROUND THE TENNIS WORLD

Objective

To teach players how to watch the ball, how to position themselves on the court, how to cover the court, and how the tennis scoring system works.

Description

This game encourages players to keep the ball in play, direct the ball to areas that will cause the opposing team to miss, and work together as a team.

Execution

The instructor forms two teams and positions players behind the service line facing each other. They use only the service-court area. Players hit the ball over the net into the opposite service court and go to the end of the line. The next player moves forward to play the return in a continuous hitting sequence. Teams score a point when opponents fail to return the ball. The first team to reach 10 points wins.

Variation

Players attempt to hit 26 shots in succession (A through Z). With chalk, the instructor marks letters A to Z around the court, progressing from easy to difficult areas. Players are behind the baseline center (T). Players start at A and progress to the next letter by using designated strokes. Players who miss, stay at that letter until they execute the stroke. The first player to Z wins.

249. VOLLEYBALL TENNIS

Objective

To promote good racket and ball control.

Description

This entertaining and challenging game mimics beach volleyball.

Execution

This game can be played with 4 or 6 players. All players are up at the net. The instructor puts the first ball into play with a gentle pop volley shot. Players must volley the ball up three times on their side before it can cross the net. Team A receives the ball and hits it three times on their side, then volleys the ball to team B on the opposite side of the net. Play continues until one team misses. If the ball hits the court, the team that let the ball hit the court loses the point. The game ends when one team gets to at least 11 points winning by 2.

250. BACK-ALLEY RACKET KING

Objective

To promote ball control, sound footwork, and shot placement.

Description

Players are limited to hitting balls back and forth inside the doubles alley. They must find a way to maneuver their feet, strokes, and bodies to keep the ball in play.

Execution

Two players take positions opposite each other in one of the doubles alleys. They use the service line as a boundary line. Players attempt to rally back and forth using only the doubles alley. Players should try to keep five balls in play. For every five balls in play, the actual game point starts. When one player accumulates 5 points, then he or she will try for 10 to 15 balls in play before the actual point starts. So the player who can accumulate 5 points after keeping 10 to 15 balls in play inside of the doubles alley will be dubbed the *Back-Alley Racket King*. After players master this game-play technique, they play a regular-scoring tennis game inside the alley. When players become comfortable with that method, they can play an entire match.

Variation

Players can hit forehand to forehand, backhand to backhand, or alternate strokes. They play a game, set, or match.

251. TORNADO TENNIS

Objective

To improve hand–eye coordination, balance, footwork, agility, and speed.

Description

Creating a game out of volleying and hitting overheads forces young players to track the incoming ball with more confidence. Young players are usually afraid to volley or hit overheads. They feel as though they are too close to the ball and it might hit them. When young players think only about playing to beat the other team, their fears of the net seem to float away.

Execution

The instructor splits up the players into two teams and positions them behind the baseline facing the net. The instructor is on the opposite side of the net with a basket of balls. The first two players sprint up to the net, spin around once, split step, hit a forehand volley, spin around in the opposite direction, hit a backhand volley, spin around again in the opposite direction, and hit an overhead. If a player can complete the entire tornado sequence without missing, he or she runs back to the baseline and tags the next player in line. The winning team is the one that first has all its members complete the sequence.

Objective

To develop hand–eye coordination, dexterity, teamwork skills, footwork, and good racket and ball control.

Description

The principle of using tiny, tight steps to play tennis is often overlooked. This game helps players feel and experience the type of footwork they need to run, hit, recover, sprint, stop, and quickly change direction during match play.

Execution

The instructor positions one or more teams behind the baseline in relay formation. The first player in the line of each team flips a ball over his or her head to the next team player in line. This player catches the flipped ball on the racket without using hands to touch the ball in any way, and flips it overhead to the next player in line. The last player in line runs to the front of the line with the ball on the racket. The lines inch forward as players change position. If a team loses control of the ball, they must start from the beginning again. Teams complete a full rotation; players return to their original positions in line. Teams see how many rotations they can make before dropping the ball.

Variation

Players can pass the ball or racket and ball between the legs, over the shoulder, or alternating over and under. They can try racing up to the net and back using this method. You can make the caterpillar into a millipede, or as long as you can make the "bug." This game is also a great warm-up when six or more players participating in a lesson.

Tip

This game is a great icebreaker for new students joining new classes. It encourages communication and teamwork. Helping players to build good teamwork skills through playing group games on the tennis court teaches players much more than just using their individual efforts to succeed or fail. Players learn that combining individual ideas and efforts and coming up with various strategic methods builds lasting friendships and good sportsmanship, and they have fun in the process.

Chapter 18

Backboard Drills

The backboard is the greatest tennis player of all time. Since it started challenging players about 70 years ago, it has never lost a match. Many top players, including Roger Federer, Pete Sampras, Chris Evert, John McEnroe, Caroline Wozniacki, Pancho Segura, and Monica Seles, have used the almighty backboard to hone their tennis skills. Many players grew up practicing for hours against a backboard—and they didn't always like this stiff competitor. Today, backboards are coming back stronger than ever.

Players will never have a better practice partner than the backboard. It never misses, it's always available to play against, it doesn't matter what level you are either. The backboard can be any size or surface as long as balls bounce and return consistently back to the player. Beginners through low intermediate players can use QuickStart red, orange, and green balls to help slow the pace of the ball coming back off the wall, or they can simply use a flat ball. Practicing against the backboard improves players' consistency, placement, depth control, spin, and power. Players of any level can benefit from practicing against the backboard. This chapter provides beneficial backboard games and drills that are fun and educational and will help players develop all parts of their game.

253. BULLSEYE BACKBOARD

Objective
To help players develop aim and consistency in serving.

Description
Serving is one of the hardest strokes to perfect in the game of tennis, but a tennis match can't start without it. To make it a consistent weapon, players must practice it and perfect it. For all serves, repetition is key.

Execution
Players draw a 2-foot (about 60-centimeter) square centered 8 inches (about 20 cm) above the net line on the backboard. Within that square, they draw two more squares of consecutively smaller sizes. The center square has a value of 15, the next square 30, and the outer square 40; the bullseye is the center square. Players can play a set rotating who serves between games.

Variation
Players can play using groundstrokes or volleys.

Tip
Players should concentrate on tossing technique and keeping the head up on the serve.

254. POPEYE

Objective
To improve reflexes and build the forearm muscles for strong volleying.

Description
Practicing volleys against the backboard is scary and daunting, but by starting slowly and hitting softly, players will gain control and confidence.

Execution
Players draw a 1-foot (about 20-centimeter) square about 1 foot above the center net line. Players move back about 1 foot away from the backboard center to start, then increase their distance until they can achieve a challenging distance of 3 feet (about 1 meter), which is the playing distance goal for proper net to volleyer distance on a regulation sized tennis court. Start volleying on the forehand or backhand side or a combination of the two. Hitting softly and with control, players hit 100 volleys in increments of 10 at a time into the square or circle, alternating between the forehand and backhand and a combination of backhand–forehand volleys. Players can practice all types of volleys using this repetitive technique. The more volleys a player can hit in a row and the harder the player can hit them, the more this drill will help build strong forearm muscles, which are needed to control hitting putaway volleys, swinging volleys, approach volleys, and half volleys.

255. FANCY FINESSE

Objective

To develop racket dexterity, feel of the ball, and coordination.

Description

Learning how to hit any type of spin and to control the pace and placement of shots requires soft hands and a gentle touch. While this drill doesn't technically use a backboard, it teaches, and builds upon, the some fundamentals as other drills in this chapter.

Execution

Players try to do this drill as many times in a row as they can, building up to a goal such as 10 times in a row. The instructor stands 6 feet (about 2 meters) away from the player either on the same side of the net or on the opposite side with a basket of balls. Players can stand in one service box or in no man's land. The instructor tosses balls up in the air to either side of the player's body (forehand and backhand sides), the player attempts to catch the ball on the racket face and then flip the ball into the basket. Once the player is comfortable, the player can attempt to catch the ball on the face of the racket on the forehand side, toss the ball from the racket to the open basket, spin around once, and attempt to catch the ball on the face of the racket on the backhand side. They can make a game of spin and catch, pass the racket under each leg catch and toss, and stand on one leg catch and toss. Each exercise should be performed one stage at a time, building to the goal of crafty, soft, fancy footwork and hands.

256. TOAST

Objective

To build players' stamina while refining their strokes and having fun.

Description

This heart-pounding game can be addictive. Not only are players learning to keep the ball going, they are also learning how to direct the ball, set up their partners if playing doubles, and to be devilish in what specific shots will cause the opponent to do or not do.

Execution

Players line up one behind the other, or they scatter around the half court. The first player can hit the ball against the backboard any place they want to get the point started. Each player only hits the ball one time, then scoots to the end of the line or gets out of the way of the next player who will hit the next shot. When players miss a shot or let the ball bounce twice, they get the first letter of the word TOAST. When players accumulate all letters, they are out of the game. The last player left standing wins.

257. PLUS OR MINUS

Objective

To help players develop the confidence and accuracy to place the ball anywhere on the court during match play.

Description

Having specific areas or targets on the practice court helps players see where to hit the ball. While working on hitting specific targets, a player is mentally practicing how to play strategic patterns, such as two forehands crosscourt, one backhand to the opposite side or one crosscourt to a player's forehand, and two to the backhand side. Practicing patterns of play helps to instill confidence and creates a smarter tennis player.

Execution

Players mark several circles and squares on the backboard, designating each target with a numerical value coinciding with a regular-scoring tennis game. They play a regular-scoring tennis game and alternate hitting shots as in regular play. Each time a player hits a circle, that player's score goes up by 15, 30, 40, or Game. If a player hits a square, that player loses a point by 15, 30, 40, or Game. Players should play sets and matches.

Variation

Players should practice all strokes such as inside forehands, slices, volleys, overheads, serves, and drop shots against the back board.

Tip

One of the best ways to control the outcome of a tennis match is to be able to control the ball and ultimately the point. By hitting to specific areas on the backboard a player is building the confidence and concentration necessary to play well. The more a player plays, the better that player will develop a feel for the ball, control of all body movements and footwork, and finesse.

258. OVERHEAD BUILDER

Objective

To help players develop early racket preparation, visual judgment, and the scissor kick technique for playing the overhead.

Description

Players learn to hit with control and confidence by continuously hitting the overhead.

Execution

Players should back up approximately 4 feet (120 centimeters) away from the backboard. Next, they must hit the ball down hard into the ground, keeping it very close to the backboard in the way a table tennis serve is started, causing it to rebound off the board as a bullet lob. This action will force the hitter to quickly turn sideways, take the racket back behind the head with the hitting elbow high above the head and the nonracket hand pointing up toward the ball. At the point of striking the ball the player will leap up off the back foot and scissor the legs in the air to help maintain balance and to develop the light, fancy footwork needed to quickly recover to hit another shot. Players must remember to practice the backhand overhead as well.

Tip

Players should work on quick early racket preparation to prepare for the overhead. They should turn their bodies sideways as soon as they hit the ball into the ground, lift the racket behind the head, and backpedal with the knees bent and the nonracket hand pointing up toward the ball.

259. MARATHON

Objective

To help players learn how to control the ball to keep it in play.

Description

Learning to keep the ball in play will help players learn to set up or build up a point, step by step, in order to win it.

Execution

Two or more players can play this game. Players position themselves 30 feet (about 9 meters) back from the backboard. Draw a target 8 inches (about 20 cm) above the center net tape line on the backboard. Player A puts the ball into play; when player B returns the ball, that ball counts as one hit. The point starts on the third ball hit into play. No winners are allowed on the first three balls in play. The first player to 15 points wins the match.

260. RACK ATTACK

Objective
To encourage aggressive play in point situations.

Description
This drill encourages players to think and move the ball around on the court. Players learn how to build points one shot at a time before pouncing on the correct shot to win the point.

Execution
Players create a playing area by marking two lines on the court 20 to 30 feet (about 6 to 9 meters) apart and perpendicular to the backboard. They also mark a line 30 to 40 feet (9 to 12 meters) from the backboard and parallel to it. Both players line up behind the horizontal line. Player A bounce hits a ball to the backboard, making the ball land in the playing area on the court. The players then alternate groundstrokes until they hit a total of three. At that point players have the option of continuing to hit groundstrokes or hitting any other type of shot, including volleys. After the first three shots, any type of shot is allowed as long as the ball rebounds off the backboard and lands in the playing area. A point is over when a player misses a shot. The first player to 21 points wins the game.

261. SUPERBALL TOUCH

Objective
To develop a feel for the ball and control of the ball when close to the net (backboard).

Description
This drill is one of the best ways for players to learn how to control the pace of the ball when attempting to hit touch volleys. Players get a sense of how to relax and use their bodies to hit touch shots.

Execution
Players should draw three or four circle targets on the backboard. Standing at arm's length from the backboard, players volley the ball, keeping the racket no more than 1 foot (about 30 centimeters) from the backboard. They vary the distance within this short range, moving along the wall and keeping control of the ball.

Variation
Players can repeat this exercise using backhand touch volleys.

Tip
When players develop a good feel for the stroke, they should try to add more backspin to the ball. This move changes the trajectory of the shot so that the ball falls more vertically after it crosses the net.

262. OOOOH NOOO!

Objective

To help develop players' confidence in hitting a variety of shots.

Description

This game develops confidence in being able to quickly change strokes, spins, and positioning on the court. Singles, doubles, or even triples can play.

Execution

Players take a position 30 feet (about 9 meters) back from the backboard. They mark a circle for each stroke and spin as they would like. Players begin play by drop hitting a ball against the backboard. If the ball lands in one of the circles, the opponent must then hit the type of stroke or spin that is written in the circle. If the player misses or hits another stroke instead of the designated stroke or spin, a point is lost. Players can use this game method to play regular-scoring games, sets, and a match, or players can play 11-point games.

Tip

Play can be quick when competing against the backboard, so players must be ready by keeping the feet moving, eyes forward, and grip loose; and they must be ready to change at the blink of an eye. Once players become more familiar with this game, they will be able to hit to any target to cause the opponent to hit any and all strokes and spins that they want.

Glossary

This is a tennis glossary. Although some of the terms may not appear in this book, players should become familiar with them if they plan to play and compete in the game of tennis. Players may hear these terms during tennis lessons and tennis tournaments.

ace—A ball served so well that the opponent has no chance to touch or return it.

ad—Short for "advantage," it is the first point scored after deuce. If the serving side scores, it is ad-in; if the receiving side scores, it is ad-out.

ad-court—The left-handed service court so called because an ad score is served there.

all—An even score (30-all, 3-all, and so on).

alley—The area on either side of the singles court that enlarges the width of the court for doubles. Each alley is 4 1/2 feet (about 1 and 1/3 meter) wide.

American twist—A spin serve that causes the ball to bounce high and in the opposite direction from which it was originally traveling.

angle shot—A ball hit to an extreme angle across the court.

approach—A shot behind which a player comes to the net.

attack drive—An aggressive approach shot.

Australian doubles—Doubles in which the point begins with the server and server's partner on the same right or left side of the court.

backcourt—The area between the service line and the baseline.

backhand—The stroke used to return balls hit to the left of a right-handed player or to the right of a left-handed player.

backspin—The ball spins from bottom to top (counterclockwise), applied by hitting down and through the ball. Also called "underspin." *See also* slice and chop.

backswing—The initial part of any swing. The act of bringing the racket back to prepare for the forward swing.

ball person—During competition, a person who retrieves balls for the players.

baseline—The end boundary line of a tennis court, located 39 feet (about 12 meters) from the net.

bevel—The tilt or slant of the racket face.

boron—An expensive, extremely durable material used to manufacture racket frames.

break service—To win a game in which the opponent serves.

bye—In competition, the situation in which a player is not required to play in a particular round.

cannonball—A hard, flat serve.

center mark—The short line that bisects the center of the baseline.

center service line—The line that is perpendicular to the net and divides the two service courts.

center strap—A strap in the center of the net, anchored to the ground to hold the net secure at the height of three feet.

check "pause"—The moment when both feet land together and "split" apart when approaching the net as the opponent is returning the ball.

chip—A modified slice used primarily in doubles to return a serve. A chip requires a short swing, which allows the receiver to move in close to return.

choke up—To grip the racket up higher on the handle.

chop—A backspin shot in which the racket moves down through the ball at an angle greater than 45 degrees.

closed face—The angle of the hitting face of the racket when it is turned down toward the court.

code, the—A supplement to the rules of tennis that specifically defines etiquette parameters such as "gamesmanship" and line call responsibilities.

composite—A racket frame reinforced with graphite, fiberglass, or boron.

consolation—A tournament in which first-round losers continue to play in a losers' tournament.

crosscourt shot—A shot in which the ball travels diagonally across the net, from one sideline of the court to the other.

deep shot—A shot that bounces near the baseline (near the service line on a serve).

default—Failure to complete a scheduled match in a tournament; a defaulting player forfeits her or his position.

deuce—A score of 40-40 (the score is tied and each side has at least three points).

deuce court—The right-hand court is called the deuce court. The ball is served there on a deuce score.

dink—A ball returned so that it floats across the net with extreme softness.

double elimination—A tournament in which a player or team must lose twice before being eliminated.

double fault—The failure of both service attempts to be good. It costs a point.

doubles—A game or match with four players, two on each team.

draw—The means of establishing who plays whom in a tournament.

drive—An offensive ball hit with force.

drop shot—A softly hit shot that barely travels over the net.

drop volley—A drop shot that is volleyed before it bounces.

earned point—A point won through skillful playing rather than through an opponent's mistake.

Eastern grip—The forehand and backhand grips presented in this text as the standard basic forehand and backhand grips.

elimination—A tournament in which a player is eliminated when defeated.

error—A point achieved through an obvious mistake rather than through skillful playing.

face—The hitting surface of the racket.

fast court—A court with a smooth surface, which causes the ball to bounce quick and low.

fault—An improper hit generally thought of as a service error.

fifteen—The first point won by a player or team.

flat shot—A shot that travels in a straight line with little arc and little spin.

floater—A ball that moves slowly across the net in a high trajectory.

foot fault—A fault resulting from the server stepping on the baseline, or into the playing court, before hitting the ball during the serve, or from a player standing beyond the sideline or touching the wrong side of the center mark before the ball is served.

forcing shot—A ball hit with exceptional power. A play in which, because of the speed and placement of the shot, the opponent is pulled out of position.

forecourt—The area between the net and the service line.

forehand—The stroke used to return balls hit to the right of a right-handed player or to the left of a left-handed player.

forehand court—For a right-handed player, the right-hand side of the court; for a left-handed player, the left-hand side of the court.

forty—The score when a player or team has won three points.

frame—The part of the racket that holds the strings.

game—That part of a set that is completed when one player or side wins four points, or wins two consecutive points after deuce.

graphite—Expensive fibers used to produce extra-strength racket frames.

grip—The method of holding the racket handle; the term given the covering on the handle.

groundstroke—Forehand or backhand stroke made after the ball has bounced while rallying from baseline to baseline or service line to service line.

gut—Racket strings made from animal intestines.

half volley—Hitting the ball immediately after it bounces.

handle—The part of the racket that is gripped in the hand.

head—The part of the racket used to hit the ball, including the frame and strings.

hold serve—To win a game in which one was server.

inside turn—For a right-handed player it is the natural turn into the tennis court after hitting a forehand groundstroke.

kill—To smash the ball down hard.

let—A point replayed because of interference; a serve that hits the top of the net but is otherwise good.

linesperson—In competition, a person responsible for calling balls that land outside the court.

lob—A ball hit high enough in the air to clear the net, usually by at least 10 feet (3 meters), and intended to pass over the head of the net player.

love—Zero or no score.

love game—A game in which the winner never lost a point.

love set—A set in which the winner has won all games.

match—Singles or doubles play consisting of two out of three sets for all women's and most men's matches, or three out of five sets for many men's championship matches and tournaments.

match point—The game point that, if won, also will win the match for a player or team.

midcourt—The general area in the center of the playing court, midway between the net and baseline. Many balls bounce at the player's feet in this area; therefore, the player can be unusually vulnerable.

midsize—A racket head of approximately 85 to 100 square inches (550 to 650 square centimeters); smaller than an oversize racket.

mix up—To vary the types of shots attempted.

National Tennis Rating System (NRTA)—A United States Tennis Association (USTA) description of tennis skills that helps the player to place himself or herself at the correct ability level from a 1.0 beginner to a world class player at 7.0.

net game—The play at net. Also called "net play."

net person—A player positioned at the net.

no ad—Scoring system in which the winner is the first player or team to score four points.

nylon—A type of synthetic racket string.

open face—The angle of the hitting face of the racket when it is turned up, away from the court surface.

opening—A court position that allows an opponent a good chance to win the point.

orthotics—An artificial material that is inserted freely into footwear to add support to the arches of the feet and align the body more efficiently.

out—A ball landing outside the playing court.

outside turn—For a right-handed player, the natural turn away from the tennis court after hitting a backhand.

overhead smash—See *smash.*

oversize—Refers to the largest of racket heads, which are 100 square inches (650 square centimeters) or more. Larger than a midsize.

overspin—See *topspin.*

pace—The speed or spin of a ball, which makes it bounce quickly.

passing shot—A ball hit out of reach of a net player.

percentage tennis—Conservative tennis that emphasizes cutting down on unnecessary errors and on errors at critical points.

place—To hit the ball to a desired area.

placement—A shot placed so accurately that an opponent cannot be expected to return it effectively.

poach—A doubles strategy in which the net player moves over to the partner's side of the court to make a volley.

point penalty system—A penalty system designed to enforce fair play and good sportsmanship.

rally—Play in exclusion of the serve.

retrieve—A good return of a difficult shot.

round robin—A tournament in which every player plays every other player.

seed—To arrange tournament matches so that top players don't play each other until the final rounds.

semi-Western grip—A forehand grip used by many players. The hand is turned on the racket handle from the Eastern forehand grip toward the right. This grip encourages extra topspin on the forehand.

serve (service)—Method of starting a point.

service line—The line that marks the base of the service court, parallel to the baseline and 21 feet (about 6 1/2 meters) from the net.

set—The part of a match that is completed when one player or side wins at least six games and is ahead by at least two games, or has won the tiebreaker.

set point—The game point that, if won, also will win the set for a player or team.

sidespin—A shot in which the ball spins to the side and bounces to the side. The sidespin slice is one of the most common types of serve.

singles—A match between two players.

slice—A backspin shot hit with the racket traveling down through the ball at less than a 45-degree angle with the court. *See also* chip.

slow court—A court with a rough surface, which tends to make the ball bounce rather high and slow.

smash—A hard-hit overhead shot.

spin—Rotation of the ball caused by hit-ting it at an angle. *See* topspin, sidespin, and backspin.

straight sets—A match in which the winner has won all sets.

string tension—Describes the tautness of the racket strings. Measured in pounds of weight.

sudden death—In no-ad scoring, when the score reaches 3-all.

synthetic gut—A racket string composed of several fibers of a synthetic material (not actually gut) twisted together.

tape—The fabric band that stretches across the top of the net; the lines of a clay court. Lead tape is weighted tape that is applied to the head of a racket to make it heavier.

tennis elbow—A painful condition of the elbow joint commonly caused by hyperextension of the elbow or by excessive wrist action in tennis play.

thirty—The score when a player or team has won two points.

throat—The part of the racket between the handle and the head.

tiebreaker—When the score in any set reaches 6 games all, a 12-point scoring system is used to determine the winner of the set. (A 9-point tiebreaker is also often used.)

topspin—Spin of the ball from top to bottom, caused by hitting up and through the ball. It makes the ball bounce fast and long and is used on most groundstrokes.

trajectory—The flight of the ball in relation to the top of the net.

umpire—The person who officiates matches.

undercut—A backspin caused by hitting down through the ball.

underspin—*See* backspin, slice, and chop.

unseeded—The players not favored to win nor given any special place on draw in a tournament.

Van Alen Simplified Scoring System (VASSS)—A no-ad, sudden death scoring system used extensively in the 1970s and 1980s. (No longer used in international competition.) The advantage point in scoring is eliminated when using this technique. The next point won after the score reaches deuce or tied at 3 all is the deciding point.

volley—To hit the ball before it bounces.

wide-body—A racket frame with a head substantially larger (thicker) than its throat.

About the Authors

Tina Hoskins-Burney is a former professional player on the Women's Tennis Association (WTA) and satellite tours and is a certified professional from the United States Professional Tennis Association (USPTA). She has trained and traveled with top pros including Arthur Carrington, Lori McNeil, Zina Garrison, and Rodney Harmon.

Hoskins-Burney has more than 30 years of experience in both playing tennis and teaching tennis to all age groups and ability levels. She has helped many young players achieve USTA rankings, find jobs as teaching professionals, and achieve college scholarships. For over 20 years, Hoskins-Burney worked as the head tennis instructor at a prestigious racket club in New Jersey before relocating to Nantucket, Massachusetts, where she continued her teaching at a private club before branching out on her own to offer instruction and equipment through The Tennis Loft.

Lex Carrington has over 20 years of experience coaching both recreational players and athletes who have gone on to play at top Division I, Division II, and Division III varsity tennis teams. He has spent the majority of his career working with junior players. In addition to several other professional players, Carrington coached Vera Zvonareva for 4 years. Achieving a career high World No. 2 by the WTA, Zvonareva was a finalist at both Wimbledon and the US Open in 2010.